THOREAU'S
ALTERNATIVE
HISTORY

THOREAU'S
ALTERNATIVE
HISTORY

Changing Perspectives on
Nature, Culture, and Language

JOAN BURBICK

University of Pennsylvania Press
Philadelphia

Copyright © 1987 by the University of Pennsylvania Press
Printed in the United States of America

Library of Congress Cataloging-in-Publication Data

Burbick, Joan.
Thoreau's alternative history.

Includes index.
1. Thoreau, Henry David, 1817–1862—Criticism and
interpretation.   I. Title.
PS3054.B87   1987   818'.309   86-30919
ISBN 0-8122-8058-X (alk. paper)

9.84

TO MY PARENTS
Eileen and Michael Burbick

Does not our country furnish antiquities as durable as any? Rocks as well grown with moss and ivy—A soil which if it is virgin—is at the same time mould—the very dust of man and nature. What if we cannot read Rome or Greece[?]

—Thoreau, *Journal*, Fall 1846

When some Vandal chieftain has razed to the earth the British Museum, and perchance, the winged bulls from Nineveh shall have lost most if not all of their features, the arrowheads which the museum contains will, perhaps, find themselves at home again in familiar dust, and resume their shining in new springs upon the bared surface of the earth then, to be picked up for the thousandth time by the shepherd or savage that may be wandering there, and once more suggest their story to him.

Thoreau, *Journal*, March 28, 1859

CONTENTS

Acknowledgments / xi

Introduction / 1

One: Mapping New Worlds / 15

Two: Framing Time / 35

Three: Views from the Walden Settlement / 59

Four: Tracks in the Sand / 83

Five: Terrestrial Rainbows / 101

Six: Regulating Eden / 123

Conclusion: Stone Fruit / 145

Notes / 151

Index / 171

ACKNOWLEDGMENTS

Scholarship has a way of branching out over the years, its shape influenced by conversations, books, and institutions. In the earliest stages of my research on Thoreau, two people stand out, Philip Rahv, whose irascible style made a difference, and Allen Grossman, whose commitment continues to provoke and sustain. At a formative point in rethinking my approach to Thoreau, I had the benefit of two academic forums. Sections of Chapter 2 were presented at the Center for the Humanities, Wesleyan University, where I was a Mellon Fellow and had the good fortune to work with Hayden White. The Summer Institute in Aesthetics at the University of Colorado provided an opportunity to experiment with my ideas about Thoreau's *Journal.*

Since coming to Washington State University I have received a number of grant-in-aid funds, a research completion grant, and a Holland travel grant. These resources facilitated crucial editing advice from Kathleen McLean and important technical assistance from a number of graduate students—special thanks to Susan Shirley, Phyllis Miller, Jim O'Neil, Enny Eshuis de Boer, and Bill Ausmus. The staffs of the Holland Library and the Inter-Library Loan Department at Washington State University also provided invaluable service. Similarly, I am indebted to the staffs of the Houghton Library, Harvard University, the Henry E. Huntington Library, the Pierpont Morgan Library, the Berg Collection of the New York Public Library, the Concord Free Public Library, and The Thoreau Lyceum.

Continued encouragement and needed criticism came from many people in the later stages of the manuscript. Richard Schneider's reactions to my work on *Cape Cod* were particularly helpful, along with the general interest of Frederick Garber and Thomas Blanding. John Hildebidle generously commented on my study and provided many thoughtful insights. I would also like to thank Peter C. Carafiol, special associate editor for *Bucknell Review,* in which an earlier version of Chapter 1 appeared. Moreover, I owe a great debt to Alex Kuo for his careful yet poetic eye. My family, of course, has been involved with this project from the start. My husband, Randy Huntsberry, kept the intellectual conversation alive, reading and questioning with a rich generosity; my daughter, Claire, has always inspired. A great debt.

Finally, I extend acknowledgment to Princeton University Press for permission to quote from *Walden*, ed. J. Lyndon Shanley (1971); *The Maine Woods*, ed. Joseph J. Moldenhauer (1972); *Early Essays and Miscellanies*, ed. Joseph J. Moldenhauer (1975); *A Week on the Concord and Merrimack Rivers*, ed. Carl F. Hovde (1980); *Journal Volume One: 1837–1844,* ed. Elizabeth Hall Witherell, William L. Howarth, Robert Sattelmeyer, and Thomas Blanding (1981); *Journal Volume Two: 1842–1848,* ed. Robert Sattelmeyer (1984); and *Cape Cod,* ed. Joseph J. Moldenhauer (to be published at the end of 1987). Also, special thanks are due the Textual Center for the Writings of Henry D. Thoreau at the University of California, Santa Barbara, for granting me access to the page proofs of *Cape Cod.* I am grateful for permission to reprint in revised form my article, "Henry David Thoreau: The Uncivil Historian," which originally appeared in the *Bucknell Review* 28, no. 1 (1983). Also, a special thanks to the Henry W. and Albert A. Berg Collection, The New York Public Library, Astor, Lenox and Tilden Foundations for permission to quote from Thoreau's "Nature Notes," containing the 1859 unpublished manuscript of "The Dispersion of Seeds."

INTRODUCTION

In the mid-nineteenth century, history was particularly significant to Americans because it explained the meaning of the new nation and predicted its manifest destiny. The history of civilized progress reassured the burgeoning American middle-class and engendered confidence in collective action. Friedrich Nietzsche was to remark later in the century that "the view into the past" hurries men "into the future, fires their courage to hold out in life a bit longer, ignites in them the hope that justice will still come, that happiness is just behind the hill which they are approaching."[1] This sense of the historical, which Nietzsche considered an illusion, if not a lie, had, however, great importance to a country in the midst of forming its geographical boundaries and its collective vision of national identity. Americans wanted a grand history, one of triumph not only over nature, but also over the decadence of Old World civilizations.

Like Nietzsche, Henry Thoreau saw the attempt to justify human actions on the basis of historical explanations of civilized progress as dangerous and false. In this sense, he was antagonistic to the historians of his day who recounted the heroic struggles of colonial America, the precious inheritance of civil and religious liberty, and the grand development of civilization in the New World. For Thoreau, a history of promise could not be found in the increasingly gluttonous needs of the civilized marketplace. Instead, Thoreau looked to the events of nature to write an "uncivil" history that both challenged the stories of civilization and accepted the implications of geologic time. No longer a background, as it was for many nineteenth-century historians, upon which to paint the progressive actions of enlightened peoples, nature became the foreground from which all human action must be perceived, justified, and understood. For civilization to turn from tragic destructiveness, the history of the natural world had to be integrated with human history. Whether the history of a Concord woodlot or a settlement at Walden Pond, Thoreau experimented with this new form of historical knowledge.

Thoreau was, of course, not alone in forwarding the cause of nature and natural history in the nineteenth century. What we need to remind ourselves of, however, is how often the description of nature in America frequently became an invitation to promote national pride in the technological advance of civilization. Particularly in midcentury, the American landscape was often valued because it contained proof of the future greatness of the emerging industrial state. In the 1852 preface to Nathaniel P. Willis's illustrated *American Scenery*, the rhetoric of historical grandeur dominated the scene. The traveler, as he "tracks the broad rivers of his own country," constantly distinguishes America from Europe and imagines the future glory of the New World.

> Instead of looking through a valley, which has presented the same aspect for hundreds of years—in which live lords and tenants, whose hearths have been surrounded by the same names through ages of tranquil descent, and whose fields have never changed landmark or mode of culture since the memory of man, he sees a valley laden down like a harvest waggon [*sic*] with a virgin vegetation, untrodden and luxuriant; and his first thought is of the villages that will soon sparkle on the hill-sides, the axes that will ring from the woodlands, and the mills, bridges, canals, and railroads, that will span and border the stream that now runs through sedge and wild-flowers.[2]

Even for American landscape painters who deeply regretted the loss of "wildness" in nature and felt its demise, civilization's triumph was both inevitable and necessary.[3] Thomas Cole, perhaps the most ambivalent of these painters, still heralded the prophetic advance of an "enlightened and increasing people." In 1835, Cole wrote, "Where the wolf roams, the plough shall glisten; on the gray crag shall rise temple and tower—mighty deeds shall be done in the now pathless wilderness; and poets yet unborn shall sanctify the soil."[4] The destiny of these New World people was not as clear to Thoreau. The marks of the plough and the building of the temple would not easily become for him signs of heroic action and the sanctification of soil.

Although Thoreau stood against these images of the landscape and rejected the myth of civilized progress, his abiding interest in historical knowledge placed him in continuity with a major American intellectual tradition. The importance of history to American thought from its colonial beginnings cannot be overstated. Stemming from the Puritan tradition in New England was the belief that history was the ground of sacred reality. Many early religious settlers of America saw little, if any, distinction between both the secular events of their communities and their exemplary individuals, and the ongoing sacred events of God. American geography was the place of both history and prophecy.[5] The establishment of American utopias and the lives of representative men provided ample evidence from which to write the explanatory stories of God's ways, hence recording a sacred history.[6]

Instead of looking for a record of sacred history in the civilized communities of men and women transplanted to American soil, Thoreau, as an heir of romanticism and the emerging natural sciences, placed history within the natural world, where he found records of a story more capable of redemption than those of civilization. To the Puritans such a move would have seemed presumptuous, if not heretical. As is well known, Anne Bradstreet, writing her famous poem, "Contemplations," made clear the fact that humans lived in a historical time to which the natural world was "insensible":

When I behold the heavens as in their prime,
And then the earth (though old) still clad in green,
The stones and trees, insensible of time,
Nor age nor wrinkle on their front are seen;
If winter come and greenness then do fade,
A spring returns, and they more youthful made;
But man grows old, lies down, remains where once he's laid.[7]

The potentially tragic story of men and their societies depended upon Scripture, grace, and providential events to redeem historical time and grant immortality. But once nature was also perceived as existing in historical (not necessarily cyclical) time, with a demonstrable story of change and decay, a providential vision of history was forced to take into account an overwhelming array of evidence, previously conceived of as suspended in time. Nature was no longer the static backdrop for the story of civilization.

By 1750, the continually emerging story of figural events began to expand into a world no longer structured by human history; in particular, geology and paleontology had significantly shattered any conventional sense of historical time. It is a commonplace in the history of ideas that by the mid-eighteenth century, nature was perceived as having a history, one that expanded extraordinarily beyond the conventional conceptions of time. As Stephen Toulmin and June Goodfield write in *The Discovery of Time,* "men were beginning to recognize that the present face of the world might carry enduring traces dating from much earlier, even prehuman times; and that, if only we could interpret them, these traces would provide evidence about the past as direct and reliable as any human tradition."[8]

The new sciences developing during the late eighteenth and nineteenth centuries that analyzed and described the natural world not only dramatically changed the concept of history for the period, but also presented new "facts" for theological explanations of the world. If nature had a history that was as crucial to human events as that of human tradition, what were the implications of this history for the sacred designs of God? The essentially tragic story of man locked in chronological time and searching for redemption through God's grace must be rewritten. By the time Thoreau committed himself to the observation and description of natural phenomena, the historical evidence for God's plan had become inextricably fused with the scenes of nature. The history of the natural world engulfed in some ways the societies of men and women; the challenge for Thoreau was to interpret this expanding sense of the historical and to find within it a sustaining vision of truth.

In his recent study, *Thoreau: A Naturalist's Liberty,* John Hildebidle argues that "Thoreau, with full knowledge, applies the methods of natural history to the reading and writing of history generally."[9] Although his study does not pursue the question "of history generally," focusing rather on the genre of the natural history essay, Hildebidle's insight applies equally to the present subject. Thoreau adapted the methods of the naturalists to write his form of history. He was not alone, of course, in attempting to reconcile natural history with a transcendental vision. Scientists such as Asa Gray and Edward Hitchcock wrote systematic essays to reconcile the findings of botany and geology with religious beliefs.[10] Natural history, like the history of Plymouth Plantation or Massachusetts Bay Colony, was under constant pressure to reveal God's design.

What would a history that privileged nature instead of civilization look like? How would it be written? Would it alter our understanding of human tradition? For instance, Asa Gray wrote in his famous review of Charles Darwin's *Origin of Species* that "the geological record, even if all displayed to view, is a book from which not only many pages, but even whole alternate chapters have been lost out, or rather which were never printed from the autographs of nature."[11] As a document of the past, nature displayed severe gaps and invited dangerous speculation. Nonetheless, to Gray it was the key book, albeit incomplete, that demonstrated not only a symbol system but a record of the duration of time. Its specific story could be traced through noting the minute variations of species. Gray insisted that the "facts" of variation and natural selection were not incompatible with theology and a developmental design of God, acting in the historical time of the natural world.[12]

Thoreau also attempted to discover the redeeming ways of God in the record of nature's duration. In constructing his history, he relied upon the descriptive techniques of natural historians to collect evidence to promote a new understanding of historical time, forcing Americans to rethink the glorified story of civilized progress. Thoreau's writings are Janus-like, running against the triumphant thinking of his contemporary civil historians, yet reaching for the sacred in an uncivil vision of historical time.

Thoreau came of age as a writer in this milieu of history that included stories of both civilization and nature. To understand his particular approach to historical knowledge, however, it is important to define all narratives of nonfiction, whether conventional history or natural history, as "fictions of factual representation," because "the process of fusing events, whether imaginary or real, into a comprehensible totality capable of serving as the object of a representation, is a poetic process."[13] We cannot merely oppose history to such art forms as the poem and the novel; we must also consider the narrative strategies of representation these forms of writing developed. The persuasiveness of historical "truth" is as dependent upon plot, figurative language, and discursive argument as are various forms of fiction writing.

In particular, both the form and content of the natural history essay and the techniques of natural description inform most of his work. Basically, Thoreau and his contemporary natural historians elevated the description of nature as the means to understand the past, and in the "particularity" of description lay the persuasiveness of their records. Unlike the naturalist, however, Thoreau emphatically insisted upon using the first person in writing his description of nature. Adhering to a romantic epistemology, Thoreau believed that both the perceiving subject and the perceived object were essential for an understanding of natural history.

Oddly enough, however, by writing natural history, Thoreau

distinguished himself from important aspects of romanticism, the great literary movement of the nineteenth century. Sacvan Bercovitch writes:

> All Romantics regarded nature as the temple of God. All of them, that is, were the heirs of natural theology—the traditional Christian view, shared by Catholics and Protestants alike, that creation is God's "other book," a Holy Writ of living hieroglyphs. The tradition leads forward to Romantic naturalism through a process of redefinition which, for our present purpose, may be simply stated. As the Bible gradually lost its authority after the Renaissance, *sola scriptura* became *sola natura*.[14]

Thoreau was typically romantic in choosing nature as his primary text, but his *style* of representing nature was dramatically unromantic. As it reached the provinces of America from England, romanticism was represented primarily through the lyric form to express its ideology—not the empirically restrictive form of natural history writing. The British romantics generally chose poetry as the preferred form to express the sacredness of nature. Despite their philosophical ties to a doctrine of organicism, the romantics, in a sense, split from the empirical sciences and natural history and denied the particularity of this history by stressing the importance of myth and the imagination. Thoreau did not.

The static book of nature as a repository of symbols and types was suitable for the post-Lockean writers from Jonathan Edwards to the Unitarians, but when nature began to be perceived as an increasingly fluid substance with classification systems subject to endless revisions, it posed a new challenge to the interpreter of *sola natura*. The hierarchies of the eighteenth century were destroyed, as competing versions of natural change gradually cohered into the theory of evolution, a tenaciously materialistic explanation of historical time. Harold Bloom is correct when he states that most romantics retreated to, or, as he would have it, found freedom in, the mind and the constituting powers of the imagination.[15] To find order and design in the flux became increasingly problematic to the poets in the nineteenth century.

Emerson in his early years as a writer expressed in *Nature* his intuitive fear of the limits of the "splendid labyrinth" of the eye and the close observation of nature; he realized that the observer could "wander without end" in the specifics of the landscape. It is not surprising that one of the most formative mystical moments of illumination within nature occurred for him within the Jardin de Plantes in Paris. Only in the humanly reconstructed world of natural things where a "grammar of plants" was visibly displayed could Emerson, the observer, have confidence that he was seeing correctly, that is, in recognizing the expression of the spirit in nature.[16] In the American tradition of romanticism, as represented by Emerson, the desire to suppress empirical evidence was particularly strong. Emerson wrote, "In a cabinet of natural history, we become sensible of a certain occult recognition and sympathy in regard to the most unwieldy and eccentric forms of beast, fish, and insect."[17] This romantic form of natural history, confined within the "cabinet" of human construction, nullified the "unwieldy and eccentric forms" of nature that threatened both the unity and tranquility of the landscape Emerson desired.

To guarantee that the metaphysical unity of the landscape and its redemptive mission remained intact, Emerson shunned "minuteness of details" in his natural history and declared in *Nature* that "matter is a phenomenon, not a substance."[18] Locke, of course, had argued for "substance" and had accordingly lessened the power of the mind in constituting sensation. Once Emerson had rendered nature instead a phenomenon, he declared in his peculiar Kantian fashion that the mind took precedence over matter and actively constructed sensation. Emerson's post-Kantian stance had additional implications, however, for the objects of sensation. Perception for Emerson often became equivalent to contemplation and necessitated the absence of both the landscape and the objects of sight. He consciously avoided description and observation as obstacles to seeing correctly. Nature was mainly a symbol, not a fact. He rejected the new sciences of the nineteenth century, which doggedly set about describing nature and all its "minuteness in detail": "Empirical science is apt to cloud the sight, and, by the very knowledge of functions and processes, to bereave the student of the manly contemplation of the whole."[19]

For Emerson, then, nature had to be viewed at a distance for its spirit and hence its redemptive story to be revealed. He insisted that the "soul holds itself off from a too trivial and microscopic study of the universal tablet. It respects the end too much, to immerse itself in the means."[20] The contemplating mind guards against the "sordor and filths of nature" by suppressing the details of observation. "The kingdom of man over nature, which cometh not with observation,—a dominion such as now is beyond his dream of God,—he shall enter without more wonder than the blind man feels who is gradually restored to perfect sight."[21]

The warnings are everywhere. Look closely, but not with the eye of the nineteenth-century observer of nature. Wholeness and tranquility will shatter against the fetish of the particular. Emerson's attitude was not unique; he shared this sensibility with the best practitioners of romantic poetry. As Northrop Frye points out, much romantic poetry placed its emphasis "not on what we have called sense, but on the constructive power of the mind, where reality is brought into being by experience."[22] Wordsworth, like Emerson, sought a "uniformity of tone and mood" that was in many ways antithetical to the observation of the landscape.

For Emerson, then, the only possible "history" of nature was a history of the mind, ideally one with universal applications. "All history becomes subjective; in other words, there is properly no History, only Biography."[23] The growth of the individual mind, however, reflects the universal flow of ideas. History becomes a manifestation of the spirit. In ironic contrast to Emerson, the empirical sciences of the nineteenth century were busy collecting in all its "minute variations" a different history of nature, one that would ultimately challenge his vision of nature as spirit.

While disregarding the cautions of Emerson not to look closely at the scenes of nature, Thoreau plunged ahead into the detailed description of natural phenomena, convinced of nature's ability to yield historical "truth" to the carefully observant individual. As part of a strong Lockean tradition that evolved with a Puritan sense of historical mission and as a contemporary of Scottish common sense philosophy, Thoreau found it difficult to reject the observation of sense data as a primary means to record both history and the duration of individual identity. American fiction writers of the period were also caught in the demands of history and the senses. Terence Martin mentions that many common sense philosophers, who argued that the imagination must be curtailed or, at least, regulated, placed the writers of fiction in an "untenable position." To these philosophers, the grand enterprise was still history: "For history orders a series of actual events, history relates the successes and failures, the hopes and fears, of actual men, [and] history, as record, is actuality in the form of language."[24] History reading was advocated as an antidote to the vogue of fiction. Defensive and fighting for space, writers like Hawthorne, Melville, and Poe claimed power for the imagination; yet they freely drew upon techniques from history writing and the empirical sciences. Emerson's call to shun the observation of the particular could not be seriously maintained as a narrative approach for either the fiction writer or Thoreau. They maintained their fascination with rendering the particulars of time and space and lingering on the problematic nature of perception.

Basically, Thoreau explored first-person description in an attempt to understand the historical truth of the natural world. History was to be found in the landscape through inventive and experimental observation. Nature existed as a force in itself that the poet must watch constantly. If nature was the most impressive record of time, then the poet must explore its recesses to find what story time could tell. This task could not be performed by blocking out the details of the landscape, but rather by rendering in language the illusion of its presence.

Thoreau, of course, did not reject romanticism as Emerson presented it to him, but he chose to perceive and describe the phenomenal world within the romantic validation of the imagination. His descriptions became the means to analyze the relationship between natural history and human civilization and to understand with different "eyes" the Puritan tradition of the civil society in which the image of America is fused with the New World kingdom. Nature, to Thoreau, was often experienced as a uniquely American landscape with its peculiar history of utopian settlements, redemptive design, and violent contact with native societies. Hence, reading the text of nature correctly, particularly that of the American landscape, demanded an extensive commitment to the processes of perception and the histories of American settlement. As a result, perception and its concomitant paradoxes, as well as conflicting stories about the American past, were woven throughout Thoreau's writings. Where Emerson hesitated, Thoreau camped down for life.

In exploring the labyrinth of the eye that Emerson feared, Thoreau came up against an unnerving sense of the phenomenal world that often challenged many of the assumptions of transcendentalism. Perception, rather than presenting a synthesis of the real and the ideal, or of natural history and human consciousness, often evoked a sense of separation between the world and the human mind. Anxiety and doubt filtered throughout Thoreau's work until in *Cape Cod* the dominating image of human perception was the eye of a drowned immigrant, filled with sand. At the same time, moments of visual epiphany dissolved the tensions of historical time into an apprehension of the beauty and design of time passing. Above all, Thoreau wrote the natural history of where he lived and journeyed, a history of the American landscape that was committed to the story of redemption. Whether it was the Concord and Merrimack rivers, the Walden settlement, the Maine woods, or the shores of Cape Cod, each geography had a history that revealed new versions of the past. How to tell this new historical story, in which the history of nature and the history of human societies were realigned, was Thoreau's persistent dream.

The literary form that best suited his purposes was first-person discourse. The autobiographical "I" was also the "I" who observed the landscape and wrote the new history of America. Unlike Emerson, Thoreau committed himself to observation and description as the means to truth. More than an essayist, Thoreau experimented with modes linking first-person discourse to the demands of description. The labyrinth of the eye led him to literary forms which were sometimes remarkably innovative. His *Journal,* in particular, testifies to his lifelong struggle with the problems of perception in a new language of description. The very "minuteness of details" that Emerson shunned was Thoreau's testing ground for the real and hence the historical. Without that minuteness of detail, the world existed only as ideas with no connection to the real. The Puritan mission to record and give account of historical time is as present in Thoreau's writings as in those of Cotton Mather.

*　*　*

In recent years, critics have found Thoreau's writings increasingly difficult to evaluate. No longer seen as the Emersonian idealist, Thoreau has been judged a contradictory, ambivalent, and even deeply ironic thinker.[25] In departing from Emerson's dictum that nature is the symbol of the spirit, he has often been seen as replacing a figurative use of nature with a more immediately experiential relationship to the natural world. James McIntosh writes: "For Thoreau the relation between fact and truth is mysterious, to be discovered by waiting and living, not to be analyzed into the categories of surface and depth. Even when a natural fact corresponds to a moral quality, it is not dismissed as superficial, as merely a 'figurative tool.'"[26]

Thoreau's writings are, then, differentiated from Emerson's precisely along the lines of the symbolic. Do we read nature as a symbol system, a means to discover the spirit, or do we, like Thoreau, relate to nature as a body within a seamless world of sensual experiences? In this reading, Thoreau becomes the sensualist who nonetheless attempts to read rightly the text of nature. But the emphasis is on Thoreau evoking "the presence of nature,"[27] not just employing a clever set of literary symbols. If judged positively, Thoreau leans away from the literariness of Emerson and toward the wildness and freedom of nature. Judged negatively, however, he appears to be a failed idealist, perhaps one whose sensuality amidst the natural landscape is inappropriate, if not perverse.[28]

Accordingly, Thoreau's "minute inspection of his own existence" in nature has often been interpreted as a sign of his parochialism.[29] It has also been taken to indicate his fall from grace and his abdication of the transcendentalist creed to read all nature as a symbol of the spirit. Sherman Paul, for instance, even though he thoroughly explicates the transcendentalist influences on Thoreau's thought, believes that, "After *Walden,* which expressed his enduring faith in the seasons, his *Journals* become increasingly a repository of scientific facts. He became an inspector of phenomena, relying more and more on manuals and guides, using a telescope, a thermometer and other measuring instruments. . . ."[30] Even though Paul stops short of judging Thoreau a "failed poet," he gives little weight to the writings after *Walden;* he evaluates technological references, particularly in passages of natural description, as indicating failed vision. For Paul, as for many critics, the poet and the naturalist are incompatible.[31]

To view Thoreau as a historical writer does not dissolve these oppositions, but it does place Thoreau's writings in a different system of critical understanding. We can no longer oppose the spirit to the body, the transcendental symbol to the natural fact, but must linger on the rhetorical methods Thoreau devised to equate description with historical revelation. In one sense, the transcendentalists knew that only in language was the battle to be fought. Philip Gura has pointed out that from the writing of *Nature* on, Emerson "believed that the revelation to the present age was that the laws of God, best expressed in human terms in the life of Christ, were also reflected through all nature and so were not just the property of men who, once upon a time, had captured Christ's 'tropes.'"[32] In this way, description is not only rendered equivalent to Scripture, but also given the status of historical truth.

If we view Thoreau as intentionally developing the art of description as the only means to present a correct history of the landscape, then his writings take on a form of continuity to the end. Even as early as *A Week on the Concord and Merrimack Rivers,* Thoreau modified a strictly transcendentalist approach to the landscape and borrowed from the natural sciences to develop new means of describing natural history. He remains, of course, a romantic in the religiously laden tradition of transcendentalism, but his brand of transcendentalism demanded the exploration of new literary forms and techniques. His epithet for the writings of at least one transcendentalist as "sublimo-slipshod" is not an idle remark. To describe accurately the "things" of nature was his lifelong pursuit.

*   *   *

Because of Thoreau's commitment to the art of description, this study gives proportionately larger weight to his *Journal* and the writings after *Walden*. Contrary to the position of many of Thoreau's critics (with the exception of Leo Stoller, James McIntosh, and John Hildebidle), it is here assumed that the naturalist and the poet were for Thoreau necessarily one, and that through this merger he carried out his desire to write uncivil history. What is absent from this study, then, is an explicit discussion of Thoreau's politics, religion, and life. Present is a constant reading of *how* he described what he saw. My method is often rhetorical, lingering on the finely tuned moments of crafting language, following the figure of speech to its completion or demise, or it is cultural, contrasting Thoreau's literary strategies with those of poets, historians, and naturalists, and linking these differences to the ideological battles of nineteenth-century America. A large part of my argument rests on the *Journal* of the 1850s. To Thoreau, the history of the natural world was not accessible from Emerson's much-praised "cabinet." The empirical testing of observation through repeated walks, assiduous note-taking, and incessant journal writing, were basic to his pursuit of the traces of time and the changing appearances of natural phenomena.

Writing in 1855, Thoreau captured this sense: "Here is self-registered the flutterings of a leaf in this twisted, knotted, and braided twine. So fickle and unpredictable, not to say insignificant, a motion does yet get permanently recorded in some sort. Not a leaf flutters, summer or winter, but its variation and dip and intensity are registered in THE BOOK" (7:140–141).[33] The record of life as a leaf over time was hence recorded in the book of nature, and this particular sense of time was enthralling to Thoreau. Without it, the dimension of history was lost and symbols became empty ciphers.

In addition, the authority for Thoreau's history and its power to persuade rested on the presence of observable evidence. Warner Berthoff defines history as "that species of narrative in which we try to describe something that happened according to the discoverable testimony about it and by means of certifiable techniques for gathering and identifying such testimony."[34] Thoreau's authority for writing the history of his settlement at Walden Pond came in part from his *Journal* between 1850 and 1854. In these intense years of gathering data about the pond and its environment, Thoreau established himself as a writer of verifiable observations. How unlike Emerson's *Nature*, which rarely described nature but established instead an attitude toward the natural world and an understanding of its proper end.[35]

With *Walden*, Thoreau attempted to find in the representative year a pattern that unlocked time and finally heralded the death of strict chronologies for natural events. All time moved forward and back to eternal spring. In his *Journal* in the spring of 1852, a period from which the journal writing was heavily incorporated into *Walden*, Thoreau asserts that for "the first time I perceive this spring that the year is a circle" (3:438). The succession of time, if properly recorded, displayed a continual return to promise. History charted this magical movement: "I would fain explore the mysterious relation between myself and these things. I would at least know what these things unavoidably are, make a chart of our life, know how its shores trend, that butterflies reappear and when, know why just this circle of creatures completes the world" (3:438). The circle of time and creation was, however, unknowable without the "chart" and the record of duration. *Walden* was built from a base of countless observations, not miniatures of discrete natural phenomena but repetitive walks over intimately familiar ground, describing the laws of succession and cracking the code of time.

After 1850, describing the landscape became a way of life for Thoreau. The task led to an endlessly renewable form of natural history. Each person in the new democratic nation had the power to apprehend the story of America: "How novel and original must be each new man's view of the universe! for though the world is so old, and so many books have been written, each object appears wholly undescribed to our experience, each field of thought wholly unexplored. The whole world is an America, a *New World*" (3:384). America became equivalent to the assumption of a point of view from which to describe the world, thereby creating new revelations.

It was on the beaches of Cape Cod that Thoreau met the most significant stumbling block to his quest for uncivil history. Description as an accurate recording device failed to discover the New World. Instead, it took on the characteristic of a sequence of "still lives" that Georg Lukacs accused all such writing of becoming: "Description provides no true poetry of things but transforms people into conditions, into components of still lives. In description men's qualities exist side by side and are so represented; they do not interpenetrate or reciprocally effect each other so as to reveal the vital unity of personality within varied manifestations and amidst contradictory actions."[36] The vitality of nature that Thoreau sought to capture in his writings was undone by death. Chronology with an ending betrayed the sense of temporal succession that returned to origin and was endless. Bodies on the shore remained mere lumps of matter.

The questioning of language and representation that went on in *Cape Cod* did, however, give Thoreau an opportunity to draw back from description and the strategies he had used to write his histories. After *Cape Cod,* Thoreau did not easily describe a circular sense of time, but pursued more intensely either the epiphany within the discrete natural phenomenon as found in the late *Journal* years, or the law of successive descriptions in the late nature essays. The language of nature, thus, takes a bifurcated route, either leading to a tremendous emphasis on how perception enters into and structures what is seen, or to an abandonment of the problem of perception for a discussion of observable natural laws.

To write uncivil history, Thoreau experimented with unorthodox historical methods. He tried to retain Emersonian idealism in the face of the nineteenth century's emerging sense of natural history. Throughout his writings we can sense not only the materialism of Darwin but the pragmatism of William James, who could find for every redemptive version of natural theology a tragic and perhaps, even worse, an ironic story. While holding onto Emerson's ideal, Thoreau found he had to reject Emerson's nature, which was too much a "cabinet" of figures for him, too much a symbol without "fact." To right Emerson's version, Thoreau committed himself to understanding not only what the eye sees, but how it sees. Only thus could he perceive paradise on earth and leave a record behind.

ONE

Mapping New Worlds

When Thoreau came of age as a writer during the 1840s, Americans in general were searching for histories that would justify their actions both at home and in Europe. The romantic historians of the period satisfied this demand, creating stories that sustained the ideal of progress, the triumph of civilization, and the necessary control of "primitive" forces. The notable George Bancroft, for instance, presented "the American past as a great play, written by God and man together, moving toward a triumphant last act in which the promises of the Christian tradition and the Age of Reason came true."[1] The conclusion to volume six of his *History of the United States of America, from the Discovery of the Continent* heralded the rise of a "new people" who through constitutional government were secure "against violence and revolution." Bancroft insisted that these new Americans had "chosen justice for their guide" and "while they proceeded on their way with well-founded confidence and joy, all the friends of mankind invoked success on the unexampled endeavor to govern states and territories of imperial extent as one federal republic."[2]

Earlier, in the 1830s, Thoreau had adhered to this sense of history, confident that his epoch, the nineteenth century, would not be "a barren chapter in the annals of the world,—that the progress which it shall record bids fair to be general and decided."[3] But, by the 1840s, this story of civilization had lost its hold on his imagination. In particular, throughout *A Week on the Concord and Merrimack Rivers*, Thoreau made a self-conscious effort not to succumb to the "decadent" stories of civilized men and women but to construct a new account that could capture the rhythm and laws of events without the facile ideology of civilized progress. The writing of this new history—an account still intent on reflecting freedom and renewal—demanded, first of all, a redefinition of historical time.

Throughout the excursion on the rivers, Thoreau as a traveler leaves behind conventional concepts of historical time, those shared by the residents of Concord and fostered by its revolutionary past, and enters into the historical time of nature. Thoreau begins the account of the 1839 trip he took with his brother by enclosing "civilized" history within a larger concept of "historicity," noting that the Concord River, as its seventeenth-century residents named it, had existed in prerecorded time. Thus, civilized history accounts for only a part of the river's history, and not the whole. Thoreau redefines history as the apprehension of time passing in which the entire natural world participates. Writing in 1778, Georges Louis Leclerc, Comte de Buffon, aptly expressed this concern for new techniques to write a history that would encompass nature:

Just as in civil history we consult warrants, study medallions, and decipher ancient inscriptions, in order to determine the epochs of the human revolutions and fix the dates of moral events, so in natural history one must dig through the archives of the world, extract ancient relics from the bowels of the earth, gather together their fragments, and assemble again in a single body of proofs all those indications of the physical changes which carry us back to the different Ages of Nature. This is the only way of fixing certain points in the immensity of space, and of placing a number of milestones on the eternal path of time.[4]

Even more striking than this new sense of nature's time, which assumes a depth fascinating to many late eighteenth- and nineteenth-century thinkers, is Thoreau's realization that the history of civilization is in no way equivalent to human history. In the study of the history of nature, entire cultures reappear on the face of the earth. For Thoreau, the history of the Concord River stands as proof of the paucity of civilized accounts because races of humans lived and died along its banks for generations before white scribes entered the river's name in their books. A journey along its banks provides, then, the opportunity to explore an expanded sense of historical time. Splitting history into "civil" and "uncivil" accounts, Thoreau aligns himself with wildness and incivility and writes a record of the past that implicitly dismantles the texts of the romantic or civil historian and casts doubt over the story of the American nation.

Thoreau maintains this antithesis between civil and uncivil throughout *A Week,* observing it not only within texts, but also in landscapes and human actions. As he does so, he critiques both the content and the form of conventional history. The implications of his counter-history, however, are not systematically apprehended within the text and, therefore, exist only as points of friction throughout the narrative. But read from a cultural perspective, in which the conventions of romantic history provide an intertextual reference, *A Week* becomes a knot of accusations against historians and an attempt to seize their power to tell the story of America.

Beneath the civil-uncivil antithesis lies Thoreau's attack on the conventional third-person form of history writing in which the historian claims to be an artist who magically recreates the past for the living. By the nineteenth century, historical fiction had become a model by which the civil historian could represent the experience of the past. Likewise, biography became a subgenre used by historians to amplify the heroic lives of individuals caught in cataclysmic moments in history.[5] Thoreau implicitly challenges the historian who attempts to present in writing the scenes of the past, based on careful familiarity with a range of historical documents, by adopting the voice of a narrator. This was the tendency of many American historians who, influenced by Sir Walter Scott's historical romances, represented the past by using novelistic techniques, adopting third-person discourse with plot, dialogue, and intense characterization.

In *A Week,* Thoreau experiments with many literary forms, such as travel guide, local history, captivity narrative, poetry, and autobiography.[6] At the same time, he comments on the methods of writing history, insisting that first-person discourse is the only legitimate *form* for historical knowledge: "But one veil hangs over past, present, and future, and it is the province of the historian to find out, not what was, but what is" (p. 155).[7] In "Monday," Thoreau advocates radical discontinuity for historical time and insists that, "the *past* cannot be *presented;* we cannot know what we are not" (p. 155).[8] He adds, further, that if "we could pierce the obscurity of those remote years, we should find it light enough; only *there* is not our day" (p. 157). The radical discontinuity of historical time does not mean that history is lost, however, only that representations of the past are based on false epistemologies.

For instance, Thoreau's skepticism about civil history is partially based on the nature of historical evidence. The historian's attempt to weave together a new text from older documents, erasing their quality as documents, is merely sleight of hand. He implicitly debunks as literary tricks the techniques of historians who artistically represent the past through the "poetic intuition of the particular."[9] The affirmation of first-person discourse as a means to write history results in a new approach to documentation. In contrast to the third-person techniques of many romantic historians, Thoreau's text is stuffed with documents that flaunt themselves as records— excerpts from local history, ecclesiastical records, town chronicles, and pre-Revolutionary captivity and Indian war narratives.[10] It also contains hundreds of quotations from classical, medieval, Renaissance, and romantic literary artists. Except for what Thoreau considers sacred texts that point to an origin before historical time and thus escape the entrapment of the "particular moment," all profane texts reflect their historical moment.[11]

Instead of suppressing the formal features of the profane document to tell the story about the past as the civil historian would, Thoreau plays upon the tension the document creates. He frames the document with first-person discourse as a means to call attention to the "subject" writing the discourse.[12] Thus, the "subject" can freely read profane documents about the past but can never forget that they are from a distant time. For instance, in "Tuesday" Thoreau copies out a letter written during the wars between the Penacooks and Mohawks, then adds as a postscript: "But now, one hundred and fifty-four years having elapsed since the date of this letter, we went unalarmed on our way, without 'brecking' our 'conow,' reading the New England Gazetteer, and seeing no traces of 'Mohogs' on the banks" (p. 221). The past is represented not only as tragically discontinuous with the present, but also as humorously distant from the "Here and Now."

Thoreau's distrust of the written historical document and his unwillingness to use it to "recreate" the past result in an affirmation of first-person discourse based upon observation. For instance, he has barely begun his record of the river when he must confront the inadequacy of documentation and the fickleness of human memory. Not only the Indians but an entire culture of fishermen lived along the Concord, leaving hardly any written documents behind. Searching for some account of these fishermen, he finds only "one brief page of hard but unquestionable history, which occurs in Day Book No. 4. of an old trader" (p. 35). Thoreau notes all the objects of trade but realizes that the recovery of the past culture is blocked by any definition of "evidence" as the written word. Faced with an ever-expanding sense of history, Thoreau recognizes that documents are fragmentary and scarce notes from the past. Any attempt to understand the Indian or fishermen's culture within the rubric of civil history is doomed.

A Week, then, attempts to validate the methods of first-person observation as the basis of a counter-history that breaks the mold of "civilized" time. Thoreau intends to reappropriate absent societies and cultures into his uncivil history, in the process telling counter-stories about the American nation. Most significantly, he finds in natural science the means to grasp the continuity between the past and present and to reconstruct the culture of the fishermen along the river. With an occasional pun and a touch of whimsy, Thoreau writes a piscatorial history that encompasses the story of the men who existed along the rivers without leaving verbal records behind.

The methods of natural history not only undermine the third-person techniques of the civil historian, but also eventually allow him to write in first-person the story of civilization along the Concord with a "plot" different from that used by the romantic historian.[13] Thoreau's observations about the shad, for example, necessarily include the story of technological growth along the river, with the proliferation of dams and factories that thwarted the instinctual drive of this migratory species and also, paradoxically, the development of the fishing culture. Thus, Thoreau employs scientific observation of species other than the human in writing uncivil history, a history interdependent with human history. Once Thoreau includes the fish in history, he produces a radically different plot from that which David Levin characterizes as the major theme of romantic historians, the spiral of human progress. Thoreau's version of man's inhabitation of the earth is tinged with tragic destructiveness; any simple redemption of time through the "progressive" actions of human individuals and communities is crossed with ignorance and doubt.

*   *   *

Thoreau's insistence on the centrality of the observer for his form of uncivil history pits him deeply against the romantic historians. His charge of elitism goes beyond their unwillingness to include vast stretches of geological time or vanished cultures; it goes to the essence of the organizing metaphors of their text. More importantly, Thoreau implicitly rejects their tendency to view the past as a *theater* of events offering a sequence of *pictures*. As Russell Nye notes, the American public "expected history to be presented as a dramatic conflict of opposing individuals, forces, or nations; the historian, like the playwright, imposed form and structure on the disorder of events, finding tension, climax, and resolution in the segments of human experience he chose to write about."[14] Accordingly, nature became "scenery," a sequence of backdrops portraying sublime and picturesque landscapes. Historians like George Bancroft and John Lothrop Motley considered themselves "painters," depicting schemes of progress and etching out "portraiture" from the actions and deeds of historical figures.[15]

Thoreau implicitly attacked the metaphors of the "theater" and the "picture" as means to frame and understand the past; they were class-bound tropes that limited and indeed falsified American history. In a criticism paralleling that directed at the civil historian, he faults Goethe in *A Week* for magnifying the theater until "life itself is turned into a stage" (p. 327). Thoreau then associates theaters with urban European life, its "kingly processions," and its aristocratic refinements, leveling a democratic, as well as Puritan, criticism against the theater metaphor. Thoreau also finds fault with Goethe's sense of nature as a sequence of pictures, a criticism which persists in his later writings on John Ruskin and William Gilpin. To read the landscape as a sequence of pictures is to transplant the cultural conventions of picture-making onto vision.[16] The pictorial code, which, as Roland Barthes points out, permeates realistic techniques of fiction,[17] was earlier used by nineteenth-century historians. In that tradition, the most accurate observer was one trained in the art of pictorial analysis. But only the elite were so trained. For Thoreau, the cultural conventions of Europe restricted the historical vision of America; he rejected the metaphors of the theater and the picture in an effort to democratize sight.[18]

Before Thoreau drafted *A Week*, he had begun to dismantle the pictorial code in his earlier essays. In a short vignette entitled "Musings," written in 1835, the natural scene is self-consciously viewed through a "little Gothic window." Clouds are "drapery" and a "truant hawk" is a "messenger from those ethereal regions."[19] The description moves toward a statement of the sublime effects of nature. But five years later in his 1840 *Journal*, nature is described as occurring around an observer located within the scene. "As I sat on the cliff today the crows, as with one consent, began to assemble from all parts of the horizon . . . as if a netting of black beads were stretched across it."[20] The observer is contiguous with the action in the scene; he is not the viewer of a framed setting.

In "A Walk to Wachusett," published in 1843, Thoreau also undercuts the theater metaphor by replacing the term "tragedy" with "scene," thus neutralizing the sense of a predictable story line.[21] More explicitly, in his climb to the summit of Wachusett, Thoreau finds not a sublime vision, but an overview of Massachusetts "spread out before us in its length and breadth, like a map."[22] Describing the topography of the land around the peak in the order of the points on a compass, he concludes that the "Yankee men" settling along the mountain's rivers are born to an unpredictable destiny. Their future is a blank; the tales of their adventures lack the sense of an ending and hence a recognizable plot. Not subject to labels like "tragedy" or "comedy," the acts of these "Yankee men" have no recognizable narrative development. Their future, and hence their story, is unknown and unknowable. All that exists is a map of events on the landscape.

When Thoreau was writing his draft of *A Week* at Walden Pond, he was also working on an essay about Carlyle. The writer of *The History of the French Revolution* and *Sartor Resartus* both amused and disturbed him. Ostensibly a tribute, Thoreau's essay is filled with ambiguities and qualifications. Carlyle falls short of the status of "poet," but his works of art introduce new ideological perspectives for Thoreau. Carlyle's writings are like "the plough, and corn-mill, and steam-engine," not like "pictures and statues."[23] Thoreau defines Carlyle's style as analogous to technological tools of labor, and opposes it to the refined techniques of the culturally educated elite. Implicit in the simile is the ideological assumption that technology gives mankind access to more objective, universal, and democratic means to articulate reality and to reach beyond the hierarchical organization of class. The Puritan hatred of "graven images" is, of course, present in Thoreau's argument, but it is wedded to the idea that the mechanics of labor are a liberating weapon against decadent elites.[24]

A surveyor since 1838, Thoreau first introduced the study of technology as a means for teaching trigonometry in his Concord school. He valued the precision that tools could give the measurement of space and was fascinated by the correlation between spatial accuracy and temporal change. He was well aware of the infinite variations in spatial coordinates caused by shifting magnetic attraction, and he found in precision surveying not only a vocation, but also figurative material for his writing.[25] In *A Week* he claims that, "If I were awakened from a deep sleep, I should know which side of the meridian the sun might be by the aspect of nature, and

by the chirp of the cricket, and yet no painter can paint this difference" (p. 319). Although many contemporary American painters
were seeking to do exactly that through precision studies of atmosphere and cloud formations, Thoreau insists that he has refined the art of observation to the point of discerning not only the
coordinates of space, but also the fluctuations of time.[26] Hence, he
is uniquely qualified to record uncivil history. His dual training as
a surveyor and a naturalist allows him to observe a natural clock
present in the topography of nature, whereby he can capture the
precise records of history. "Being in time" replaces the stage and
the picture frame with a new technology of seeing. A highly idealized seeing, deeply utopian in intent and American in purpose, it
contains an implicit desire to level aristocratic class distinctions.

*　*　*

In *A Week,* then, Thoreau as uncivil historian rejects the "dream of
painting" and the "theater of heroic actions" in favor of counter-
metaphors of an egalitarian nature. Drawn to the techniques of
observation pioneered by the natural sciences and the technologies
of cartography and surveying, Thoreau experiments with perception and its representation.[27] As E. H. Gombrich and twentieth-
century philosophers of language point out, there is never an
absolute sense of apprehending an object or an ideologically free
text. There is only a "discrimination" within the perceptual field
and a subsequent encoding of this "discrimination" in language.
For Thoreau, the historian as first-person observer replaces the
playwright who artistically recreates the theater of the past. The
picture gives way to the *map* in a movement toward democratizing
the history of the American landscape.[28]

Although *A Week* contains nature descriptions that conform to
picturesque and sublime conventions, cartography provides the
book's major metaphor for the apprehension of space. From the
opening pages, the landscape is viewed topographically. The uncivil historian charts geographical space before he enters events
into the narrative. After Thoreau discusses the etymology of the
Concord River, he describes the river according to its location in a
space that is not pictorial, with foreground and background, but
mapped:

> "One branch of it," according to the historian of Concord, for
> I love to quote so good authority, "rises in the south part of
> Hopkinton, and another from a pond and a larger cedar

swamp in Westborough," and flowing between Hopkinton and Southborough, through Framingham, and between Sudbury and Wayland, where it is sometimes called Sudbury River, it enters Concord at the south part of the town, and after receiving the North or Assabeth River, which has its source a little further to the north and west, goes out at the north-east angle, and flowing between Bedford and Carlisle, and through Billerica, empties into the Merrimack at Lowell. (pp. 5–6)

Once situated in the space of the map, a highly idealized perspective that takes its coordinates from the axes of the earth, the description jumps its focus from a metaposition to a perspective on the river's banks, recording measurements, agricultural uses, and wildlife from within the scene, not from without. Thoreau conveys a sense of enveloping plenitude along the banks of the river at Bound Rock:

Many waves are there agitated by the wind, keeping nature fresh, the spray blowing in your face, reeds and rushes waving; ducks by the hundred, all uneasy in the surf, in the raw wind, just ready to rise, and now going off with a clatter . . . gulls wheeling overhead, muskrats swimming for dear life, wet and cold . . . cranberries tossed on the waves, and heaving up on the beach, their little red skiffs beating about among the alders;—such healthy natural tumult as proves the last day is not yet at hand. (p. 7)

Highly metonymical in presentation, the style accumulates units of action, as opposed to arrangements of things, for a sense of ceaseless motion. As Kenneth Burke would say, Thoreau's description focuses on the "Act"; flux surrounds the observer but does not engulf him, because he has the map to guide and order the description.[29]

In an earlier essay, Thoreau commented on how the entomologists, by giving us the insect's view of nature, proved that "nature" could stand up against the scrutiny of its details.[30] Viewed metonymically, nature revealed no "interstices," no gaps or emptiness betraying signs of disease or death. Similarly, only a view inside the landscape can perceive its historical continuity and record a sense of regeneration through time. The sequences of matter in motion that Thoreau describes as occurring at Bound Rock are grouped according to water, air, and earth, all revolving around the position of the observer.[31] They constitute a catalogue of sequential moments that defies the pictorial foreground/background organization of space.

Thoreau also finds in this technology of seeing a means to defeat the finality of death by the assumption of new points of view within nature that produce "evidence" of regeneration. These "new views" he considers more accurate and persuasive than the romantic historian's bankrupt vision of victory over natural and societal restraints. In this way, perception of the landscape becomes the means to reassert a positive sense of growth without the ideology of "civilized" progress. In "Friday," the last chapter of A Week, Thoreau describes the autumnal moment of nature and its associations with death and silence while he dreams of regeneration:

> Sitting with our faces now up stream, we studied the landscape by degrees, as one unrolls a map, rock, tree, house, hill, and meadow, assuming new and varying positions as wind and water shifted the scene, and there was variety enough for our entertainment in the metamorphoses of the simplest objects. Viewed from this side the scenery appeared new to us. (p. 349)

The "scene-shifter" acts as an observer who carefully orders his journey by the sequential unfolding of nature envisioned as map. The map with its fixed topographical arrangement orders the ceaseless angles within the scene, caused by the natural "metamorphoses of the simplest objects," and the shifts in point of view made by the observer. Infinite points of view are possible at any point along the map, but the progression through the scene is always based on a metaposition, possible only through a technology of seeing. This dialectic allows for the apprehension of the "new" within nature, producing "evidence" of life as ceaseless renewal.

As Thoreau returns to the Concord shore at the end of A Week, a sense of triumph over the passage of time is reinforced by the instruments of technology:

> Almost any *mode* of observation will be successful at last, for what is most wanted is method. Only let something be determined and fixed around which observation may rally. How many new relations a foot-rule alone will reveal, and to how many things still this has not been applied! What wonderful discoveries have been, and may still be, made, with a plumb-

line, a level, a surveyor's compass, a thermometer, or a barometer! Where there is an observatory and a telescope, we expect that any eyes will see new worlds at once. (p. 363)

Despite his occasional fear that science, with its precision tools, could cause mechanical descriptions of nature, Thoreau sees the potential that technology holds for space and time, particularly when space and time are envisioned in flux, in a state of continuous metamorphosis. Technology can redeem time and space from chaos and can lead to a new relationship between man and nature that holds the promise of infinite angles of vision and a new form of history. But the observer who so views nature must be both distanced from the scene and immersed in it with intense mobility at any point on the idealized grid of the map.

Theoretically, this new historian is immune to the concept of a fixed, American historical plot because the act of observing within the natural landscape is an experience of incessant change. What Thoreau refers to in A Week as the grand "scene-shifter" of nature confuses the narrative line to be plotted along the American rivers. Writing about his own river account, he concludes, "Whether it might have proved tragedy, or comedy, or tragi-comedy, or pastoral, we cannot tell" (p. 114). The structural topography of a scene as a map can be described and fixed, and the accumulation of details at any point along the scene can be recorded; but that scene cannot take final shape, in terms of inherited cultural conventions, as a "theater" or a "picture" framing human behavior. Rather, the uncivil historian must abandon such story lines and rely instead, as an individual "subject," on the continual apprehension of discrete events that instill a sense of historical continuity.

Also at stake in Thoreau's resistance to "plot" is an implicit belief that romantic historians are bent on composing a story of nationhood that is a half-truth. Thoreau considers the civil historian, at his worst, to be, like the American pioneer, an opportunist and a conqueror, not the creator of national history and national pride, but the "white man, pale as the dawn, with a load of thought." After buying the Indian's hunting grounds and burying his bones, only to forget their location and, later, to plow them up, the white man comes with "a list of ancient Saxon, Norman, and Celtic names, and strews them up and down this river,—Framingham, Sudbury, Bedford, Carlisle, Billerica, Chelmsford,—and this is New Angleland, and these are the new West Saxons, whom the Red Men call, not Angle-ish or English, but Yengeese, and so at last they are known for Yankees" (p. 53). Although the Yankee's history superficially is a story of obedience to the laws of trade and the "improvement" of nature,[32] Thoreau perceived the blood and violence underneath.

Besides nature, the Indian is indeed the specter of Thoreau's uncivil history, as are the Hannah Dustans and Captain Lovewells that fought them to the death. Civil history becomes for Thoreau a story of political victory and gardening, a record of the demise of the wild and the ironic advance of debility. Uncivil history is a perpetual reminder that at the root of the national saga lie the smashed brains of Hannah Dustan's infant. But Thoreau's history does not clearly conform to the tragic mode.[33] Instead, the vanished societies serve as warnings against the triumphant stories of the romantic historians.

It is only when Thoreau imagines what a "universal history" might look like that he envisions a developmental model for race and culture, but, even then, he places the present in an ambiguous position. He finds that "historical stories" of his contemporaries, when read carefully, belie a progressive ideal and indicate that man may not be so near the apex of development as one would like to imagine. In fact, the future, though potentially glorious, is difficult to imagine and impossible to know. At these moments, Thoreau doubts whether historical truth provides "wisdom" about humankind at all and speculates that perhaps only mythic truth can provide a vision of "progress."[34]

Nonetheless, in writing his uncivil history, Thoreau advocates technological methods of observing nature that he hopes can generate a redemptive vision of time. The historian with his mode of first-person discourse provides the new "facts" by which this history is created. Once space is apprehended as a map, the individual observer functions within its skeletal measurements to describe an accumulation of events that demonstrate the plenitude and health of nature. Along his route on this map, Thoreau enters "events" which may be either elaborations of first-person description, as we have seen, or extended passages of reflection. His method of organizing reflection is similar to Emerson's, stringing allusions like beads around a number of transcendental commonplaces. As such, it reinforces the primacy of first-person inspiration and intuition and joins with observation to legitimate the methods of the uncivil historian. Only in this way can Thoreau return to the romantic motif of progress and regeneration that the civil historians vehemently proclaimed.

*   *   *

What Thoreau continually describes in *A Week,* once he has established the mapped journey, is what he calls the "vestige," or any object bearing the marks of cultural or natural time. The properly trained observer can discern "facts" about the past by "reading" such vestiges as the discarded clay pipes of a fisherman or the twisted vines of a plant. Hence the "vestige" becomes to the uncivil historian what the document is to the civil historian. Thoreau assumes that, even without written records, all societies and natural phenomena have left traces of their presence on and in the earth.

Thoreau values the vestige primarily because it can be observed and described by a "subject." Thus, people whose lives are not recorded in books have left behind traces of their presence that are accessible to the living. In a sense, they have written their "history," but they leave to the living scribe the deciphering of the vestige's meaning. To Thoreau, the farmer without his Virgil nevertheless writes "on the face of the earth already, clearing, and burning, and scratching, and harrowing, and plowing, and subsoiling, in and in, and out and out, and over and over, again and again, erasing what [he] had already written for want of parchment" (p. 8). Thus, the text of human action is the earth; the material traces on its surface become the legitimate basis of uncivil history, which includes classes and societies both neglected and suppressed by civil historians. All that is needed is the correct interpreter of these nonverbal texts. Nature and the cultural objects within it become the authoritative book of history, recording not only its own presence but the historical presence of humankind. For instance, the Indian, the ever-absent personage of *A Week* whose trace is nonetheless pervasive, is found by merely sifting through a shovelful of dirt from the banks of the Concord. Arrowheads are as important to Thoreau's vision of the American past as the documents of the Revolutionary War.

Thoreau's records of material traces of previous cultural and natural change then become the generating foci of his description. The apprehension of time by such vestiges as a cluster of stones, an arrowhead, or marks on a tree, forms the locus of associations. These associations are culled from memory, mythology, or local history and hence can evolve into passages of reflection. The vestige includes within itself, then, a physical sign from the past, and it acts as a fossil would for Cuvier. In it and through it the past unfolds and manifests itself to speculation and association.

Ironically, however, as Thoreau became increasingly aware, the vestige too must be deciphered; and because it also must be encoded in language, it forces Thoreau into versions of history he either cannot write or wants to suppress. When he comes upon some carpenters repairing a scow along the Merrimack River, he writes, "The whole history of commerce was made manifest in that scow turned bottom upward on the shore" (p. 216). But Thoreau stops short of "reading" the scow; instead, he associates the boat with other sailing vessels from Ovid's *Metamorphoses* and Alexander Henry's *Travels and Adventures in Canada,* through which association he offers the possibility of writing a "new history" based on boat-building, "as ancient and honorable an art as agriculture" (p. 216). This time what emerges is not an uncivil history but a gesture to its potential.

Farther up the Merrimack, Thoreau comes upon the potholes at Amoskeag Falls, vestiges he reads in terms of their purely natural causes:

> A stone which the current has washed down, meeting with obstacles, revolves as on a pivot where it lies, gradually sinking in the course of centuries deeper and deeper into the rock, and in new freshets receiving the aid of fresh stones which are drawn into this trap and doomed to revolve there for an indefinite period. . . .(p. 247)

Clearly this vestige signifies for Thoreau vast stretches of geological time and is physical evidence that the landscape has altered dramatically. He finds that a "thousand feet above these rivers" there are ledges with "stones still in them," showing that "the mountains and rivers have changed places" (p. 248). This overwhelming depth of time cannot be reflected in civilized history.

Thoreau implicitly assumes that from the partial vestige the trained reader can infer the whole text of history. The vestige, both natural and cultural, becomes, then, the synecdoche from which to reconstruct the uncivil history. But the story this vestige contains is problematic in the text. While the potholes, for instance, may indicate the immensity of nature's "historicity," they also teach the "lesson" of doomed action, fated "Sisyphus-like" to revolve "until they either wear out, or wear through the bottom of their prison, or else are released by some revolution of nature" (p. 247). They could point to a purely "naturalistic" origin for creation: "By as simple a law, some accidental by-law, perchance, our system itself was made ready for its inhabitants" (pp. 248–249). Hence, the vestiges might signify order and design, but the purpose of the design is at odds with a redemptive vision of nature. As Thoreau moves closer to describing vestiges and the traces of time, he has increasing difficulty extracting a plot that is in accord with his desire for renewal and regeneration.[35] In this instance, it is not merely a matter of finding "evidence" in that landscape which discounts the stories of the romantic historians. Rather, the methods of natural science produce "facts" that also defy a redemptive vision of time. Thoreau's hope to discover "new views" by which to understand the infinite "promise" of the American landscape are frequently blocked by the discoveries of the uncivil historian.

Thoreau insists, however, that Americans must claim the vestiges found on the American landscape, for without the "ruins" of European civilization, American historians must look into the "dust and primitive soil" for an understanding of the history of America. As an uncivil historian, Thoreau is as concerned as his contemporary civil historians are to isolate what is distinctly American about the history of the New World. A story of violence, it is also a story of time gaps, which force transplanted Englishmen and -women to face the kind of societies they had relegated to the distant past. While the European historian must dig down through layers of Rome, Greece, Carthage, and Babylon for the past, the American historian arrives quickly at the remains of Indian culture and the inscriptions of time on nature's face. "Historicity" takes on a depth never before imagined by the American historian. The near and the far collapse into one material trace. The lichens on the rock, like the Indian burial stones, are the hieroglyphs of an American past that demand a new set of eyes to read their meaning. Antiquity becomes infused in the American landscape. "The walls that fence our fields, as well as modern Rome, and not less the Parthenon itself, are all built of *ruins*" (pp. 250–51).

It is not surprising, then, to find Thoreau carefully selecting his vestiges. For instance, in the leaves of New England trees, "old runes . . . are not yet deciphered." Thoreau turns to "catkins, pinecones, vines, oak-leaves, and acorns; the very things themselves, and not their forms in stone" (p. 251). The reader of the landscape selects only the forms of life that contain within themselves the potential for crucial life functions such as reproduction or transpiration. Hence the purpose of "change" in the vestige is directed toward renewal. In the most transcendental "event" on the river journey, the "subject" can gaze on the organic vestige and with his "poet's eye . . . detect the brazen nails which fastened Time's inscriptions, and if he has the gift, decipher them by this clue" (p. 250). But the plot Thoreau wants to decipher is one of regeneration and growth. He apprehends time most successfully in a form of nature that is renewable *in itself.* As Thoreau pursues his method of empirically describing vestiges, however, he is often left with the "what" of signification in abeyance. Only the method to achieve this state of "truth" is consistently pursued.

As an uncivil historian Thoreau is searching for new methods to discover "signs" in the natural world that ultimately "tell" the story of redemption, the triumph over limit and fate. He often writes of health triumphant over disease rather than life over death, with health as the symbol of regeneration, reproduction, and growth. But as he immerses himself in time and develops his historical method, he also pulls away from the apprehension of time in the landscape, rejecting historical time altogether, and finding his redemptive vision instead in a static reconstruction of the natural world:

It is a scene which I can not only remember, as I might a vision, but when I will can bodily revisit, and find it even so, unaccountable, yet unpretending in its pleasant dreariness. When my thoughts are sensible of change, I love to see and sit on rocks which I *have* known, and pry into their moss, and see unchangeableness so established. I not yet gray on rocks forever gray, I no longer green under the evergreens. There is something even in the lapse of time by which time recovers itself. (p. 351)

Here, in order to discover redemption "even in the lapse of time," Thoreau sets the scene with ever-gray rocks and ever-green vegetation, the direct opposite of the method he has devised for deciphering "Time's inscriptions" within the natural world. Now, the "subject," through a ritual of repetition, revisits the scene that signifies permanence, reassured that life is not merely a sequence of discontinuous moments. The "there and then" is experienced in the "here and now" because the landscape remains fixed even if the "subject" reading the landscape has altered. Flux and change are nowhere etched in this landscape.

Absent is the sentiment that would lead Thoreau to write toward the end of *A Week,* "The landscape contains a thousand dials which indicate the natural divisions of time, the shadows of a thousand styles point to the hour" (p. 319). Here, like many contemporary American painters and scientists, Thoreau sometimes accurately describes aspects of natural change through meteorological transformations. His fascination with material vestiges as access to past events borders on an attempt to collapse time present and time past into one moment of observation, thereby heightening the sensation of "being in time." Perhaps this attempt is the major motive underlying the entire trip on the Concord and Merrimack rivers, that is, to enter the stream of time on its inevitable course.[36]

In *A Week,* Thoreau also suppresses the vestige and the sensation of "being in time," fearing imprisonment by time and doubting his ability to find redemption within its limits. He exclaims that "We will not be confined by historical, even geological periods, which would allow us to doubt of a progress in human affairs" (p. 158). Yet, although Thoreau dreams about the elevation of men to gods, he must conclude that "we do not know much about it" and returns to his sacred texts for consolation.

When Thoreau remembers his climb to Saddleback Mountain, he exults because, having risen above the mist, he could "shut out every vestige of the earth, while I was left floating on this fragment of the wreck of a world, on my carved plank in cloudland" (p. 188). Only then does he find "revealed" the "new world into which I had risen in the night, the new terrafirma perchance of my future life" (p. 188). Strangely enough, in this world, "As there was wanting the symbol, so there was not the substance of impurity, no spot nor stain" (p. 188). Without the vestige and time's inscriptions in the symbol, Thoreau is truly free to imagine transcendence, a place without change, and hence, death.

Thoreau goes even further in the last chapter of *A Week,* "Friday," to subvert the efficacy of the vestige. He rhapsodizes upon things beyond observation and description:

Indeed, all that we call science, as well as all that we call poetry, is a particle of such information, accurate as far as it goes, though it be but to the confines of the truth. If we can reason so accurately, and with such wonderful confirmation of our reasoning, respecting so-called material objects and events infinitely removed beyond the range of our natural vision, so that the mind hesitates to trust its calculations even when they are confirmed by observation, why may not our speculations penetrate as far into the immaterial starry system, of which the former is but the outward and visible type? (pp. 385–86)

Intuition without and beyond sensation becomes ironically the final haven for the "observer." This call for Emersonian transcendentalism, where nature is mainly the symbol of the spirit, ends in a fairly clear rejection of the body. "I have interest but for six feet of star, and that interest is transient. Then farewell to all ye bodies, such as I have known ye" (p. 387). Thoreau is now in direct conflict with his earlier rhetorical question: "Is not Nature, rightly read, that of which she is commonly taken to be the symbol merely? (p. 382)." Ultimately, he falters on the question of whether nature is the symbol of the spirit or the spirit itself. The former leads him into the idealism of Emerson, typified by a sentence near the end of *A Week:*

Two herons, *Ardea herodias,* with their long and slender limbs relieved against the sky, were seen travelling higher over our heads,—their lofty and silent flight, as they were wending their way at evening, surely not to alight in any marsh on the earth's surface, but, perchance, on the other side of our atmosphere, a symbol for the ages to study, whether impressed upon the sky, or sculptured amid the hieroglyphics of Egypt. (p. 390)

As impressions or sculpture, the herons transform from moving creatures to static symbols that signify or point to the spirit. They typify the way in which the transcendentalist would "read" the text of nature, but they also lead to a method of interpretation beyond change and becoming. Thoreau's quest to describe the vestige and reconstruct an uncivil history is, however, one with his desire to define nature, not as a mere repository of "figures," but as the ground of being within which change can be apprehended. The marks of time on a leaf or a stone contain time past and imply time future in the present. Their significance is within their being, not beyond it. But since vestiges are observed by a "subject," they still have to yield their significance within the codes of language. Thoreau cannot rid the "vestige" of its "plot." And the story it signifies does not necessarily point to regeneration, but perhaps to deterioration and death. In this sense, the vestige is still trapped within the language and culture of the "subject" who observes its presence in nature. As a result, Thoreau is frequently forced to suppress the vestige in order to maintain his "plot" of regeneration.

This dilemma becomes most acute at the end of *A Week*, when Thoreau develops the opposition between sound and silence. Earlier in the text, the journey was seen as a quest to recover the healthiness of sound and to find within the river's current the movement of time and the basis of what he called a *"sound* state" (p. 42). By the end, however, the power of regeneration does not have its source in sound, but in silence. Instead of positing a space beyond nature and the senses, Thoreau splits nature into compensatory forces in order to establish regeneration. No longer in the sound of the stream but in the "under-current" is found the "evidence" of "strength and prolificness." The pure space of silence, then, transcends the incursions of time and history. More important, this space of silence is beyond language and interpretation: "It were vain for me to endeavor to interpret the Silence. She cannot be done in English. For six thousand years men have translated her with what fidelity belonged to each, and still she is little better than a sealed book" (p. 393).

But Thoreau hardly recognizes this space of pure regeneration, in a sense the source of all creation, before he expresses his terror of its reality. To enter the silence is tantamount to annihilation. Thoreau hypothesizes that to dive into the "under-current" would mean that the "reader" would disappear beneath the surface, lost to words and human society. To dive into the timeless space of silence is to dive into death. Thoreau, therefore, differentiates himself from the sacrificial "reader," preferring instead to act like "Chinese cliff swallows," clutching onto the surface, "feathering" their "nests with froth." Confined to the surface "bubbles" and not the depth of silence, however enticing it may be, he ends his journey by leaping "gladly on the shore" and seeing in the Concord mud the outline of his boat's keel, the trace of time passing on the surface of the earth. Thus, Thoreau ends *A Week* with a return to the motif of the vestige. He fastens his boat to the "wild apple-tree, whose stem still bore the mark which its chain had worn in the chafing of the spring freshets" (p. 393). The imprint of the rope, like the marks of language, he finally recognizes as the necessary boundary of life and, consequently, as his vision of history.

* * *

In *A Week* Thoreau tries to forge the uncivil history of America, retelling captivity and Indian war narratives as he travels across old battlegrounds, jotting down graveyard epitaphs and records from the daybooks of ordinary citizens as he comes across their deserted homesteads. Nostalgically longing for a bardic voice, he seeks to undermine the civil historian's sense of the past as theater and his view of nature as picture. He expands the definition of "history" while democratizing the means for the historian to apprehend the past. Substituting his own dictum for recording "time," he finds in the scenes of nature and the technologies of the nineteenth century a means to revise the civil historian's "stories" of the past.

But Thoreau's method of discovering historical facts often defies his desire to plot the story of regeneration and the redemption of nature. The American landscape becomes a highly unstable repository of texts and figures which, no matter how persistently Thoreau attempts to "rightly read" them, do not yield the story of promise. As a result, in *A Week* Thoreau periodically retreats from history in favor of sacred texts and mystical illumination as the means to grasp human continuity and the redemption of time. To read *A Week* is to experience a philosophical tug of war. As the text pulls in the direction of time and history, it yearns for silence. As it hunts for what can be seen and described, it impulsively attempts to stand beyond the senses and fate. But, most importantly, it forces us to look again at what is indeed uncivil about the American past.

T W O

Framing Time

In *The Savage Mind,* Claude Lévi-Strauss conducted a searing analysis of historical knowledge, claiming that history does not "escape the common obligation of all knowledge, to employ a code to analyse its object, even (and especially) if a continuous reality is attributed to that object. The distinctive features of historical knowledge are due not to the absence of a code, which is illusory, but to its particular nature: the code consists in a chronology. There is no history without dates."[1] Taken as a whole, Thoreau's journal writings stand as a monument to chronology. Whether he is attempting to describe the discrete events of a particular day or extract from dated notes, over an extended period of time, a representative day, week, or year, Thoreau remains essentially committed to this code of historical knowledge.

If, as Thoreau states in *A Week,* "the province of the historian is to find out, not what was, but what is," then the journal entry, a method of writing "periodic in composition,"[2] becomes a constant exploration of the "present" that offers him a literary form suited to his historical mission. By 1850, Thoreau is beginning to record consistently his daily walks in the woods of Concord and to describe perceptual epiphanies signifying redemption. This chapter focuses on the *Journal* of 1850 to 1854, in particular the springs of 1851 and 1852, when Thoreau develops his techniques of describing minute natural events that are to him "signs" of spring.[3] Over a period of days or weeks, he records, for example, the startling effects of moonlight, the display of gossamer on the river banks, and the opening of water lilies to the warmth of the sun.

Breaking natural history into discrete and sequential units of time slows down Thoreau's search for redemption. In the *Journal,* an individual natural event is visited, observed, and described repeatedly, yielding the "truth" of the event over time. Thoreau is surprisingly self-conscious about the suitability of the *Journal* for his needs as an uncivil historian. Whereas *A Week* is set in opposition to the conventions of romantic history, the *Journal* is contrasted to the form of the essay. Thoreau comments that even though Emerson, Montaigne, and Plutarch wrote successful accounts of private and public experience, their method was often incompatible with his intention. Reflecting on the advantages of the journal over the essay, he writes: "Perhaps I can never find so good a setting for my thoughts as I shall thus have taken them out of. The crystal never sparkles more brightly than in the cavern. . . . The truth so told has the best advantages of the most abstract statement, for it is not the less universally applicable."[4]

Although Thoreau regrets his shortcomings as an essayist, he suggests a rationale for his journal writing. Both Thoreau and the essayist write in first-person discourse, the only linguistic mode of truth for Thoreau, but the essayist does not link the language of the "I" with an index of time.[5] The "wildness" of form that Thoreau desires is contingent upon a particular conception of time that such essayists violate, thereby potentially removing their work from historical "truth." Thoreau also writes that the essay form provides "no proper frame" for his entries. "Mere facts and names and dates communicate more than we suspect" (3:239).[6] What the essayist might consider notational has for Thoreau the possibility of meaning. The index of time becomes a necessary sign representing the presence of the historical.

In Thoreau's *Journal,* then, an individual entry with its days and dates becomes a metronome splitting experience, fragmenting the sense of continuity into days, hours, and minutes. Steeped in the exacting demands of measured time, the *Journal*'s structure, even though it is mechanically mimetic, becomes for Thoreau an indicator of historical truth. In a sense, chronological time and the repetition of acts become his fetish. Historical experience and aesthetic representation are indelibly bound within units of time. Days and dates become in themselves communicators of history; they signal progression and index change. In the *Journal,* then, more than in any of his other writings, we can analyze what Thoreau means by historical time. We can understand how he attempts to record time passing in the natural world.

Critics have demonstrated that Thoreau did not write spontaneous accounts of what he observed in nature, but rather painstakingly revised narratives of individual excursion and descriptions of natural phenomena.[7] My interpretation, however, is not concerned with the question of spontaneous or revised writing but instead with how and why an individual journal entry is fundamentally presented as bounded within a temporal sequence. Thoreau's *Journal*, with its meticulous dating, signals the breakage of time into units of perception or, to use his word, "nows" that constitute his sense of history.

Measured, chronological time not only is a means to signal historical events; it also indexes for Thoreau a "truth" about how consciousness as well as perceptual events occur. In the *Journal* Thoreau writes, "thoughts written down thus" can be "printed in the same form with greater advantage than if the related ones were brought together into separate essays. They are now allied to life, and are seen by the reader not to be far-fetched" (3:239). Because Thoreau experienced consciousness as basically occurring within time, the literary form must represent this apprehension. Also, Thoreau implies that a "thought" is an already coherent linguistic unit that exists sequentially and is severed from other "thoughts." Written down in their order of occurrence, the verbal records represent not only the thoughts, but also the spaces between them.

In contrast, the essayist applies a cognitive trick while composing, gathering together "related" thoughts and making coherent wholes out of separate moments of consciousness. But if the goal is a record of life, conceived of primarily as acts of consciousness within time, then the order of occurrence, the "thought" as it appears in time as a chronological sequence, becomes crucial to Thoreau's criteria of art and history. Hence, artifice for Thoreau is basically an attempt to defeat time through a violation of temporal sequence. The essayist "forgets" this sequence of consciousness and rearranges "thoughts" to create the illusion of wholeness. In this way, like the romantic historian, he is a trickster and a "civil" artist who imposes culturally learned forms onto consciousness. The "uncivil" artist, however, locked into a more exacting exploration of first-person discourse, is obligated to preserve the basic apprehension of consciousness as a sequence of "acts," entrapped within units of time.

An explicit chronological frame and the repetition of acts, the essence of the journal form, are the aesthetic expressions of simplicity and historical truth for Thoreau. Only when this form signals and indexes time can time be redeemed. Observing nature and its vestiges is ultimately a means to undo the debilitating march of chronological time. But the rules of this convention demand an exhausting commitment to the sequential records of consciousness. Although an individual journal entry fixes the "moment" in its consecutive order, the entry itself, in its most successful form, defeats the chronology in indexes.

For instance, Thoreau writes in his *Journal* that on October 9, 1851, at about 2 P.M., the witch hazel blooms and its leathery-colored, yellow leaves remind him of spring. The witch hazel, as the sign of autumn, nonetheless evokes memories of spring in the observing mind, which thereby undercuts the sense of time as a linear chronology. Thoreau writes, "All the year is a spring." Hence, time, when it is broken into parts and the world of appearances is examined within these measured units, actually contains sub-indexes pointing back toward origin and not forward toward death. The smallest unit of temporal sequences contains "evidence" defeating sequence, although, in this instance, the "evidence" results from remembered associations of the observer with springlike blossoms of the witch hazel. Thus, the "acts" of consciousness and perception ultimately transcend sequence and analogically connect the present with both the lived past and the potential future. The historical events of nature do not merely move forward, like chronological time, toward death and decay, but have a more essential "index," signaling cyclical renewal and regeneration.

Hypothetically, then, the "ideal" journal entry would contain two necessary but paradoxical features: first, a time "frame" that explicitly indexes the historicity of the event, and second, an apprehension of the event that points toward the possibility of breaking chronology as an index of death. Each miniature event becomes a dialectic between time and timelessness, the historical and the transcendent. The ideal journal entry that serves to redeem time, however, is merely a model of aesthetic intent, not a description of Thoreau's actual *Journal*. As Thoreau begins his exhaustive observation of natural phenomena in temporal sequence, he is drawn further into an analysis of perception itself and its constitutive role in consciousness. In his attempt to describe accurately natural events, he confronts the divisiveness of temporal sequence and the complexity of perception. Although the new historian's methods are based primarily on first-person description, these very methods have their own limitations.

* * *

Thoreau began keeping his *Journal* on October 22, 1837, three months before he graduated from Harvard College. Up until the late 1840s, it was basically a collection of aphoristic and philosophical statements on life, literature, and religion. Quotations from Goethe, Coleridge, Oriental religion, and the classics abound. Despite moments of "local color" and folk-philosophizing, the early *Journal* reflects minimal efforts to record the events of the day or to describe the natural landscape as it appeared at a particular moment in time. Views of nature, when they occur, are highly strained and riddled with literary allusions:

> Here on the top of Nawshawtuct, this mild August afternoon, I can discern no deformed thing. The prophane haymakers in yonder meadow—are yet the haymakers of poetry—forsooth Faustus and Amyntas. Yonder school-house of brick, than which near at hand nothing can be more mote-like to my eye, serves even to heighten the picturesqueness of the scene.[8]

As Thoreau takes more interest in description, he first maintains the attitude of the "pictorial" view, limiting what is seen to a stationary observer. By 1845, however, the *Journal* includes descriptions of individual natural phenomena such as the sound of bullfrogs on a summer evening and the actions of a tortoise. "The tortoises rapidly dropped into the water, as our boat ruffled the surface amid the willows. We glided along through the transparent water, breaking the reflections of the trees" (1:447). This strikingly beautiful passage describes the activity of a natural phenomenon as observed by a moving perceiver, located in space at a particular moment in time, a technique we have already seen him develop in the late 1840s in *A Week*.

As it develops, the *Journal* becomes for Thoreau the literary form in which he can extensively explore the use of a moving perceiver. Within a measured sequence of time, space opens up cartographically from the standpoint of the perceiver: "I saw Fair Haven Pond with its island, and meadow between the island and the shore, and a strip of perfectly still and smooth water in the lee of the island. . . . As I looked on the Walden woods eastward across the pond, I saw suddenly a white cloud rising above their tops . . ." (2:107). No longer stationary, the perceiver now rotates or moves. Foreground and background are less important than the angle of vision as the observer looks out from a specific geographical location that changes over time: "Now at *very earliest* dawn the nighthawk booms and the whip-poor-will sings. Returning down the hill by the path to where the woods [are] cut, off I see the signs of the day, the morning red. There is the lurid morning star, soon to be blotted out by a cloud" (2:387).

In the *Journal*, this new precision in viewing space within a cartographical grid and a unit of time is wedded to a recognition of the illusory quality of seeing. By 1851, Thoreau notes that the view from Mount Tabor varies significantly from the mapped space: "I saw the same deceptive slope, the near hill melting into the further inseparably, indistinguishably; it was one gradual slope from the base of the near hill to the summit of the further one, a succession of copse-woods, but I knew that there intervened a valley two or three miles wide, studded with houses and orchards and drained by a considerable stream" (2:187). A singular view does not comprehend the measured space between objects, but presents as contiguous those spaces that are actually miles apart. The single view, then, distorts mapped space.

In fact, early in 1852, Thoreau claims that all perception, when scrutinized, proves intensely momentary: "The mirage is constant. The state of the atmosphere is continually varying, and, to a keen observer, objects do not twice present exactly the same appearance. . . . The prospect is thus actually a constantly varying mirage, answering to the condition of our perceptive faculties and our fluctuating imaginations. . . . It is a new glass placed over the picture every hour" (3:291). The act of perception is volatile, dependent upon both the material conditions of sight and the human imagination. Thus, perception over time not only involves significant risks for the uncivil historian, but also demands an exacting commitment to the process of seeing. Constant vigilance is necessary to refine the faculty of sight.

Given the extreme transiency of perceptual events, Thoreau develops a style of description in the *Journal* that balances the stability of spatial grids with the fleeting effects of time: "As I look down the railroad, standing on the west brink of the Deep Cut, I seem to see in the manner in which the moon is reflected from the west slope covered with snow, in the sort of misty light as if a fine vapor were rising from it, a promise or sign of spring" (3:340). Such epiphanies, drawing an analogy between the specific natural event and the promise of spring, are intensely fragile acts of human perception and imagination, demanding exact orientation in space.

The daily walk, structured as a mapped excursion over time, becomes a major organizing device of Thoreau's journal entry. At various specific locations on the walk, perceptual epiphanies occur:

There are bars or rays of nebulous light springing from the western horizon where the sun has disappeared, and alternating with beautiful blue rays, more blue by far than any other portion of the sky. These continue to diverge till they have reached the middle, and then converge to the eastern horizon, making a symmetrical figure like the divisions of a muskmelon, not very bright, yet distinct, though growing less and less bright toward the east. (2:473–74)

Epiphanies are also triggered by specific sounds, such as those produced by what Thoreau calls "dream frogs" or the magical humming of the telegraph harp, and by sudden smells, such as those caused by the breaking of a sassafras twig or the odor of water lilies (4:12–14; 3:219; 3:373; 4:235).

Frequently, Thoreau begins his journal entries that describe a sustained excursion with a general geographical itinerary and a starting time, such as "7.30 P.M.—To Conantum," or "Walked to Walden last night (moon not quite full) by railroad and upland wood-path, returning by Wayland road" (2:378; 2:248). He then structures the action around several key locations on this route. For instance, on August 8, 1851, he makes observations at Hubbard's Wood, on the road at the causeway, on Conantum, and on the bridge below. The reader can often trace the walk on a map. Changes in position as the observer moves are synchronized with changes in the atmosphere and light. As in *A Week*, the familiar points along the mapped journey become the skeletal structure of permanence, organizing the dramatic variations in the landscape.

Thus, by 1851, the *Journal* is no longer a collection of inspirational ideas, but has become a preserve of redemptive epiphanies locatable in both space and time. On the evening of June 11, 1851, after making observations at the sand-bank in the Deep Cut, the old pigeon-place field out of the Deep Cut, and the upland terrain above the field, Thoreau records the following moment:

I now descend round the corner of the grain-field, through the pitch pine wood into a lower field, more inclosed by woods, and find myself in a colder, damp and misty atmosphere, with much dew on the grass. I seem to be nearer to the origin of things. There is something creative and primal in the cool mist. This dewy mist does not fail to suggest music to me, unaccountably; fertility, the origin of things. An atmosphere which has forgotten the sun, where the ancient principle of moisture prevails. It is laden with the condensed fragrance of plants and, as it were, distilled in dews. (2:237)

The movement through the topography of Concord imparts what Barthes and other structuralists call the "reality" effect.[9] Enough details of time and place accumulate to create the illusion of the "here and now." This reality of time and place is then made contingent on both history and transcendence. The "origin of things" becomes "nearer" to human time and space. It projects the walker back in time and space to an original moment at one with all living phenomena.

The entire entry of June 11 is not, however, confined to this one excursion. It also contains excerpts from Darwin's travel account of the *Beagle* and extensive passages of philosophical reflection, cut adrift from any particular walk. An individual journal entry rarely functions as a whole to achieve an integrated aesthetic effect, but usually is a conglomerate of things, notes on individual phenomena, references to readings, and comments on local people or events. It can, however, also contain a carefully written excursion account that attempts both to map and to render transcendental a historical event.

Walking becomes the means for both physical ecstasy and spiritual transcendence. Like Wordsworth, Thoreau can "recover the lost child" he becomes in the woods without "any ringing of a bell" (3:324). It is in the topographical relationship between the body of the perceiver, the angle of perception, and the context of space that uncivil history is written. Gazing over Dudley Pond, Thoreau sees "coarse mazes of a diamond dance seen through the trees" (3:97). The walk becomes the vehicle by which the "eye" positions itself in relation to the natural world and seeks out dynamic views: "My eye wanders across the valley to the pine woods which fringe the opposite side, and in their aspect my eye finds something which addresses itself to my nature. . . . I am sure that my eye rested with pleasure on the white pines, now reflecting a silvery light, the infinite stories of their boughs, tier above tier, a sort of basaltic structure, a crumbling precipice of pine horizontally stratified" (3:131). The movement of the eye, continually positioning and repositioning itself in space, changing its angle of perspective, resting momentarily and then moving through the structure of the map, is recorded in Thoreau's *Journal* with poetic force in the springs of the early 1850s. In these years, the act of perceiving the landscape becomes one with the redemption of time.

*   *   *

Although Thoreau continually attempts to distinguish between poetic and scientific description in his *Journal,* it is clear from his reading of and allusions to naturalists that his demand for "accuracy" in description is stylistically similar to nineteenth-century natural history writing.[10] Reading Asa Gray and Charles Darwin in 1851, Thoreau records in his *Journal* examples from their technical descriptions of natural phenomena. He is interested in the naturalists' need to record "minute variations" in species and sometimes even corrects their descriptions and improves them with more details.[11] Basically, the naturalist observes phenomena by breaking down the natural object into functional parts. The object exists within a grid of separate functions such as reproduction or respiration, but within each function exists an array of parts.[12] Once perceived according to a functional schema, the object is subject to metonymical splitting.

This style of natural description, by which an object is perceived only as a sequence of parts in relation to a specific function, decreases the object's potential as a source for analogizing, and thereby reduces the possibility for a dialectical relationship between the perceiver and the object. The effect of the object on the perceiver is insignificant to the description. But for Thoreau, who wants his writings to have the status of both history and art, a dialectical model involving both the perceiver and the perceived is essential. Hence, when he attempts to distinguish himself from the naturalists, he insists upon the crucial parts both the imagination and consciousness play in perception. He analyzes natural description by focusing not only on the object perceived, but also on the process of perceiving it.

A good way to demonstrate this difference is through a comparison of Charles Darwin's description in *The Voyage of the Beagle,* which Thoreau was reading and transcribing into his *Journal* in 1851, and a journal entry of this period.[13] Darwin's method of observation is to analyze skeptically the "appearance" of a natural phenomenon, as he does in seeking the causes for phosphorescence in the ocean. To Darwin, naive observers simply reason from "appearance" to causal explanations, as do the sailors on board the *Beagle* who attribute the rapid flashing of phosphorescence to the motion of a large fish. Darwin examines instead the conditions for the appearance of phosphorescence, not phosphorescence itself, and speculates that a function such as respiration is its cause. But to get to this conclusion, Darwin maintains a steady skepticism of "appearances" and avoids linking analogically one appearance with another.

In observing phosphorescent light on Walden Pond, Thoreau is equally skeptical about "appearance" as a reliable category of experience, but instead of focusing on the conditions that would link together other instances of the light's appearance, he analyzes how the "appearance" varies over time and through space within the confines of a single journal entry. In a sense, he conducts experiments on the *act* of perceiving, rather than on the object of perception. On June 13, 1851, Thoreau walks toward Walden Pond by way of Hubbard's Path, mapping his movement so as to give a sense of his approach through topographical space. "Walked to Walden last night (moon not quite full) by railroad and upland wood-path, returning by Wayland road" (2:248). This abbreviated itinerary is expanded as the entry unfolds by specific locations at Deep Cut and Hubbard's Path. "As I approached the pond down Hubbard's Path, after coming out of the woods into a warmer air, I saw the shimmering of the moon on its surface, and, in the near, now flooded cove, the water-bugs, darting, circling about, made streaks or curves of light" (2:251–252). Thoreau then records various misperceptions about what he is seeing and begins to note that what the "I" observes depends not only on the alertness and experience of the observer, but also on the distance from the observer to the object.

Description of the intensity of the moon's light as opposed to its reflection on the water becomes progressively relative as Thoreau notes how interdependent the perception of an object is with the field surrounding the object. Switching away from the "I," he writes, "one would have said they [the reflections of the moon in the water] were of an intenser light than the moon herself; from contrast with the surrounding water they were" (2:252). The logical inference that reflections of an object cannot be brighter than the object itself breaks down in face of the intensity of the reflection as it is contained within a background. Because an object is contiguous to other objects within a field, the ability to perceive it depends upon that field. Human vision situated in space and time is determined not only by physiology, but also by a field of vision. By holding constant in an almost classical sense the unities of time and space, Thoreau maps the event, shifting the variable of distance in order to observe the process of perception, and thereby renders as inherently *contextual* the nature of sight.

In this 1851 journal entry, the first six sentences move the observer nearer to the light on the water, making sight relative. But Thoreau jumps beyond observations in the process of perception when he imagines a hypothetical "eye," capable of apprehending the object by transcending the spatial and temporal limits of the individual observer. Because "appearance" is dependent upon the observation of an individual set of eyes placed within a specific time and place, it is strictly limited. Change is what the eye records as it moves in space and time. Thus the apprehension of an individual object becomes dependent upon the mind as well as material conditions. But this exacting metamorphosis of perception does not lead Thoreau to disavow appearance or to postulate a grid of functions behind appearance, as Darwin does, but encourages him to *imagine* multiple points of view. Perception, then, is essentially dialectical, in that it occurs only as a product of both the material context of the perceived object and the imagination. Thoreau writes, "To myriad eyes suitably placed, the whole surface of the pond would be seen to shimmer, or rather it would be seen, as the waves turned up their mirrors, to be covered with those bright flame-like reflections of the moon's disk, like a myriad candles everywhere issuing from the waves" (2:253). One must note, however, that this "imagining" still has a component of materiality. The observer transcends the space of an individual set of eyes by multiplying the angles of vision surrounding the perceived object.

Thoreau goes on to rephrase this speculation as a hypothetical proposition, writing that if "there were as many eyes as angles presented by the waves, the whole surface would appear as bright as the moon" (2:253). These "eyes" positioned in relation to the angles of the waves on the water would finally "see" the reflections of the moon and be able to describe the object accurately. Thoreau elaborates on the visual effect of this chimerical scene: "these reflections are dispersed in all directions into the atmosphere, flooding it with light" (2:253). The observer finally dissociates himself from an individual set of eyes and describes the imagined vision of unrestricted perception, transcending the limits of time and space.

In the next sentence, however, Thoreau undercuts the inventive quality of his imaginary "eyes" by switching to a different agent for what is seen: "The water reveals itself." After taking the reader through a tightly knit web of perceptions and pushing perception through the door of speculative vision, he reverses the process by attributing all this "power" to the "water itself." The myriad points of view that are created by the perceiver's imagination are not locked in the solipsism of the individual mind, but are also seen as a function of the object. Hence, a dialectic exists between human imagination and the natural world. Thoreau hesitates to sever one from the other in an attempt to retain the reference to the object. Instead, he links the "power" of perception with both the expanding power of the human imagination and the restricting agency of the phenomenal world.

By lingering on what Darwin and other natural historians take for granted, namely, how the "eye" sees the object, Thoreau refutes the stability of naive observation. By analyzing the relativity of vision and describing the shifts in the perceptual relationship, he carves out a space for his "poetic" description of the object. Unlike Darwin, Thoreau finds any thread of commonality between separate perceptual events almost impossible to sustain because identical conditions never recur to allow the same observation.

Change is all the "eye" perceives, and change so fundamentally pervades all observation that no "eye" can literally add up its observations and induce the whole. The effect of the whole is gained only through an act of imagination. To assume "myriad eyes" is to break all time and space positioning and to fuse the object into a mental image. The description the "I" writes is dependent upon an exhaustive perceptual analysis. The space for the "I" is ultimately carved out, but only after an acceptance of the material restraints on perception.

If perception is constituted by the physiology of the eye and contextual constraints, then the human imagination becomes even more necessary for the description of perceptual events. What the "eye" sees must be continually filtered through the reflective imagination. Thoreau's concept of the imagination is hardly, however, a refuge away from the intricate processes of perception, but a mental force in dialectical relationship with them. Again, only in this way can the record of perceptual events describe both history and art. Further, in the entry of June 13, 1851, Thoreau illustrates the achievement of this merger:

> As I entered the Deep Cut, I was affected by beholding the first faint reflection of genuine and unmixed moonlight on the eastern sand-bank while the horizon, yet red with day, was tingeing the western side. What an interval between those two

lights! The light of the moon,—in what age of the world does that fall upon the earth? The moonlight was as the earliest and dewy morning light, and the daylight tinge reminded me much more of the night. There were the old and new dynasties opposed, contrasted, and an interval between, which time could not span. Then is night, when the daylight yields to the nightlight. It suggested an interval, a distance not recognized in history. Nations have flourished in that light. (2:249–50)

The journal form indicates that this entry records the events of a specific time and place; yet the event itself destroys the frame of time, as the rhetorical question "In what age of the world does that fall upon the earth?" makes clear. Walking in the geography of Walden, Thoreau presents himself as struck by the light that re-defines historical time. The rise and fall of civilizations pales in relation to the sustaining power of this light. On June 13 at the Deep Cut, Thoreau observes the light that transcends the pettiness of "civil" history. Natural light becomes the agent by which time is redeemed from the tragic stories of human societies. This light, however, must exist not only in the imagination of the observer, but in the landscape as a perceptual event. To Emerson's assertion that "America is a poem in our eyes; its ample geography dazzles the imagination, and it will not want long for metres,"[14] Thoreau would add that the "dazzle" is possible only after an extensive com-mitment to the processes of perception and a recognition of the historical nature of the perceptual event.

* * *

Thoreau's need for a dialectical relationship between the perceiver and the perceived often results in a tenuous and unsettling ap-proach to the world of matter. If there exists historical evidence for redemption, then Thoreau must not move too quickly from describing the material conditions of a perceptual event to the drawing of imaginative associations from it. Even though he admits that the imagination constitutes what is seen, he often writes *as if* analogies and symbols were *caused* by the object, not the imagina-tion. For instance, the *Journal* often reveals him to be preoccupied with a particular natural phenomenon for a period of days or weeks. The dreamy sound of bullfrogs and toads or the display of gossamer on the river banks is observed and described over a se-quence of days. In the summer of 1852, Thoreau becomes fasci-nated by water lilies opening to the warmth of the morning sun.

The entry of July 4 begins on a note of timelessness: "I hear an occasional crowing of cocks in distant barns, as has been their habit for how many thousand years. It was so when I was young; and it will be so when I am old" (4:179). These events are endlessly repeatable in the landscape and impart a permanence to nature.

But then the mapped event proceeds to a specific destination, "to Conantum, to see the lilies open." Events are linked to the movement of the walker through the woods: "I hear a little twittering and some clear singing from the seringo and the song sparrow as I go along the back road, and now and then the note of a bullfrog from the river" (4:179). Mostly sound and visual impressions are strung along the skeletal trail. By the time Thoreau has moved from his yard, down the Back Road to the Corner Road—only halfway to Conantum—he has heard at least eight specific sounds of birds and toads and has seen three distinct changes in the atmosphere. The gradual shift in the atmospheric conditions of the sky is described in relation to the approach of dawn.

The mapped walk is intended to foreshadow the final event, the observation of the water lilies. In this entry, Thoreau momentarily loses the sense of simultaneity of action and regresses to indexing events only according to measured time. He notes that "the last traces of day have not disappeared much before 10 o'clock, or perchance 9.30, and before 3 A.M. you see them again in the east,—probably 2.30,—leaving about five hours of solid night, the sun so soon coming round again" (4:180). But he quickly builds up again the sense of expectation before arriving at Conantum right before the moment of dawn:

> A nighthawk squeaks and booms, before sunrise. The insects shaped like shad-flies (some which I see are larger and yellowish) begin to leave their cases (and selves?) on the stems of the grasses and the rushes in the water. I find them so weak they can hardly hold on. I hear the blackbird's *conqueree,* and the kingfisher darts away with his alarum and outstretched neck. Every lily is shut. (4:181)

As he records the moments before the approach of dawn, extended analogies develop from the exacting observations of atmospheric conditions. With this moment fixed in time and space, Thoreau associates the "sight of the first cool sunlight now gilding the eastern extremity of the bush island in Fair Haven, that wild lake" (4:181) with Hades, spring flowers, the pollen of sun, and the coolness of innocence. The changes in light as perceived by the eye of observation and imagination build toward a transcendental climax: the description of the water lily. But this description fails miserably as a conveyor of historical redemption:

> Carefully looking both up and down the river, I could perceive that the lilies began to open about fifteen minutes after the sun from over the opposite bank fell on them, which was perhaps three quarters of an hour after sunrise (which is about 4.30), and one was fully expanded about twenty minutes later. When I returned over the bridge about 6.15, there were perhaps a dozen open ones in sight. It is very difficult to find one not injured by insects. Even the buds which were just about to expand were frequently bored quite through, and the water had rotted them. You must be on hand early to anticipate insects. (4:182–83)

Thoreau's method as an uncivil historian undoes the epiphany. Atmospheric conditions as they exist at the eastern extremity of the pond at dawn trigger correspondences, but a lily riddled with insect holes is *in itself* totally inappropriate as a historical sign of transcendence. If anything, it is an ironic counter-symbol of death and decay. Poe, Melville, or Hawthorne would have delighted in the ironic play afforded by such opposition between purity and decay, but Thoreau is left with a measured record of the event in time and space, bereft of analogies and any hint of redemption. The mind as a technological recording device continues, but not as a generator of poetic allusions. Although Thoreau cannot deny the event, he can dismiss its importance. In fact, the lily's state of material decay is interpreted not as evidence of nature's mortality, but only as a physiological event caused by unfortunate timing.

The moral reminder, "You must be on hand early to anticipate insects," guards against the disappointments of vision. Occasionally, Thoreau comments on this myth of the perfect moment in his *Journal:* "There is a moment in the dawn, when the darkness of the night is dissipated and before the exhalations of the day commence to rise when we see things more truly than at any other time. The light is more trustworthy, since our senses are purer and the atmosphere is less gross. By afternoon all objects are seen in mirage" (3:354). This ideal temporal instant, ephemeral yet obtainable by human eyes, militates against the material conditions of natural phenomena unsuited to redemptive analogies.

Despite this myth of the ideal moment, to compensate for his inability to "see things more truly," Thoreau brings home "a dozen perfect lily buds" which gradually expand in a large pan of water at his home. Through manipulation, they open: "I touch the points of their petals, and breathe or blow on them, and toss them in. They spring open rapidly, or gradually expand in the course of an hour,—all but one or two" (4:183). Removed from the natural scene, perfection is possible. But this perfection has no relationship to the grid of time and space apprehended within the atmospheric conditions of nature. The object is no longer contextual; hence, for Thoreau it is not historical in an *original* sense.

Also, it is not only in his home experiment that Thoreau attempts to realize the "historicity" of the transcendental symbol. In the *Journal* both before and after recording this walk, he engages in extended reminiscences of earlier visions of lilies. One week before, for instance, he had written, "It is pleasant to remember those quiet Sabbath mornings by remote stagnant rivers and ponds, when pure white water-lilies, just expanded, not yet infested by insects, float on the waveless water and perfume the atmosphere" (4:162–63). In memory, the lilies can become symbols of both innocence and fertility. They are capable of conveying moral truths such as that found at the end of Thoreau's 1854 essay, "Slavery in Massachusetts," where the lily transcends the decay of its environment to shine forth in perfection.

Thoreau's analysis of human perception as a limited mode of apprehending the fleeting signs of redemption in the landscape can lead to a counter-reality to actual vision. In such a case, as in *A Week*, dream experience and memories of childhood become juxtaposed with the constantly changing phenomenal world. Thoreau writes, "I am conscious of having, in my sleep, transcended the limits of the individual, and made observations and carried on conversations which in my waking hours I can neither recall nor appreciate. . . . On awakening we resume our enterprise, take up our bodies and become limited mind again" (3:354).

In the *Journal*, however, Thoreau continues to describe the acts of consciousness, which are to him interdependent with perceptual events in nature, and, further, he begins to describe in depth the psychological processes of perception. These "perceptual events," such as the effect of light and reflected light, often provide rich material to develop a dialectical relationship between the mind and nature because they focus on the *act* of perception. But other material objects, such as the water lilies which themselves might signify transcendental analogies, defy the transcendental experience. Matter in decay mirrors back a world without epiphany and thus signifies a break in the ability of the mind to analogize, to make uncivil history out of natural events.

*   *   *

Perry Miller, in his classic essay, "From Edwards to Emerson," writes: "What is persistent, from the covenant theology (and from the heretics against the covenant) to Edwards and to Emerson is the Puritan's effort to confront, face to face, the image of a blinding divinity in the physical universe, and to look upon that universe without the intermediacy of ritual, of ceremony, of the Mass and the confessional."[15] In this sense, Thoreau's techniques as an uncivil historian follow the religious tradition of American Puritanism. His attempts to see correctly and describe accurately the natural environment are merely another means to unite history and redemption. But Thoreau's efforts to refine description into a sacred art become enmeshed in the complexity of perceptual processes, forcing him to recognize, at best, a dialectic between the perceiver and the object of perception—at worst, a rift between vision and the natural world. What begins to confront Thoreau during the 1850s is not only the complexity of perception but also the status of language in natural description. Miller's statement emphasizes the Puritan drive "to confront, face to face, the image of a blinding divinity in the physical universe." But once achieved, how is this vision to be made known to others? In what manner will it be recorded or described? Even more problematic, how is language always present within the metaphor of a "face to face" experience?

As a journal writer, Thoreau grappled with the function of language in creating an entry.[16] This difference between nature and language is most acute in the *Journal* because of Thoreau's conception of each entry as a record of the acts of perception and consciousness. How then does language enter into the relationship between the eye, the object, and the mind? On one level, Thoreau self-consciously values the role language plays in creating the journal entry. He justifies language as a notational memory device, guaranteeing the empirical and historical status of his text. On his excursions around Concord, Thoreau collects field notes in preparation for his journal entries. William Ellery Channing calls Thoreau's notebook his "invariable companion," into which "must go all measurements with the foot-inch which he always carried, or the surveyor's tape that he often had with him. Also all observations with his spyglass (another invaluable companion for years), all conditions of plants, spring, summer, and fall, the depths of snows, the strangeness of the skies,—all went down in this notebook."[17] Channing is amazed that Thoreau can expand these jottings into extended journal entries.

In order to make the transformation from field note to narrative entry, Thoreau required a lapse of time between the event and its notational record and the extended journal entry. He is explicit about his method: "I succeed best when I *recur* to my experience not too late, but within a day or two; when there is some distance, but enough of freshness" (4:20). Ideally, then, a journal passage reinforces the dialectic between the event as an empirically observable phenomenon and the event as a product of the refining imagination. In this synthesis of field note and recollection, Thoreau posits a belief that language helps to fuse the historical event with the recollection of the event in consciousness. Thoreau's desire to write both history and "poetry" are "guarded" by this conception of language. He clearly insists on this process as a journal writer, hoping that his ideas will not be "overthrown by the first wind" but will penetrate into the "womb of things."

To guard against absorption within the "womb of things," however, Thoreau evokes the mental process of recollection. A basic metaphor by which he justifies his concept of the composing process is that of reflection: "I find some advantage in describing the experience of a day on the day following," he writes. "At this distance it is more ideal, like the landscape seen with the head inverted, or reflections in water" (6:207). The physical reflection of a scene is analogous to the mental reflection, existing a step beyond perception—the kind of reflective process, with its cognitive and imaginative faculties, that Thoreau needs in order to fuse the "ideal" with the "real."

The metaphor of the reflection becomes increasingly important in the middle journal years between 1850 and 1854. In the fall of 1853 on a walk to Swamp Bridge Brook, Thoreau describes the image of weeds on the water: "What lifts and lightens and makes heaven of the earth is the fact that you see the reflections of the humblest weeds against the sky, but you cannot put your head low enough to see the substance so. The reflection enchants us, just as an echo does" (5:517). The reflection, achieving what is physiologically impossible, functions as the means to overcome the limits of direct perception and to enhance it by casting the perceived real object, the weeds, against the ideal background of the sky.

In 1854, Thoreau carefully formulates an entry based on a walk with Channing:

> A warm, thawing day. The river is open almost its whole length. It is a beautifully smooth mirror within an icy frame. It is well to improve such a time to walk by it. This strip of water of irregular width over the channel, between broad fields of ice, looks like a polished silver mirror, or like another surface of polished ice, and often is distinguished from the surrounding ice only by its reflections. I have rarely seen any reflections . . . so distinct, the stems so black and distinct; for they contrast not with a green meadow but clear white ice, to say nothing of the silvery surface of the water. Your eye slides first over a plane surface of smooth ice of one color to a water surface of silvery smoothness, like a gem set in ice, and reflecting the weeds and trees and houses and clouds with singular beauty. The reflections are particularly simple and distinct. These twigs are not referred to and confounded with a broad green meadow from which they spring, as in summer, but, instead of that dark-green ground, absorbing the light, is this abrupt white field of ice. (7:82–83)

The complexity of perception makes the reflection of objects a welcome relief. The process of reflection selects individual elements out of the perceptual field and places them in the foreground against a unified background. While the busyness of a "broad green meadow" obscures the individual twig, the "white field of ice" heightens through sharp contrast the perception of the object. If the perception of objects must exist within a context, then the reflection is a means to control the context, hence simplifying the fuzziness of human vision and guarding against absorption in the labyrinth of the eye. Likewise, the human mind and language function to simplify and delineate those aspects of the object that represent its "truth" and, in this instance, its beauty.

In a later journal entry, Thoreau realizes more completely the tension between the worlds of the real and the ideal and proposes a new strategy to integrate the two. "I would fain make two reports in my Journal, first the incidents and observations of to-day; and by tomorrow I review the same and record what was omitted before, which will often be the most significant and poetic part. I do not know at first what it is that charms me" (9:306). Although lists of natural phenomena and technical data become increasingly frequent, in these middle journal years, Thoreau favors the journal entry as a synthesis of field notes and recollection.[18]

In the entry, then, language serves a dual function—to insure a text that is both empirically valid and imaginatively refined. But language entails as many pitfalls as does perception. While the quagmire of perception exists on the surface of Thoreau's *Journal*, underneath lies the even more unsettling question of language as an impure medium that distorts perception and further distances the uncivil historian from the "face to face" encounter with the natural world. When Thoreau took up the *Journal* as an appropriate literary form for his vision of historical time, its use continually strained his understanding of language. The journal entry in its ideal form reflects the dialectic between time and timelessness; the perceiver in an exact moment within the geography of America and the transcendent powers of the imagination. In other words, the journal required a "natural" or "transparent" language, that is, one shaped not by history and culture, but by the force of universal consciousness. In order for natural description to have the status of a record that reveals redemptive history, language itself must not be trapped within the historical.

Thoreau's attitude toward the language of the journal can be traced as far back as his college years. As a student, he imagines the journal as a mind-machine, accurately transcribing ideas "as they occur" on a blank sheet of paper. Thoreau writes: "Hence, could a machine be invented which would instantaneously arrange on paper each idea as it occurs to us, without any exertion on our part, how extremely useful would it be considered."[19] He implicitly described the journal as a perfectly mimetic mechanical apparatus, eliminating both the effort and effect of the human hand and human will. The ideal journal script is the product of a recording technique that magically erases the mark of the pen and hence the traces of culture. The fantasy envisions a neutral box or space that would preserve the "natural" arrangement of the flow of ideas as they appear at their moment of generation.

The ground of possibility for Thoreau's mind-machine would seem to require that ideas as they appear in the mind already be linguistic structures, but the "arrangement" of these structures can easily become upset and distorted by "human" interference, or the "human" process of signification. Paradoxically, though Thoreau urges one to keep a journal to record what is "spontaneous" in his experience, his image of the mind-machine points to the limits of writing. The machine replaces the hand to insure a perfect transcript, severing writing from its cultural and historical roots and the distorting process of human signification.

Another instance of Thoreau's concern about the ability of language to convey accurate description comes sixteen years later when he is in the midst of his most aesthetically successful journal writing:

> It is a rare qualification to be able to state a fact simply and adequately, to digest some experience cleanly, to say "yes" and "no" with authority, to make a square edge, to conceive and suffer the truth to pass through us living and intact, even as a waterfowl an eel, as it flies over the meadows, thus stocking new waters. First of all a man must see, before he can say. (3:85)

Thoreau begins with a series of urgent directives for writing his *Journal.* He stresses the experiential basis of perception and writing and, by implication, their moral basis in an ideology similar to what Sacvan Bercovitch finds at the heart of the American tradition of perception: "First of all a man must see, before he can say."[20] And again, "As you *see,* so at length will you *say.*" Right perception, then, is a prerequisite of correct saying.

The previous journal entry also describes the process of perception and language through the metaphor of digestion. The object is not only seen but taken in and incorporated. Writing becomes commensurate with the ability to "conceive and suffer the truth to pass through us living and intact, even as a waterfowl an eel, as it flies over the meadows, thus stocking new waters." The digestive analogy, operating as a prerequisite for "true" writing on the level of declaration, becomes anything but that on the level of description, because the eel, passing through a waterfowl, is excreted intact. The waterfowl merely conveys the eel; it does not absorb or assimilate it. The waterfowl, like the mind-machine and hence the writer, must transport truth through language, but without tainting it by history or culture. Instead, the historical event must be purely lifted from the stream of experience, transmitted through a transparent language, and recorded as sacred or uncivil history. Paradoxically, however, the metaphor of the waterfowl suggests both the violence of consumption and the inevitability of death as necessary stages in the digestive process, while at the same time it suppresses them by the image of the eel "living and intact." However much an eel may look like feces, Thoreau cannot allow the possibility of excrement upon the scene of writing. The eel, then, represents the perfect figurative substitution for an impossible problem—how to base writing on the experience of being in the world, not only its perception but its incorporation, and yet repress death and decay as necessary stages of being in history. Paradoxically, the writer must taste but not destroy.

In his *Journal,* Thoreau laments the fact that words are subject to distortion. "Things are said with reference to certain conventions or existing institutions, not absolutely." Words, like eels, are apt to be transformed radically by their journey through the world or the stomach. But here, what distorts the perfect script, that is, words said "absolutely," are "conventions and existing institutions." When writing conforms to culture, it destroys authenticity.

The desire for a transparent perceiver, the perfect uncivil historian, becomes one with the desire for a transparent language, a monosemic system of communication that is artless and transcultural. For Thoreau, a perceptual event rightly described is the spirit. It is an eternal presence, resisting the transformations of time and space and therefore of culture. Early in his *Journal,* Thoreau writes, "A word which may be translated into every dialect, and suggests a truth to every mind, is the most perfect work of human art; and as it may be breathed and taken on our lips, and, as it were, become the product of our physical organs, as its sense is of our intellectual, it is the nearest to life itself" (1:370). But as "human" art, such words enter into a problematic relationship to both the writer and the world. The question for Thoreau is how to write an uncivil history free from the distorting lens of language entrapped in history and culture. For Thoreau, "a fact truly and absolutely stated is taken out of the region of common sense and acquires a mythologic or universal significance." Ideally it is possible to "say it and have done with it" and to "express it without expressing yourself" (3:85). Once achieved, the style of this language would be oracular, "in which the matter is all in all, and the manner nothing at all" (3:86).

To have the perfect journal entry in which time is undone by accurate description of eternal truths, an "artless" language is necessary, with "manner" consigned to the bin of artifice. The means to acquire this "universal" language Thoreau usually describes by a perceptual analogy: correct seeing leads to correct saying. The implication is that when Thoreau perceives correctly, his writing testifies to the regenerative potential of the American landscape and the American self.

But inherent in the descriptive passages that elaborate the scene of writing are both an error in perception that prevents "celebratory" rhetoric and lingering doubts about language itself as a transparent medium. The scene of writing can become instead a place of distortion and excrement. Error cannot be kept from the eye of the beholder, for it adheres to the very medium of communication—language itself. The dream of a purely "natural" language that transcends art is tainted with images of dirt and decay.

Death stalks Thoreau even as he attempts to outwit it in the journal form. He subdues chronological time only to confront the paradoxes of language, an enigma he faces throughout his writings. The ideal of accurate description that synthesizes the real and the ideal proves elusive; his passages on journal writing often hint at failure and confused purposes, rather than achieved glory. But whatever the limits of the journal form and Thoreau's conception of language, in the *Journal* he experiments boldly with the recording of perceptual events, moments in time that crystallize into signs of promise and renewal. The *Journal* as periodic composition, anchored in the boundaries of dates and exact time, is still the necessary base from which to write uncivil history.

THREE

Views from the Walden Settlement

In both *A Week on the Concord and Merrimack Rivers* and the *Journal,* Thoreau travels beyond civilization and enters the historical time of nature, reclaiming not only vast amounts of unrecorded history, but also vanished cultures. In *Walden,* this clear opposition between nature and civilization diminishes. In writing the history of his settlement at Walden Pond, Thoreau attempts instead to reconcile himself to the necessities of culture, that is, restraints he can distinguish from civilized entrapments, and to record his most sustained vision of redemptive history. Like John Stuart Mill and Thomas Carlyle, Thoreau separates culture from civilization. In 1838, Mill writes that the "culture of the human being had been carried to no ordinary height, and human nature had exhibited many of its noblest manifestations, not in Christian countries only, but in the ancient world, in Athens, Sparta, Rome; nay, even barbarians, as the Germans, or still more unmitigated savages, the wild Indians, and again the Chinese, the Egyptians, the Arabs, all had their own education, their own culture. . . ."[1] As such, the concept of culture allows for a comparative analysis of human societies and a leveling of the progressive ideals of civilization. As Raymond Williams notes, in the nineteenth century, culture became "the court of appeal in which real values were determined, usually in opposition to the 'factitious' values thrown up by the market and similar operations of society,"[2] that is, by the mechanistic, industrial workshop that was civilization.

At Walden, Thoreau establishes a culture that both critiques civilization and validates the redemptive history of Walden Pond. In this culture, nature is not severely harnessed or pushed to the boundaries of the civil, but is the essential foundation of the cultural. Accordingly, this history moves beyond the individual observation of nature to the description of a cultural plan, enhancing the observation of redeemed time. Encompassing accounts of geographical sites, economies of the household, species arrangements and the psychological process of perception, *Walden* delineates a cultural space in nature, setting its geographical boundaries as tightly as John Winthrop and William Bradford did for their utopias.[3] Walden, a spot on a map and a cultural entity, becomes the "sedes," or seat, from which the uncivil history of the natural world can be fully known.

In this pursuit, Thoreau departs radically from the excursion motif found in *A Week* and the *Journal*. He still favors first-person discourse and observation in *Walden,* but he abandons the pattern of the lone traveller leaving civilization and immersing himself in the wild in order to return home with his account of redemptive history. In *Walden* Thoreau confronts the materiality of culture and the economics of the household. Even though the Walden settlement represents a culture of only one, through it Thoreau reassesses the necessary points of alignment between human and natural structures.[4] More than the construction of a symbol sequence or a myth of creation that stresses the "constant theme" of "spiritual awakening," *Walden* analyzes the material dimensions of culture and its effects on history, perception, and ultimately, language.[5]

In establishing the culture of Walden, Thoreau begins by reconstructing its economic history. The observer of redemptive history who walks through nature is no longer free merely to see and describe; now the site of observation must first be understood and analyzed. The initial step in settlement for Thoreau involves a purification of the foundations of culture that rest on human labor. Illusory needs must be exposed and eliminated. Each item of a new economy, a system of organizing the household, must be analyzed and judged. True necessities must be recognized as such and acquired through "free labor." Accordingly, for the first eighty pages of *Walden*, Thoreau acts as an accountant, constructing a system of labor that requires the least amount of days to accomplish. The worth of each "commodity" must be measured: "the cost of a thing is the amount of what I will call life which is required to be exchanged for it, immediately or in the long run" (p. 31).[6] Consumption must be rationalized and made accountable so that the amount of labor needed for purchases may be determined. The freeing of time, a prerequisite of the new culture, and the moral adherence to voluntary poverty are the goals for this economy of one.

Once he has cleared a space, the individual then erects a house capable of sustaining "human culture," where his actions will not be hampered by the debilitating demands of a fickle civilization. The material structure of the house guards against the intrusions of civilization and fosters the continuous perception of nature. In one sense, Thoreau's hut is like Martin Heidegger's concept of a dwelling, in which "to dwell, to be set at peace, means to remain at peace within the free, the preserve, the free sphere that safeguards each thing in its nature. *The fundamental character of dwelling is this sparing and preserving.*"[7] But unlike Heidegger, Thoreau has an empirical need to assert a particular geographical site, which leads him to a pragmatic consideration of space. There is, as Thoreau remarks, no cleared land left in America nor even suitable homes to purchase. Everything must therefore be rethought and restructured on space already claimed before human culture can be renewed. "Before we can adorn our houses with beautiful objects the walls must be stripped, and our lives must be stripped, and beautiful housekeeping and beautiful living be laid for a foundation: now, a taste for the beautiful is most cultivated out of doors, where there is no house and no housekeeper" (p. 38). The major activity of *Walden* is to build a house and to cultivate the soil, that is, to produce a human culture where health, free labor, and productivity abound. In this way, *Walden* is more a fable of the renewal of culture than a "fable of the renewal of life."[8] The house must become the "sedes" from which the apprehension of nature can commence and continue over time. "With this more substantial shelter about me, I had made some progress toward settling in the world. This frame, so slightly clad, was a sort of crystallization around me, and reacted on the builder" (p. 85).

When nature is viewed from the cultural site, however, a paradoxical relationship between nature and culture results. The house provides both a "settling" into the world and a necessary but acceptable entrapment: "I found myself suddenly neighbor to the birds; not by having imprisoned one, but having caged myself near them" (p. 85). The house, like the body, becomes an inevitable limit from which nature is beheld: "Wherever I sat, there I might live, and the landscape radiated from me accordingly" (p. 81). Thus, the site constitutes perception and adds an additional enclosing structure to the materiality of the body.

Once the site is established, its geographical features are essential to the new relationship between nature and culture that is to be explored:

I was seated by the shore of a small pond, about a mile and a half south of the village of Concord and somewhat higher than

it, in the midst of an extensive wood between that town and
Lincoln, and about two miles south of that our only field
known to fame, Concord Battle Ground; but I was so low in
the woods that the opposite shore, half a mile off, like the rest,
covered with wood, was my most distant horizon. (p. 86)

In this instance, the site of the cabin, which is analogous to the "I"
of the speaker, necessarily restricts all attempts to perceive the natural world to the limit of a half-mile horizon. All objects are confined within the structure of this spatially contracted vista. To build
a house in the woods is to accept these additional limits as necessary.

In contrast to the walker with a moving point of view, the settler,
though he wanders out from and back to the site, must affirm these
limits of fixed space. In *Walden,* Thoreau juxtaposes movement and
stasis, underscoring the advantages of each. In "Where I Lived,
and What I Lived For," the settler gains freedom by walking around
his site, constantly varying his angle of vision and rotating on the
axis of charted space. When Thoreau views the landscape from a
"hill top near by" southward across the pond, he can change the
view by "standing on tiptoe" or shifting "in the other directions."
What is seen from this bounded view provides then figure/ground
reversals for familiar objects. "When I looked across the pond from
this peak toward the Sudbury meadows, which in time of flood I
distinguished elevated perhaps by a mirage in their seething valley,
like a coin in a basin, all the earth beyond the pond appeared like
a thin crust insulated and floated even by this small sheet of intervening water, and I was reminded that this on which I dwelt was
but *dry land*" (p. 87).

When Thoreau walks around his site, multiple points of view
open up paradoxical visions. The land can become the "figure" in
the "ground" of the water, whereas "ordinary" apprehension reverses this perception. Land is usually dominant, water the variant,
but when the angle of viewing is carefully perceived, objects flip
back and forth, changing and inverting frames. Mobility leads to
an understanding of perception that is densely contextual.

But when the settler is confined within the house and limited in
the ability to assume physically different points of view, he relies
on the mind to understand the phenomenal world. Thoreau realizes that the body always limits sight, but the house pushes the
limits further. "Though the view from my door was still more contracted, I did not feel crowded or confined in the least. There was

pasture enough for my imagination" (p. 87). In the house, where sight is restricted to the view from either a door or a window, Thoreau still opens up the apprehension of his world through threads of association from remembered experiences or readings. Basically an association machine, the mind is allowed the time and leisure to make connections within confined space. The house then becomes the site from which the products of culture emerge. Indeed, for Thoreau it serves precisely this purpose; it is where he composes *A Week* and the first draft of *Walden*.

Reading, sounds, and solitude also blend in the house to create a sense of authentic human culture. First, the house is justified by its conduciveness to communication with the writings of poets and other thinkers. "My residence was more favorable, not only to thought, but to serious reading, than a university; and though I was beyond the range of the ordinary circulating library, I had more than ever come within the influence of those books which circulate round the world, whose sentences were first written on bark, and are now merely copied from time to time on to linen paper" (p. 99). Preferable to the church and the institutions of learning, the house becomes the site of cultural enhancement, the place to sift through language and the classical works of varied civilizations. The shell around the observer encourages the perceiver to become a reader of written texts, what are to Thoreau the "choicest of relics," more "universal than any other work of art" (p. 102). The materiality of the book and the stasis required of the reader necessitate a fixed spot denied the saunterer.

Second, in the house, Thoreau is forced to explore more intensely senses other than sight—in particular, his sense of hearing. Even though he consistently shows throughout his journals an interest in the sounds of both the forest and its adjacent technological intruders such as the railroad and the telegraph pole,[9] in "Sounds," Thoreau juxtaposes confined sight with the expansiveness of hearing:

As I sit at my window this summer afternoon, hawks are circling about my clearing; the tantivy of wild pigeons, flying by twos and threes athwart my view, or perching restless on the white-pine boughs behind my house, gives a voice to the air; a fishhawk dimples the glassy surface of the pond and brings up a fish; a mink steals out of the marsh before my door and seizes a frog by the shore; the sedge is bending under the weight of the reed-birds flitting hither and thither; and for the last half hour I have heard the rattle of railroad cars, now dying away and then reviving like the beat of a partridge, conveying travellers from Boston to the country. (p. 114)

The sounds of the railroad with its sublime technology as well as the noise of the pigeons permeate the space of the house. Later, the noise of wagons over bridges, the melancholy hooting of owls, and the abrasive baying of dogs filter through the evening air. Thoreau freely moralizes about what he hears and continues his apprehension that the world is not limited by the enclosed frame of a window; confined space still permits both sense experience and the play of the mind.

Third, while the house protects against the ravages of nature, its placement in the woods permits a perception of the culture embedded within nature that leads to a sense of well-being in solitude, dispelling the ennui of village life. Thoreau's house in the midst of the woods exudes an "infinite and unaccountable friendliness all at once like an atmosphere sustaining me, as made the fancied advantages of human neighborhood insignificant . . ." (p. 132). Nature is valued as the "perennial source of life" and the keeper of all "universal, vegetable, botanic medicines." A culture, whether of one or many, must sustain this fundamental perception of encompassment by the noncultural. As long as culture is based solely on an arrangement of human affairs, institutions, and commodities, it is prone to sickness and malaise. Only in the site within the woods can solitude and self be thoroughly explored. Culture in this way leads to self-knowledge. Paradoxically, the house becomes the site from which to grasp the essential doubleness of the human mind. Within the house one becomes conscious of the self as a "human entity; the scene, so to speak, of thoughts and affections; and [I] am sensible of a certain doubleness by which I can stand as remote from myself as from another" (p. 135). Even though the house becomes what Gaston Bachelard calls a "center of concentrated solitude"[10] from which true culture, in the sense of the awakening of the soul, is made possible, it reinforces a split between matter and spirit. In effect, Thoreau attributes to the "scene" many characteristics of the self. "Thoughts and affections" can be considered qualities of the mind, but now they become characteristics of a "human entity," existing within a particular geographical and cultural space. In a sense, Thoreau creates a mind within a mind that is able to distance itself from the cultural space enclosing it.

Establishing the house itself, however, provides a necessary distance from which to look at both the nature of the woods and the culture of the village. In "Visitors," Thoreau asserts that society does not require physical closeness. Men and women may choose to live next to each other, but out of a fear that goes beyond that of the storms of nature. Village culture is predominantly a "league for mutual defence." War and criminality are the hidden motives behind community. Hence, Thoreau senses the dangers of village life: "The old and infirm and the timid thought most of sickness, and sudden accident and death" (p. 153). Also, when he saunters in the village, it appears like "a great news room" (p. 167) or an advertising agency: "Signs were hung out on all sides to allure [the traveller]; some to catch him by the appetite, as the tavern and victualling cellar; some by the fancy, as the dry goods store and the jeweller's; and others by the hair or the feet or the skirts, as the barber, the shoemaker, or the tailor" (p. 168). The commodities and labor of the town are premised on seduction and material gratification. How unlike the labor of the bean-field, whose end is to perceive nature as a garden set in the wilderness and to give back to man both time and thought. "Haste and heedlessness," products of large farms and villages, are the veneers of nineteenth-century cultural arrangements.

In the first half of *Walden*, then, Thoreau traces the building of the house and its advantages to the cultural life of its inhabitant, contrasting the civilization of the village with the cultural life in the woods. But what is to be gained in terms of writing uncivil history by such elaborate preparations? How does the house or its idea contribute to a vision of redeemed time? Most importantly, what the house makes possible is the observation of natural events over extended periods of time. Thoreau as settler begins to think less in terms of the unique moment than in terms of a representative year that captures the "laws" of natural sequence. The discrete moment is not as important as the observable repetition of events that might signify a pattern of change and hence a law of redemption.

The second half of *Walden*, accordingly, explores further the advantages to the inhabitant of a house within nature where he can "camp down" amid natural phenomena and observe their minute details over time.[11] More densely descriptive, the latter part of *Walden* concerns itself not only with the psychological processes of perception, as do those sections of the *Journal* (1850–1854) from which much of *Walden* is drawn, but with the inference of laws from various observations. The description of seasonal changes dominates as the approach of spring is described through the landscape.[12] In particular, by means of repeated trips back and forth from the house to the woods, Thoreau observes the melting of the pond and deduces general laws about its shape. The saunterer turned settler has a more effective base from which to conduct the experiment of seeing and writing uncivil history.[13]

Hence, by becoming a settler, Thoreau attempts to merge the perception of redeemed time with laws about the sequence of natural events. He is serious when he writes in the early pages of *Walden* that "when one man has reduced a fact of the imagination to be a fact to his understanding, I foresee that all men will at length establish their lives on that basis" (p. 11). It is not enough to imagine; Thoreau must also know. In the second half of *Walden*, the settler measures and surveys the landscape, validating not only intuition, but also reason.[14]

Before Thoreau develops fully the laws he discovers at Walden Pond and describes its uncivil history, he includes two episodes that comment on and implicitly critique his settlement efforts. As Thoreau begins to describe in greater detail the natural environment around his house, he continues to reflect on the basic problems of cultural life. "Baker Farm" and "House-Warming" pose significant questions about the relationship between the individual and cultural space, whose virtue is a protective, simplifying structure for human life, and whose terror is a stifling entrapment for the human spirit. "Baker Farm" begins with Thoreau rambling through the woods around his house, visiting the sacred landscape of birches and lichens. Observing a "rainbow's arch" about his shadow, he plays with the idea that he is "one of the elect." The walker-saint, however, is abruptly tested when he comes upon John Field, an immigrant Irishman, and his disheveled home. Thoreau attempts to educate Field by telling him about his own labor-saving life style, his voluntary poverty and abstinence, and his efficient and cheaply built home, but the conversation halts in face of the cultural differences between the men. Thoreau blames the "culture of an Irishman" for the immigrant's entanglement within exploitive labor, a demanding family, and misdirected material desires for things such as "tea, and coffee, and meat every day." Faced with the paradox of the immigrant seeking an illusory freedom in America, Thoreau has to redefine the vision of "the only true America" as "that country where you are at liberty to pursue such a mode of life as may enable you to do without these [tea, and coffee, and meat], and where the state does not endeavor to compel you to sustain the slavery and war and other superfluous expenses which directly or indirectly result from the use of such things" (p. 205). Creating America means more than claiming new geographical space: to Thoreau it also involves a radical departure from the material and economic expectations of the inherited culture. Thoreau's utopia of one at Walden Pond stands against cultural determination, and his plea to "live simply" is ultimately a stance against cultures that manufacture false needs and their accompanying military systems that breed on material gratification.

But Thoreau clearly admits how inapplicable his vision of cultural space is to the family of John Field. They stare back at him, sigh, and go on with their lives. An exemplary saint Thoreau is not. As solution to the relationship between culture and nature, he produces only a statement of self-justification, not a realistic blueprint for cultural reform.[15] Sensing his ineffectualness, Thoreau fights back with a call to "adventure": "Grow wild according to thy nature, like these sedges and brakes, which will never become English hay. . . . Let not to get a living be thy trade, but thy sport. Enjoy the land, but own it not. Through want of enterprise and faith men are where they are, buying and selling, and spending their lives like serfs" (pp. 207–208). Thus, Thoreau forsakes the model of the settler with his newly constructed house as a persuasive reply to Field's life; instead, he implicitly returns to the model of the saunterer who escapes the constrictions of the debilitating demands of culture by travel.

In "House-Warming," however, Thoreau returns to the need for the specific settlement of *Walden* through a discussion of masonry and a utopian dream. Preparing for winter, he constructs the chimney of his hut along carefully planned lines and considers "that, if it proceeded slowly, it was calculated to endure a long time" (p. 241), even beyond the life of the main structure. The addition of fire is another justification for Thoreau's cultural space: "I now first began to inhabit my house, I may say, when I began to use it for warmth as well as shelter" (p. 242). Thoreau does not abandon the need for settlement because of John Field's dilemma. Indeed, he expresses an even more extravagant plan for house-building.

In this chapter Thoreau's dream vision of the ideal cultural space combines simplicity of design and intent with "enduring materials" to create a "golden age" for men. The settlement of his dreams, like the chimney, would be built for permanence and protection. A shelter for the "weary traveller," it contains "all the essentials of a house, and nothing for house-keeping" (p. 243). Not the built and abandoned hut for one, it is a continuing structure for community habitation, "where some may live in the fire-place, some in the recess of a window, and some on settles, some at one end of the hall, some at another, and some aloft on rafters with the spiders, if they choose" (p. 243). Nothing here is hidden from sight, except perhaps the shifting shadows on the ceiling. It is a house "where you can see all the treasures of the house at one view . . ." (p. 243). The objects that constitute cultural space are all seen by one set of eyes. A perfect correspondence exists between the limits of individual spatial perception and the world beheld. No gothic mansion haunts Thoreau's landscape, no obsessions with drawers, chests, closets, and secret spaces.[16] Instead, he dreams of a culture based upon the simplicity of individual vision, by which both matter and vision enjoy an enduring stability. The ideal cultural space is where "you can see so necessary a thing as a barrel or a ladder, so convenient a thing as a cupboard, and hear the pot boil, and pay your respects to the fire that cooks your dinner and the oven that bakes your bread, and the necessary furniture and utensils are the chief ornaments" (p. 244). This vision of cultural utopia, though imitated on a small scale by Thoreau's house, extends beyond a stance of radical individualism to one of community. As such, it provides a commentary on the Walden settlement.

*   *   *

While "Baker's Farm" and "House-Warming" indicate the limits of Thoreau's cultural experiment, from "The Ponds" until the end of *Walden,* Thoreau describes the paradoxes of perception and the search for laws. In particular, the perception of color, a topic engrossing his attention during the 1850s, epitomizes for him the complex relationship between the eye and the object. In "The Ponds," Thoreau records the intensely varied effects of light on the surface of the pond, and how shifting the point of view and contextual frame produces different color tones.[17] The psychological and contextual processes of vision focus his attention. Basically, Thoreau fixes the apprehension of color to the variable of distance—close at hand the Concord water looks one way, at a distance, another. Atmospheric conditions, he adds, greatly affect the view from a distance. He then describes the color of the water from varying points of view: first, from a boat, second, from a hill-top, and third, against different backgrounds such as the shore or the railroad sand-bank. In this section, Thoreau also develops a description from a single view: "I have discerned a matchless and indescribable light blue, such as watered or changeable silks and sword blades suggest, more cerulean than the sky itself, alternating with the original dark green on the opposite sides of the waves, which last appeared but muddy in comparison" (p. 177). But he also recognizes that "Walden is blue at one time and green at another, even from the same point of view" (p. 176). As an instance of viewing, Thoreau stresses the comparative and metamorphic apprehension of color. Color is totally dependent on context, defined by its relationship to other colored shapes of both nature and culture, its distance from the eye, and the general atmospheric conditions. The world the eyes behold is in constant flux.

Yet, as Thoreau uncovers these slippages between the eye and the object and the limits of the individual view, he is again drawn to a language system and a technique for vision that attempt to create stability for viewing the landscape. As in his earlier writings, Thoreau clearly links the perception and description of Walden Pond with cartographical grids that posit a point of view beyond that of the individual observer. No longer a particular site viewed from a limited position, the pond is described through the familiar figurative device of the map developed in both *A Week* and the post-1850 journal entries:

> It is a clear and deep green well, half a mile long and a mile and three quarters in circumference, and contains about sixty-one and a half acres; a perennial spring in the midst of pine and oak woods, without any visible inlet or outlet except by the clouds and evaporation. The surrounding hills rise abruptly from the water to the height of forty to eighty feet, though on the south-east and east they attain to about one hundred and one hundred and fifty feet respectively, within a quarter and a third of a mile. (pp. 175–76)

To visualize this description, the reader must also construct a map and imagine the relative three-dimensional shape of the pond. Measurement again becomes a key trope for Thoreau's description of nature, and the settler, in his repeated walks from the site, brings the tools and technologies of culture to create the mapped perception of the pond, at once a static and transcendent view.

Increasingly in *Walden*, Thoreau's desire for cultural stability within the natural world goes beyond the real or imagined house. Culture invades the very act of perception as he attempts to find laws and principles in the natural world. Perhaps Thoreau's developing awareness of the inherent instability of perception accounts for his constant use of technological grids, derived ironically from the culture of nineteenth-century America, to fix space and time and to describe meticulously the verifiable laws that emerge during the second half of *Walden*. These technologies, like the hut at the pond, also become temporary shelters against disorientation in a natural world of constant flux. Like the house, they become necessary frames from which to behold the world, deduce its laws, and write its redemptive history.

"House-Warming" provides a good example of how Thoreau's observations are interwoven with the technologies of the nineteenth century and are necessary to his search for laws. It contains not only the ideal vision of culture and a recognition of the fluidity of perception, but also a method to stabilize observations structured by measured grids of space, a strict adherence to observations along a temporal index, and the final assertion of laws logically induced from empirical data. When Thoreau begins to describe the ice on the pond, the result is essentially a catalogue of different views based on distance variables between the eye and the object. Atmospheric conditions contribute to what is seen to such an extent that they become constitutive of perception. But Thoreau then shifts to a more systematic description of the ice:

> If you examine it closely the morning after it freezes, you find that the greater part of the bubbles, which at first appeared to be within it, are against its under surface, and that more are continually rising from the bottom; while the ice is as yet comparatively solid and dark, that is, you see the water through it. These bubbles are from an eightieth to an eighth of an inch in diameter, very clear and beautiful, and you see your face reflected in them through the ice. There may be thirty or forty of them to a square inch. There are also already within the ice narrow oblong perpendicular bubbles about half an inch long, sharp cones with the apex upward; or oftener, if the ice is quite fresh, minute spherical bubbles one directly above another, like a string of beads. (pp. 246–47)

Placement in relation to the eye, and the apprehension of shape within measured grids of space structure the description of the ice. Thoreau continues in this fashion for another page and a half. By settling near the frozen ice he has the unique opportunity to describe in detail an object that is somewhat static over a certain period of time. Its changes fluctuate less than, say, the colors of Walden Pond or the reflection of the moon on the water; but another purpose underlies Thoreau's examination of the air bubbles' shape, size, and distance from the surface of the ice. Over a period of time, all these descriptions permit Thoreau to induce a theory about the thundering sound of ice when it melts. "I inferred that the infinite number of minute bubbles which I had first seen against the under surface of the ice were now frozen in likewise, and that each, in its degree, had operated like a burning glass on the ice beneath to melt and rot it. These are the little air-guns which contribute to make the ice crack and whoop" (p. 248).

By holding constant the description as single frames over a period of time, Thoreau discovers a principle of succession to account for the sound of the pond. Only by building a house in the woods and thence observing the natural phenomena over time can Thoreau employ natural description to arrive at potential *laws* by which to apprehend the world. In this process, imagination is secondary to the ability to observe, order, and describe natural phenomena in temporal sequence, an ability which through the uses of measurement and reason produces a theory or law that explains a natural event. Again, the discovery of this law seems to be a necessary prerequisite to the writing of uncivil history. The observer of natural events is asked to do more than witness a redemptive moment; he or she must understand the sequence and verifiable patterns leading up to any sign of rebirth.

This process of inducing a "law" from careful observation becomes even more imperative when Thoreau comes to determine the shape of Walden Pond. "As I was desirous to recover the long lost bottom of Walden Pond, I surveyed it carefully, before the ice broke up, early in '46, with compass and chain and sounding line" (p. 285). Thoreau first recounts folk stories about Walden Pond's bottom, but then proceeds on the premise that the bottom can be discerned and fixed spatially. "I fathomed it easily with a cod-line and a stone weighing about a pound and a half, and could tell accurately when the stone left the bottom, by having to pull so much harder before the water got underneath to help me. The greatest depth was exactly one hundred and two feet . . ." (p. 287). This factual knowledge of limit, however, still urges Thoreau on to applaud the pond's depth. "I am thankful that this pond was made deep and pure for a symbol. While men believe in the infinite some ponds will be thought to be bottomless" (p. 287). But Thoreau's method undermines the belief in the infinite. He has to assume that the pond's depth can be measured.

A major distinction must be made between Thoreau's attempt to fix the depth of Walden Pond, an issue of concern to such critics as Walter Benn Michaels and Joseph Allen Boone, and his urge to predict where the deepest point could be in any pond and fix the *shape* of the bottom.[18] It is in pursuit of a mapped geometrical grid that the possibility of inducing a natural law emerges. Thoreau begins to work from the depth to chart the dimensions of the pond. "In one instance, on a line arbitrarily chosen, the depth did not vary more than one foot in thirty rods; and generally, near the middle, I could calculate the variation for each one hundred feet in any direction beforehand within three or four inches" (p. 288). Thoreau sketches carefully the grid of measurement and then notices a pattern for his calculations. "When I had mapped the pond by the scale of ten rods to an inch, and put down the soundings, more than a hundred in all, I observed this remarkable coincidence. Having noticed that the number indicating the greatest depth was apparently in the centre of the map, I laid a rule on the map lengthwise, and then breadthwise, and found, to my surprise, that the line of greatest length intersected the line of greatest breadth *exactly* at the point of greatest depth . . ." (p. 289). Only after a hundred calculations have been carefully made and correlated on the grid of the map does a general "law" appear that could geometrically predict the point of greatest depth in a body of water.

Thoreau tries out his theory on White Pond with fair success, but he does not practice his surveying techniques on other bodies of water. Instead, he develops his understanding of theory and reconciles it with his experiments in point of view. Thoreau speculates that "if we knew all the laws of Nature, we should need only one fact, or the description of one actual phenomenon, to infer all the particular results at that point" (p. 290). But he is fully aware that only a "few laws" are known and puts the blame for this ignorance on the fact that individuals are confined to "instances which we detect." Nature, of course, is a system of stable laws without "any confusion or irregularity." The basic problem of knowledge comes from the necessary limitations of human perception. "The particular laws are as our points of view, as, to the traveller, a mountain outline varies with every step, and it has an infinite number of profiles, though absolutely but one form. Even when cleft or bored through it is not comprehended in its entireness" (pp. 290–91). The traveller in constant motion can never penetrate through variation to law or absolute form. But implicitly, perhaps, the settler with his incessant return to the same phenomena over time, his use of tools, and his reasoning skills can come closer to the "laws" of nature.

Thoreau attempts to record the minute variations "with every step" in his *Journal*, but in *Walden* he methodically tries to induce an "absolute" law for predicting depth through the collecting and analyzing of sequenced observations. The shape of Walden Pond cannot be "seen" by the individual in the scene. Only on paper where the pond is drawn by "the scale of ten rods to an inch" can the shape be represented. Map-drawing is hence a dominant trope for the book.[19] It is as important to Thoreau as the apprehension of the symbolic in nature. It demands understanding and reason. It suggests order and intelligence.

In addition, Thoreau uses his discovery about the "law" of Walden's shape to analogize moral behavior. The character of a man, likewise, can be charted, "but draw lines through the length and breadth of the aggregate of a man's particular daily behaviors and waves of life into his coves and inlets, and where they intersect will be the height or depth of his character" (p. 291). Observable patterns, then, are applicable not only to nature, but to human actions as well. Thoreau continually hopes that his observations will correlate with the dimensions of moral character, and that measurements in nature will become measurements in man. Intending to bring more accuracy to ethical vision, Thoreau looks to nature to find more precise ways of talking about the dimensions of character.

Once Thoreau links his discoveries about nature with human behavior, however, he comes back to the experiment of viewing the natural world without precise moral analogies. Ironically, his observations often lead to a perception of flux, not order, in nature. For instance, in "The Pond in Winter," he detects the instability of the earth's surface through the tools of the surveyor: "While I was surveying, the ice, which was sixteen inches thick, undulated under a slight wind like water" (p. 292). Ice, an example of solid water, is now seen from a different point of view to move like a fluid substance. What appears to be is not. With his relatively crude instruments of vision, Thoreau notes the inability to fix matter in space. "At one rod from the shore its greatest fluctuation, when observed by means of a level on land directed toward a graduated staff on the ice, was three quarters of an inch, though the ice appeared firmly attached to the shore" (p. 293). Through technology Thoreau demonstrates that the stability of the earth is basically an illusion. Not only does the viewer walk through nature constantly changing the point of view and hence the object seen, but, theoretically, the object could be constantly moving also. Thoreau speculates on an apprehension of space and matter inimical to visual certainty. "Who knows but if our instruments were delicate enough we might detect an undulation in the crust of the earth?" (p. 293). The mirage quality of sight again is foremost. Thoreau cannot help but record that vision plays with reality. "Sometimes, also, when the ice was covered with shallow puddles, I saw a double shadow of myself, one standing on the head of the other, one on the ice, the other on the trees or hillside" (p. 293). Doubleness exists not only within the mind but in the act of perception, implying a complex relationship between objects and their context against which naive observations dissolve. Variation becomes then an unnerving reality threatening all attempts to write uncivil history.

Despite his observations on fluctuating matter, "The Pond in Winter" demonstrates how Thoreau attempts to use the map as a form of representation that stabilizes space and gets beyond the inherent problems of the individual view. That view may be able to delve into imaginative associations for what is seen and open up the world to others; but many views must be recorded systematically before any "law" of nature emerges, preparing the way for a more verifiable description of the pond's history.

Walden's climactic "Spring" chapter is usually interpreted as a tour de force for Thoreau's mythopoetic or symbolist method, whereby sequences of images such as "ice-thaw-flux" become "symbols of gradual transformation," or a natural event such as the "thawing of the sand and clay bank" becomes a model of "mythmaking."[20] Before any description of redeemed time or epiphany is possible, however, speculation on natural laws must provide an underpinning for the scene of spring. For instance, the temperature differences between Walden and Flint's ponds provide Thoreau empirical data to speculate on why Walden Pond is so late in melting. He also supports his earlier observations on the ice and asserts a causal explanation for the "thundering of the pond": "The cracking and booming of the ice indicate a change of temperature" (p. 301).

The melting of the ponds is, of course, on one level, a symbol to Thoreau of redemption and immortality. He views the return of spring to the frozen earth with wonder as well as scientific calculation. But he cannot resist ordering the occurrence. He lists the dates of the thaw in various years and considers them verification of the first "signs of spring." Thoreau values Walden Pond in particular because it "indicates better than any water hereabouts the absolute progress of the season, being least affected by transient changes of temperature" (p. 299). Walden becomes, then, a reliable predictor of spring and hence implies a principle of succession, guaranteeing rebirth. Walden Pond "has its law to which it thunders obedience when it should as surely as the buds expand in the spring. The earth is all alive and covered with papillae. The largest pond is as sensitive to atmospheric changes as the globule of mercury in its tube" (p. 302). An enormous water clock and thermometer, Walden Pond acts like precision technology, signaling the law of rebirth.

Thoreau's continual desire to record the signs of spring as both symbol and law is nowhere more apparent than in the *Journal* for the years between 1851 and 1854, when he is also revising the *Walden* manuscript. Out of all the various recorded "signs," Thoreau selects the thawing of the sand and clay in the deep cut by the railroad to culminate his epiphany of spring. In "The Pond in Winter," he indicated the potential of matter to become fluid; now he achieves that potential in the transformation of inorganic substance into organic. But the motion of the sand flow does not indicate the limit of individual perception or the difficulty of inferring a natural law. Instead it becomes part of a system of tropes that triumphs in the paradoxical vision of the inorganic become organic.

Thoreau is initially concerned with recording how the sand assumes "the forms of sappy leaves or vines, making heaps of pulpy sprays a foot or more in depth, and resembling, as you look down on them, the laciniated lobed and imbricated thalluses of some lichens . . ." (p. 305). The point of view from above looking down on the sand flow establishes the physical relationship between the eye and the natural phenomena. The correspondences that develop between the sand and leaves, vines, and thalluses are not between a natural object and a mental analogy; for Thoreau the correspondence is *in* matter. The sand *itself* resembles vegetation so that the analogies exist in the horizontal world of the material. Thoreau observes in the vestige of the sand flow a visible paradox, inorganic matter in organiclike forms. If earlier the earth's fluidity has signified a relentless movement in matter, here the movement signifies design. Not merely in motion, the earth's thawing adheres to both a principle of resemblance with vegetative forms and a sequence of ordered stages:

> When the flowing mass reaches the drain at the foot of the bank it spreads out flatter into *strands,* the separate streams losing their semi-cylindrical form and gradually becoming more flat and broad, running together as they are more moist, till they form an almost flat *sand,* still variously and beautifully shaded, but in which you can trace the original forms of vegetation; till at length, in the water itself, they are converted into *banks,* like those formed off the mouths of rivers, and the forms of vegetation are lost in the ripple marks on the bottom.
> (p. 305)

The sand flow moves according to a principle of successive shapes, providing an organizing principle for the description: "strands," "sand," and "banks" become the named stages for the progressive melting of the railroad banks. Thoreau infers that a principle of design activates all substance, no matter how seemingly inorganic. All shapes are hence reduced to one prototype, the leaf; and the language or grammar of the leaf and its law of developmental formation permeates the structure of matter. Unlike the potholes at Amoskeag Falls, the "plot" of this vestige represents a law of rebirth, not annihilation. All matter moves in regenerative patterns. This language of successive shapes is, then, as much a law to Thoreau as a symbol of redemption. "No wonder that the earth expresses itself outwardly in leaves, it so labors with the idea inwardly. The atoms have already learned this law, and are pregnant by it" (p. 306). The reduction to the leaf as prototype, or the original pattern of creation, is, of course, a desire for the vision of growth and regeneration as the principles underlying both the organic and the inorganic, hence both life and death. By spanning both, it nullifies the finality of death for Thoreau.

The law and symbol found in natural observation is then predictably applied to the structure of human nature, thus holding onto the moral dimensions of both. "What is man but a mass of thawing clay?" (p. 307). All nature, then, is the product of a primary idea that in itself reveals the promise of growth and redemption: "it seemed that this one hillside illustrated the principle of all the operations of Nature. The Maker of this earth but patented a leaf" (p. 308). Although the use of illustrative analogy would have been considered unreliable evidence of natural law by contemporary natural historians,[21] for Thoreau this apprehension of the prototype in the shape of the clay becomes proof that matter is not "inorganic," and hence cannot die. All life is part of a continual cycle of change and rebirth. The earth's "throes will heave our exuviae from their graves" (p. 309). Accordingly, the uncivil history of the earth also defies death:

> The earth is not a mere fragment of dead history, stratum upon stratum like the leaves of a book, to be studied by geologists and antiquaries chiefly, but living poetry like the leaves of a tree, which precede flower and fruit,—not a fossil earth, but a living earth. . . . (p. 309)

The ancient "book of nature," augmented with the romantic concept of organicism, also implies for Thoreau a rejuvenated form of history writing which as "living poetry" yields only the plot of renewal, uncovered in the sequence leaf, flower, and fruit. The earth as historical text conveys a principle of time that destroys the concept of death.

This law of regeneration, witnessed in both organic and inorganic matter, rests in part on the measuring of units and the fixing of dates for Walden's freezing and thawing. In order to write "Walden was dead and is alive again," the sentence toward which the entire text gravitates, Thoreau carefully describes the sequence of events that necessitate the rebirth of the pond. The settler at Walden is foremost a surveyor and collector of data, correlating the phenomena of spring into a dominant pattern that shapes a representative year.

Thoreau ends the "Spring" chapter by insisting upon the historical nature of his account: "Thus was my first year's life in the woods completed; and the second year was similar to it. I finally left Walden September 6th, 1847" (p. 319). A record of both an actual and representative year, in which Thoreau observed and described the vision and law of redemption, *Walden* becomes a masterpiece of uncivil history. For the most part, this history of Walden Pond is based upon what Thoreau calls the "hard bottom and rocks" of reality, that is, the necessity for "having a *point d'appui*, below freshet and frost and fire, and place where you might found a wall or a state, or set a lamp-post safely, or perhaps a gauge, not a Nilometer, but a Realometer, that future ages might know how deep a freshet of shams and appearances had gathered from time to time" (p. 98). And these instruments for registering "how real is real" involve nineteenth-century technologies for fixing the space and time of uncivil history throughout a significant amount of the descriptive passages in the final chapters of *Walden*.

*   *   *

Ironically, however, the ending of *Walden* practically obliterates the methods of the settler who with his "Realometer" both measures and witnesses uncivil history, and revives, almost in opposition, the saunterer who bathes in the "wildness" of nature. In the "Spring" chapter after Thoreau proclaims the rebirth of the pond, he nonetheless lingers on the fact of death. Pointing to the "pure and bright" light that fills the wild river valley, he declares that its existence proves immortality: "All things must live in such a light. O Death, where was thy sting? O Grave, where was thy victory, then?" (p. 317). This somewhat anticlimactic section, which shifts from the defeat of death through the cyclical process of rebirth to the victory over death by the traditional religious concept of immortality, changes the focus of the "Spring" chapter. Thoreau's rhetorical questions turn the chapter away from the image of the settler of Walden whose vision is aided by culture, to focus on the familiar wanderer in the woods whose vision is free from civilized restraints.

What follows this section is an exhortation to explore the wildness and not stagnate in the village. This passage, contained in the earliest version of *Walden*, restates the simple opposition between civilization and nature and practically forgets the intervening cultural basis of observing natural phenomena over time.[22] Basically an antisurveying plea, this paragraph stresses the nostalgia of an unmeasured apprehension of both space and time. "At the same time that we are earnest to explore and learn all things, we require that all things be mysterious and unexplorable, that land and sea be infinitely wild, unsurveyed and unfathomed by us because unfathomable" (pp. 317–18).

Moving even further from the importance of both law and symbol as the basis of uncivil history, the next section substitutes for a discussion of natural law, drawn from repeated observations, a description of natural excess. A limitless vigor becomes the means to declare redemption: "I love to see that Nature is so rife with life that myriads can be afforded to be sacrificed and suffered to prey on one another; that tender organizations can be so serenely squashed out of existence like pulp,—tadpoles which herons gobble up, and tortoises and toads run over in the road; and that sometimes it has rained flesh and blood!" (p. 318). Here, death is undone by the proclivity of the natural world to reproduce: "Poison is not poisonous after all, nor are any wounds fatal" (p. 318). Through negation and hyperbole, death is described as subsumed by the excessive cycles of destruction and reproduction. Rebirth, as a law underpinning carefully documented changes in the pond and the sand flow, recedes in importance.[23] The lessons of careful observation seem particularly irrelevant to this vision of nature's fecundity. Thoreau proclaims that both the slaughter of the individual and the species appear like "universal innocence" to the "wise man."

Even more emphatically, the "Conclusion" begins with the plea to leave civilization to regain health and the senses, reverting to the model of the saunterer who wanders beyond all boundaries and grids to the essential "healthy-minded" and ecstatic vision of the natural world. This chapter is filled with directives to "Explore thyself" and "Say what you have to say, not what you ought." And it contains the vision of the artist of Kouroo, who becomes the master of worldmaking by basically transcending time and hence history and culture: "As he made no compromise with Time, Time kept out of his way, and only sighed at a distance because he could not overcome him" (pp. 326–27). His commitment to crafting the perfect art object finally leads to triumph: "And now he saw by the heap of shavings still fresh at his feet, that, for him and his work, the former lapse of time had been an illusion . . ." (p. 327). Undoing his commitment to observe in the history of the earth "evidence" of redemption, Thoreau instead posits the art object and its maker as the sole place of worldmaking: "When the finishing stroke was put to his work, it suddenly expanded before the eyes of the astonished artist into the fairest of all the creations of Brahma. He had made a new system in making a staff, a world with full and fair proportions; in which, though the old cities and dynasties had passed away, fairer and more glorious ones had taken their places" (p. 327). The labor of the artist who strives for perfection is the final cause of all worldmaking. The patient crafting of the art object becomes the means to transcend time and space, and within the work emerges a "world of full and fair proportions." Only the text of *Walden,* but not the Walden settlement, can transcend time. Thoreau attributes this worldmaking power to both the artist and Brahma. In so doing, he retains his transcendental need to conflate human and divine creativity and abandons the naturalistic technology of observing and surveying. Brahma, not redeemed culture, is the ultimate creative force for Thoreau.

In this way, the artist of Kouroo is the American romantic whose role, as Charles Feidelson has pointed out, is to find the symbol constitutive of meaning.[24] By possessing imagination and intuition, the artist transcends the world of illusion, and hence matter and history, to join with a divine force in worldmaking. Symbols and myths function in similar ways for the artist as structuring devices that are universal and not tied to particular cultural visions. In this way they are perceived as transhistorical. Whether Thoreau gathers his symbols from nature, where they become for him a universal language,[25] or culls them from myth, where they share in the "characteristics of traditional myth," with universal features,[26] the myth or symbol reading of *Walden* ends in a triumph over any historical or cultural account.

In the "Conclusion," then, Thoreau develops a series of arguments and images that refute his methods of natural observation and undermine his attempts at fusing law and epiphany, reason and imagination, history and poetry. Significantly, the "Conclusion" has more in common with his essay "Walking," which Thoreau reworked for a period of eleven years as a popular lecture, and which can be read as a companion piece to *Walden*, if not its literary alter ego. In it, Thoreau insists on a solely "poetic" apprehension of nature that excludes any systematic collection of observations and measurements: "a successful life knows no law."[27] Excluding understanding and reason from the walk, Thoreau asserts that "the highest that we can attain to is not Knowledge, but Sympathy with Intelligence." He adds that "man cannot *know* in any higher sense than this, any more than he can look serenely and with impunity in the face of the sun: 'You will not perceive that, as perceiving a particular thing,' say the Chaldean Oracles."[28]

Walking becomes a religious exercise that acts as an antidote to the suicidal impulses of city life, allowing one to return to the body and the senses, but it does not entail building a house or determining the fundamental necessities of culture. Hence, walking implies a shedding of all culture to apprehend the necessary "awakening" into wisdom. "So we saunter toward the Holy Land, till one day the sun shall shine more brightly than ever he has done, shall perchance shine into our minds and hearts, and light up our whole lives with a great awakening light, as warm and serene and golden as on a bankside in autumn."[29] Religious enlightenment has no prerequisite in the methods of observation and science. It is not necessary to measure the depth of Walden Pond and discern the shape of its bottom; in "Walking" it is only important to look at

nature through the mist. "These farms which I have myself surveyed, these bounds which I have set up, appear dimly still as
through a mist; but they have no chemistry to fix them; they fade
from the surface of the glass, and the picture which the painter
painted stands out dimly from beneath. The world with which we
are commonly acquainted leaves no trace, and it will have no anniversary."[30] What must be erased is exactly the cartographical grid
that fixes geography and imparts a precision to the landscape; sympathy, not understanding, is demanded. Nature in this instance
exists also outside of time, and its traces cannot be measured or
fixed. How different this is from the attempts in *Walden* once and
for all to establish the depth of the pond and to insist upon the
ability to understand the shape of the bottom.

In contrast to "Walking," *Walden* does, however, contain both the
strategies of the settler and the saunterer. Even though Thoreau
lauds in the "Conclusion" the accomplishments of the artist of Kouroo, whose work transcends history and culture, he betrays a meth-
odology and a justification for culture that places tremendous
importance on the physical and psychological process of perception and the significance of reason. The intuitive force of the artist
may partake of the divine, but the patient collector of empirical
observations and laws remains an integral part of Thoreau's worldmaking.

In "Brute Neighbors," Thoreau asks, "Why do precisely these
objects which we behold make a world?" (p. 225). His techniques
of description in the second half of the text explore the dialectical
relationship between perception and worldmaking. As Nelson
Goodman writes, worldmaking frequently consists of "taking apart
and putting together, often conjointly: on the one hand, of dividing wholes into parts and partitioning kinds into subspecies, analyzing complexes into component features, drawing distinctions;
on the other hand, of composing wholes and kinds out of parts
and members and subclasses, combining features into complexes,
and making connections."[31] Not merely a product of an ecstatic
vision, worldmaking employs the fundamental processes of perception, reason, and analysis. But for Thoreau at the end of *Walden*, the intricate processes of worldmaking are subsumed by the
intuitive force of the child of Brahma. The artist's power of creation, conceived of primarily as a flight from civilization, takes over
instead.

The "Conclusion" ends with the parable of a folk story, proph-
esying transcendent rebirth. Heated by the warmth of an urn, an

egg deposited in the aged furniture of a Massachusetts farmer is finally transformed into a "beautiful and winged life" (p. 333). The triumph of vision comes only by shedding the "many concentric layers of woodenness in the dead dry life of society" (p. 333), and by a return to the simple opposition between nature and civilization. Transcendence becomes the dominant movement, away from society and its "trivial and handselled furniture," and immortality is reassured through the metamorphosis of the egg: "Who does not feel his faith in a resurrection and immortality strengthened by hearing of this?" (p. 333). The traditional religious language of parable also reinforces the ending's spiritual message. What is forgotten, however, is the search for a cultural site within which visions can grow. In the end, the mission of enlightenment supersedes the problem of settlement:

> I do not say that John or Jonathan will realize all this; but such is the character of that morrow which mere lapse of time can never make to dawn. The light which puts out our eyes is darkness to us. Only that day dawns to which we are awake. There is more day to dawn. The sun is but a morning star. (p. 333)

Presented mainly as a problem of consciousness and not the creation of redeemed culture, the ending lines dwell on the image of a light that has its source in both divine and human consciousness.

The Walden settlement, however, lingers; its careful observations still provide an essential index for tracing the history of the pond and for understanding its cyclical fluctuations as both symbol and law of rebirth. Despite Thoreau's "Conclusion," the site at Walden Pond proves remarkably useful as a place to separate the pitfalls of civilization from the necessities of culture. The building of a house, clearing of a field, and planting of beans are accomplished with attention to the historical processes of nature and remembrance of the vanished cultures of the New World: "in the course of the summer it appeared by the arrowheads which I turned up in hoeing, that an extinct nation had anciently dwelt here and planted corn and beans ere white men came to clear the land . . ." (p. 156). Thoreau's field, like his homestead, found ground on which to build culture, connecting him with the human history of the soil and with the regenerative forces of nature.

FOUR

Tracks in the Sand

In *Cape Cod,* Thoreau dissembles and inverts our expectations, writing within the first two pages: "I did not see why I might not make a book on Cape Cod, as well as my neighbor on 'Human Culture.' It is but another name for the same thing, and hardly a sandier phase of it." (p. 3)[1] Unlike *Walden,* in which Thoreau finally creates a sense of transcendence through the worldmaking powers of the artist of Kouroo resulting in an individual vision beyond culture and history, the text of *Cape Cod* is equated with "Human Culture." By the final chapter, "Provincetown," Thoreau juxtaposes representations of this sandy geography from French, Dutch, English, and Norse cultures in such abundance that the reader is left with the ironic grit of cultural relativism rather than transcendence on his hands.

Many critics, however, have judged *Cape Cod* not as ironic but as dissociative, where the transcendental enterprise of fusing fact and symbol fails.[2] While not denying the split between fact and symbol in Thoreau's descriptions, this chapter instead explicates *Cape Cod* as a text of either forceful irony or simmering doubt; above all, it does not read *Cape Cod* as a failed artistic vision. Rather, Thoreau is both master and victim of his writing experiment as he attempts to assert an ironic solution for the problems of representing nature and writing uncivil history.

In the initial chapter, "The Shipwreck," a blend of actual experience and dream, the language of both redemption and defeat converges. At its center is the account of the drowned Irish girl, who exists as mere exposed matter: "bone and muscle . . . quite bloodless—merely red and white," like the "hard sienitic rocks" that caused her death (p. 6). The material world of the girl's body becomes inorganic, and yet blatantly part of nature, without evidence of regenerative potential. A victim of the wreck of the *St. John,* on a historical journey to the promised land of America, the young immigrant has eyes "wide-open and staring . . . , yet lustre-less, dead-lights; or like the cabin windows of a stranded vessel, filled with sand" (p. 6), unable to witness New World wonders.

Perception, the means to an accurate description of the natural world which would in turn signify regeneration and renewal, is undone by the shipwreck, which, like Emerson's Fate, cuts across human action, defying its goals. Thoreau's eyes also become "lustreless, dead-lights." He describes the scene with chilling detachment, reluctant to admit the dimension of compassion and the concomitant threat of death. When he does describe the scene, he consigns the victims to a realm beyond history. In the face of such loss, Thoreau voices his version of Carlyle's "Everlasting No!" He writes, "No, no! If the St. John did not make her port here, she has been telegraphed there. The strongest wind cannot stagger a Spirit; it is a Spirit's breath. A just man's purpose cannot be split on any Grampus or material rock, but itself will split rocks till it succeeds" (pp. 10–11). Dead bodies and the world of matter and history have no place in the life of the Spirit. *Here* is split from *there,* and belief in a celestial promised land replaces the failure to realize redemption on earth.

Thoreau's evocation of images of splitting is not, however, unique to *Cape Cod,* although here is Thoreau's most severe apprehension of a fissure between man and natural history. The "Ktaadn" essay of *The Maine Woods* contains a similarly disturbing vision of matter without regenerative potential.[3] It is appropriate to examine this essay in relation to "The Shipwreck," in an attempt to see when and why Thoreau retreats to a language of dissociation. The comparison also underscores how much bolder and more experimental is *Cape Cod's* solution to a dissociative description of the natural world.

In 1846, three years before Thoreau's first trip to Cape Cod and while he was still living at Walden Pond, he climbed Mt. Katahdin in the wilderness of Maine, a feat previously accomplished by only a few other white men.[4] Thoreau's purpose in penetrating the wilderness is, he states early in the essay, to place himself in a landscape where "one could no longer accuse institutions and society, but must front the true source of evil."[5] And the account of his lone ascent to the summit of Mt. Katahdin is cast in terms of mythological force. The mountain resembles "the creations of the old epic and dramatic poets, of Atlas, Vulcan, the Cyclops, and Prometheus. Such was Caucasus and the rock where Prometheus was bound. Aeschylus had no doubt visited such scenery as this. It was vast, Titanic, and such as man never inhabits."[6] Onto this hostile scene, Thoreau projects the voice of a female god, similar to the local legend in which the Indian god Pomola punished intruders to the mountain home:

> She seems to say sternly, why came ye here before your time? This ground is not prepared for you. Is it not enough that I smile in the valleys? I have never made this soil for thy feet, this air for thy breathing, these rocks for thy neighbors. I cannot pity nor fondle thee here, but forever relentlessly drive thee hence to where I *am* kind.[7]

Nature, then, is split into separate functions, those of a good mother of the valleys and of a terrible mother of the alien mountain top who offers no consolation, love, or aid. In the latter, a total opposition exists between matter and spirit.

But in a subsequent description of the descent from the summit, this split becomes interiorized into the self. It begins with a contradiction. The untrodden landscape is "no man's garden, but the unhandselled globe." Thoreau adds, however, that "it were being too familiar even to let his bones lie there—the home this of Necessity and Fate. There was there felt the presence of a force not bound to be kind to man. It was a place for heathenism and superstitious rites,—to be inhabited by men nearer of kin to the rocks and to wild animals than we."[8] These wild men and animals, however, are easily identified with the body and the self. In this desolate mountain landscape, Thoreau is undone by the link of matter to matter. He stands in awe of his body:

> . . . this matter to which I am bound has become so strange to me. I fear not spirits, ghosts, of which I am one,—*that* my body might,—but I fear bodies, I tremble to meet them. What is this Titan that has possession of me? Talk of mysteries!— Think of our life in nature,—daily to be shown matter, to come in contact with it,—rocks, trees, wind on our cheeks! the *solid* earth! the *actual* world! the *common sense! Contact! Contact! Who are we? where* are we?"[9]

The split also resides within the human frame; though the essential identity of the "I" is spirit, it inhabits the material world of the body, the ultimate mystery of existence. With bodies we are linked to necessity and fate; hence, the fronting of nature leads to a recognition of a split within the observer. Thoreau experiences himself as two separate forces, matter and spirit. His body, like the earth's surface, is at once terribly strange and all too familiar. As Emerson had written in *Nature:* "Philosophically considered, the universe is composed of Nature and the Soul. Strictly speaking, therefore, all that is separate from us, all which Philosophy distinguishes as the NOT ME, that is, both nature and art, all other men and my own body, must be ranked under this name, NATURE."[10] This definition which Thoreau inherited is based on a dissociation between soul and body. Once Thoreau recognizes himself as an extension of the material world, the split is irrevocably internalized.

By the essay's end, however, this fractured vision of nature and self transforms. Within the structure of a single question the cruel stepmother dissolves and her dissociative powers vanish:

> Who shall describe the inexpressible tenderness and immortal life of the grim forest, where Nature, though it be mid-winter, is ever in her spring, where the moss-grown and decaying trees are not old, but seem to enjoy a perpetual youth; and blissful, innocent Nature, like a serene infant, is too happy to make a noise, except by a few tinkling, lisping birds and trickling rills?[11]

This question is the turning point for the essay. The ancient, dark forest and the forbidden summit grow younger as the essay progresses until nature manifests only the beneficent force of life, perpetually young and permanently innocent.

Everything that follows is triumphant; nature becomes "a place to live" as well as "a place to die and be buried in! There certainly men would live forever, and laugh at death and the grave. There they could have no such thoughts as are associated with the village graveyard,—that make a grave out of one of those moist evergreen hummocks."[12] The essay raises this sense of renewal to the national level, with America as the consummate example of youth: "While the republic has already acquired a history worldwide, America is still unsettled and unexplored. Like the English in New Holland, we live only on the shores of a continent even yet, and hardly know where the rivers come from which float our navy."[13] With hope and promise dominating both the political and psychic landscape, "Ktaadn" ends with the triple feat of rejuvenating nature, self, and America.

In contrast, the natural world, America, and the body are in danger of dissolution at the opening of *Cape Cod:*

Why care for these dead bodies? They really have no friends but the worms or fishes. Their owners were coming to the New World, as Columbus and the Pilgrims did; they were within a mile of its shores; but, before they could reach it, they emigrated to a newer world than ever Columbus dreamed of, yet one of whose existence we believe that there is far more universal and convincing evidence—though it has not yet been discovered by science. . . . (p. 10)

The regenerative potential of the would-be American self is here severed from the American landscape and hence from redemptive history. It is dissociated from the methods of natural science and displaced from the historical time of nature. Once the political image of the landscape as uniquely American appears, the language of redemption based on empirical description gives way to a declaration of hope, a dream world Columbus did not understand.

Typically, however, Thoreau does not let the dissociation between matter and spirit stand without qualification. He salvages bits and pieces from the landscape and reasserts the image of regeneration within the material world. The chapter ends with Thoreau's return to the scene of the shipwreck at a later time, when the traces of the tragedy are no longer visible on the landscape, to collect "evidence" of the regenerative potential of the landscape. Bathing in the sea, he finds on the rocks of death "basins of fresh water left by the rain" from which he views "the most perfect sea-shore" that he has ever seen (p. 14). Beauty now dominates the scene of former terror; its name, Pleasant Cove, is no longer ironic. The transformed ocean is as "beautiful as a lake," incapable of terror and destruction. "Not a vestige of a wreck was visible, nor could I believe that the bones of many a shipwrecked man were buried in that pure sand" (p. 14). This scene of tranquility, of still, crystalline water merging with pure sand, prevails over the initial violence of the waves to end the chapter in peace, reinserting the methods of natural history in order to describe a vestige which signals regeneration. Studying the "fantastically worn rocks," Thoreau observes the "stripe of barnacles" reminiscent "of some vegetable growth, the buds and petals and seed-vessels of flowers. They lay along the seams of the rock like buttons on a waistcoat" (p. 13).

This passage has extremely significant associations with dreams and previous events in Thoreau's life which illuminate the meaning that is suppressed here—a meaning that unsettles his efforts to

write redemptive history about the shores of Cape Cod. The barnacles that resemble vegetative forms also resemble the "buttons
on a waistcoat," an image that appears twice in the *Journal*, within
a rare account of a dream and within a description of the search
for Margaret Fuller's body on Fire Island. An analysis of these two
Journal passages in relation to "The Shipwreck" chapter underscores how severe the images of splitting and mind-body dissociation are in *Cape Cod*. On October 26, 1851, Thoreau records the
following dream:

> I awoke this morning to infinite regret. In my dreams I had
> been riding, but the horses bit each other and occasioned end-
> less trouble and anxiety, and it was my employment to hold
> their heads apart. Next I sailed over the sea in a small vessel
> such as the Northmen used, as it were to the Bay of Fundy,
> and thence overland I sailed, still over the shallows about the
> sources of rivers toward the deeper *channel* of a stream which
> emptied into the Gulf beyond,—the Miramichi, was it? Again
> I was in my own small pleasure-boat, learning to sail on the
> sea, and I raised my sail before my anchor, which I dragged
> far into the sea. I saw the buttons which had come off the coats
> of drowned men, and suddenly I saw my dog—when I knew
> not that I had one—standing in the sea up to his chin, to warm
> his legs, which had been wet, which the cool wind numbed.
> (3:80–81)

With horses fighting for control, the dream begins with a sense
of anxiety and fear, juxtaposed with an image of adventure and
freedom as Thoreau sails in a ship like those of the "Northmen," a
reference that recurs in *Cape Cod*. In the *Journal*, Thoreau speculates that perhaps his name was connected with the Thors of Norway, who first traveled to the North American continent and
worked their way down the coast to New England. Recording a
part of Samuel Laing's account of their journeys, he pictures them
as men of action and discovery who succeed against indeterminable
odds—the heroes, the "supermen" of an earlier epoch.[14]
But the next image in his dream transports Thoreau back into
his own "pleasure-boat" where he sees two distinct objects, the "buttons" of "drowned men" and his "dog." The former clearly refers
to Thoreau's search in July of 1850 for the remains of Margaret
Fuller, who had drowned in a shipwreck off Long Island. His *Journal* records the incident:

I have in my pocket a button which I ripped off the coat of the Marquis of Ossoli on the seashore the other day. Held up, it intercepts the light and casts a shadow,—an *actual* button so called,—and yet all the life it is connected with is less substantial to me than my faintest dreams. This stream of events which we consent to call actual, and that other mightier stream which alone carries us with it,—and what makes the difference? On the one our bodies float, and we have sympathy with it through them; on the other, our spirits. (2:43)

Here, as in *Cape Cod,* Thoreau describes a split reality where the world of the body and the "actual" are less important than the "mightier reality," bodiless and immortal. By so doing, Thoreau severs nature and the spirit in a most untranscendentalist manner.[15] Vestiges signaling redemption should be found in the historical text of nature and the body. But before the dead body all redemptive history stops.

Also, in his dream, Thoreau first is a Northman, crossing the sea in an act of adventure. But back in his "pleasure-boat," he comes upon the evidences of death. The "buttons" of drowned men in *Cape Cod* are oddly linked to a symbol of the barnacle, a "seed-vessel," capable of regeneration. In the "seed-vessel," the actual signifies growth and renewal, but in the "button," contrarily, it signifies limit and inconsequence. Linked together in "The Shipwreck," they demonstrate how the "vestige" or evidences of the spirit in the landscape can point opposite ways, both to the spirit and to death. In the very act of describing the landscape, Thoreau compounds the text, creating a symbol system that has no easy sequence of correspondence between matter and the spirit; instead, it suggests an irreconcilable split, a fissure in the seam of uncivil history. The dream continues to delineate this split, describing the flesh one moment as "the organ and the channel of melody" and the next, on waking, as "not the thoroughfare of glorious and world-stirring inspirations, but a scuttle full of dirt, such a thoroughfare only as the street and the kennel, where, perchance, the wind may sometimes draw forth a strain of music from a straw" (3:81–82).

The revulsion of the flesh differs significantly from Thoreau's objectification of it in *Cape Cod.* The bodies on the beach are objects, not of revulsion or fear, but of almost anatomical interest, even though we know from what Thoreau writes that such sights can cause death in the beholder. Characteristically, Thoreau qualifies the dream and the shipwreck account with visions of redemption. After he records the dream, he continues to search for a protean self that, by its elusiveness, can never become static or dead. After the shipwreck description, however, he searches for evidences of the spirit, producing the condensed image of the "buttons," signifying both death and life.

The most important consequence of this split within the description of the vestige is how it disturbs not only uncivil history but also Thoreau's concept of language and the representation of the natural world. After the initial chapter that portrays grief and catastrophe, Thoreau begins to analyze the gap between the description of the landscape and the landscape itself. The dissociation that the text displays on the level of the image becomes a self-conscious problem that Thoreau confronts as a writer of travel accounts. If there exists a split between matter and spirit, there also exists a split between matter and language.

* * *

Cape Cod opens with a warning: "My readers must expect only so much saltness as the land-breeze acquires from blowing over an arm of the sea, or is tasted on the windows and on the bark of trees twenty miles inland after September gales" (p. 3). The grist of the sea is not to be found in Thoreau's account. Indeed, the thing represented always remains elusive and distant. Throughout *Cape Cod*, Thoreau calls attention to the nature of representation and its relationship to human culture. Scattered comments alert anyone who travels through the text to tread with care his "sandy" account.

In general, we can characterize *Cape Cod* as a first-person narration like his previous works, proceeding along two distinct levels. On the one hand, it is a first-person travel account that is distilled from various journeys Thoreau made to the Cape. On the other hand, like *A Week,* it is a weaving of previous representations of a specific geography by other writers into the journey narration. But unlike his earlier writings, irony dominates the text. To understand Thoreau's increasing use of irony, the reader must pay close attention to the transitions between these two levels, where he bridges the gap by direct commentary to the reader. Through these authorial comments, he creates a set of lenses by which to view the account, and in so doing explores the ironies of human representations of nature.

Critics of *Cape Cod,* however, rarely concern themselves with Thoreau's use of narrative form, preferring instead to read the text at the level of content and then to assess Thoreau as an American romantic, intent upon reconciling fact with symbol. That reconciliation is usually perceived as occurring in the text when Thoreau's descriptions of nature, usually on the level of the journey narrative, lead to a pattern of figuration involving an extended metaphor or simile. The natural "fact," then, allows a play of figuration, and the description moves to a new level of meaning, one with metaphysical, moral, or aesthetic significance.

Because Sherman Paul's writings have determined the epistemological basis of subsequent articles on *Cape Cod,* it is best to start with his view of the book as another of Thoreau's efforts to confront "natural facts" and to distill "spiritual discovery" from them.[16] These "vistas of discovery" then become the "framework of the narrative."[17] Paul discusses the correspondence between fact and symbol, or fact and spiritual reality, as rooted in the transcendentalism of Emerson's *Nature,* and based upon a familiar nineteenth-century theory of language by which the name "always stood for a thing."[18] In this sense, to name an object correctly was to unpack its spiritual or symbolic significance. Naming connected one not only to the thing but to the spirit. Mario L. D'Avanzo and Martin Leonard Pops, writing on *Cape Cod* after Paul, share a similar hypothesis. Pops says that as Thoreau's "eye is on the fact, his mind's eye is simultaneously on the symbol, concentrated on the All, beyond Man's limited understanding of what is really Evil and what Good. Such is Thoreau's capacity for dialectical synthesis."[19] Even though Pops feels Thoreau is frequently unable to synthesize in *Cape Cod,* the critical questions are couched in the same language. A critic like James McIntosh, however, who sees few successful "romantic correspondences" in *Cape Cod,* argues that Thoreau, unable to fuse fact and symbol, retreated to a "wilful but purposeful inconsistency," producing no final answers but only a "succession of different attitudes" toward nature as fact and nature as symbol.[20]

All of these critics of *Cape Cod* treat Thoreau as either a successful American romantic or a failed one and would agree that the text cannot exist apart from the romantic desire to see the symbol in the fact. But in the shifts between narrative levels in *Cape Cod* there resides a layer of meaning that pulls at the very nature of the romantic enterprise. In one respect, *Cape Cod* is an exploration of the very possibility of writing an account of the Cape at all. After the first chapter, in which uncivil history splinters against the associations of death, the text consistently plays with the conventions of representing nature, periodically startling the reader with the reminder that the description is significantly different from the thing represented, that representations are as dependent upon culture and history as upon poetic inspiration.

In one of these transition moments in chapter 3, "The Plains of Nauset," Thoreau begins extended comments on representation. The chapter opens by evoking the narrative time of the journey: "The next morning, Thursday, October 11th, it rained as hard as ever, but we were determined to proceed on foot, nevertheless" (p. 24), continuing the story of the journey down the Cape which has proceeded two days. But, Thoreau quickly interrupts the journey narration with quoted material from ecclesiastical history. After having passed by and described Millennium Grove, he launches into the story of Rev. Samuel Treat, continues with text extracts from Treat's sermons, and adds another story about how the same sermon read by Reverend Treat and his father-in-law, Mr. Willard, elicited totally opposite effects, the meaning of the sermon coming not from the meaning of the words but from the manner of delivery. Read by Mr. Willard, a man who "possessed a graceful delivery, a masculine harmonious voice," all the terror and fear of Reverend Treat's delivery vanished. Thus, Thoreau gives the reader an example of how meaning is often dependent upon the medium of delivery instead of the content of his words.

Thoreau then relates the manner of Reverend Treat's death and adds the following instructions:

> The reader will imagine us, all the while, steadily traversing that extensive plain in a direction a little north of east toward Nauset Beach, and reading under our umbrellas as we sailed, while it blowed hard with mingled mist and rain, as if we were approaching a fit anniversary of Mr. Treat's funeral. We fancied that it was such a moor as that on which somebody perished in the snow, as is related in the "Lights and Shadows of Scottish Life." (p. 40)

These stage directions to the reader are both humorous and revealing. Thoreau entreats us not to forget that the journey narrative, his walk along the beach with his companion, William Ellery Channing, continues, and that the events occurring a few pages back are still in progress, regardless of his fun in relating the story of Reverend Treat's journey on Cape Cod. His aside is ironic precisely because the reader by this point has forgotten for the moment that Thoreau is narrating a story about himself walking across the plains of Nauset, and has let go of the vision of Thoreau holding Reverend Treat's history under his umbrella as he trudges through the rain. The Treat extracts have established their own narrative temporality. When Thoreau shifts to the invented temporality of the journey account, he uses the transition to juxtapose the separate temporal orders.

In addition, Thoreau also wants us to imagine his walking *as if* it were in accord with the anniversary of Reverend Treat's funeral. He goads the reader to blend extract and reported event. And it is clear that the extract has irrevocably altered the "real" journey event of walking. The reader is watching Thoreau create a new walk, one that is not a transcription of a walk taken, but a synthesis of representations resulting from having "walked" through a specific number of pages quoting Reverend Treat. In this sense, the walk is constructed by the text.

Thoreau also informs the reader that as he and his companion trudge in funereal fashion across the plain, they fancy the scene like the one described in the "Lights and Shadows of Scottish Life." Like Mark Twain, Thoreau presents a world where boys read adventure stories and girls read romances and then go on to construct reality according to these not-so-innocent narratives. Thoreau, of course is not as satirical and antiromantic in ideology as Twain, but clearly he is poking fun at the point that the subject being described as a natural "fact" is neither a "fact" nor "natural." In this instance, its very nature is constructed by a previously read text. The mimetic character of natural representation is called into question. We are watching Thoreau laugh at the very enterprise of representing the plains of Nauset.

Later in this chapter, when Thoreau begins to quote from Latin eulogies of Cape Cod ministers, he invents his own linguistic praise:

> But, probably, the most just and pertinent character of all, is that which appears to be given to the Rev. Ephraim Briggs, of Chatham, in the language of the later Romans: "*Seip, sepoese, sepoemese, wechekum*"—which, not being interpreted, we know not what it means, though we have no doubt it occurs somewhere in the Scriptures, probably in the Apostle Eliot's Epistle to the Nipmucks. (pp. 42–43)

This section of the "Plains of Nauset," which involved Thoreau in a squabble with George William Curtis, an editor of *Putnam's*

Magazine,[21] shows how the scene of writing is as much a part of *Cape Cod* as is the geographical scene. Creating nonsense and laughing at the sanctity of the biblical quotation, Thoreau presents himself as a writer daring to "fancy" reality out of mere wordplay in which sacred as well as profane texts are parodied.

The chapter ends with a curious aside to the reader: "There was no better way to make the reader realize how wide and peculiar that plain was, and how long it took to traverse it, than by inserting these long extracts in the midst of my narrative" (p. 43). Critics have sought for symbolic meaning in these words. D'Avanzo claims that since "the church imposes a rigid uniformity on man's spirit and is therefore cognate with the dreary, unvarying plains," the extracts correspond symbolically with the natural fact of the plains.[22] But instead of a "symbolic" reading, this study proposes that Thoreau again draws the reader's attention to the inability of the account to mirror simply the plains of Nauset. We laugh at his attempt to reconcile nature and its representation. Thoreau has created his own narrative temporality in his book, and its relationship to his actual walks is basically amusing.

In *Cape Cod* Thoreau repeatedly backs away from description where we would expect it and instead comments on the difficulty of describing. Perhaps the less familiar landscape of the desert-beach impressed on him that seeing is a learned and therefore a partially cultural activity. Thrown into the environment of Cape Cod without the eyes of its native residents, he confronted the relativity of sight and the dependence of sight on experience. As Richard J. Schneider points out in an essay on Thoreau's optics, Thoreau in *Cape Cod* is particularly taken by illusions in which "the truth of a visual perception often seemed to be more in the distortion or illusion caused by the intervening atmosphere than in the actual substance being viewed."[23] When Thoreau is on the beach, he is confronted with the perceptual difficulties of mirages and unmeasurable distances, but back in Concord writing *Cape Cod*, he is faced with the intervening distortion of any representation of the Cape.

At one point in the journey narration where we would expect a mapped description of a panoramic view of the beach similar to those found in *A Week* and *Walden*, Thoreau instead writes: "It was not as on the map, or seen from the stage-coach; but there I found it all out of doors, huge and real, Cape Cod! as it cannot be represented on a map, color it as you will; the thing itself, than which there is nothing more like it, no truer picture or account; which you cannot go further and see" (p. 50). Language, maps, and pictures, like atmosphere and the effect of light, mediate between the writer and the object represented. Instead of reflecting a moment in a romantic artist's "failed vision," this passage shows how Thoreau is acutely aware that representations of nature are more complex than he previously recognized and that these gaps, rather than creating silence in the transcendentalist, provoke both humor and irony.

After he writes about the disjuncture between the thing or natural fact and its representation, Thoreau again comments to the reader that, "though for some time I have not spoken of the roaring of the breakers, and the ceaseless flux and reflux of the waves, yet they did not for a moment cease to dash and roar, with such a tumult that, if you had been there, you could scarcely have heard my voice the while . . ." (p. 51). Again the reader is the straight man for Thoreau's humor. Unable to keep in mind the mental image of the ocean as well as the acoustical tape of the waves, the distracted reader is prodded by a schoolteacherish Thoreau not to forget the scene of nature while he is deliberately distanced from it.

Thoreau goes on to discuss the relationship between the sounds of nature and the sounds of words. "I put in a little Greek now and then, partly because it sounds so much like the ocean—though I doubt if Homer's *Mediterranean* Sea ever sounded so loud as this" (p. 51). He adds in a footnote that we "have no word in English to express the sound of many waves, dashing at once . . ." (p. 51). However, Thoreau's Greek words are more than an elaborate attempt at onomatopoeia. His flippant tone of adding Greek "now and then" undermines the seriousness of the attempt. The Greek words are a reminder of another way of representing the ocean, one belonging to a Hellenic past and its traditions of cultural representations.

To those readers who want an account of Cape Cod, particularly a romantic one in which descriptions of natural landscape lead to statements about its symbolic significance, these "digressions" are simply intolerable. But if we enter into the ironic texture of *Cape Cod* and its consistent humor, we may observe a well-educated writer play with the filters through which we view and hence represent nature.

By the time Thoreau wrote *Cape Cod,* he was familiar with the major conventions of literary representations of nature. He had read Edmund Burke, William Gilpin, and Udevale Price and was therefore aware of the sublime, the beautiful, and the picturesque as styles of representing natural landscape. In fact, between 1852 and 1854, Thoreau had read at least eight works of Gilpin on the picturesque.[24] In addition, he was better acquainted with the naturalist and historical accounts of Cape Cod than with the Cape itself. In this sense, the text comes at the end of a long tradition of natural history writing.

To those readers familiar with a Thoreau who is always trying to throw off the traditional ways of seeing and instead write a new vision of the American landscape, *Cape Cod* must indeed seem like a strange text. In no other work, except perhaps *A Week,* does he call attention so repeatedly to the filters through which we look at nature. He does not find all filters equally good, for he does admit a hierarchy of truths. For instance, when he compares the views of the Greeks and the naturalists on the ocean, he writes: "We looked on the sea, then, once more, not as ἀτρύγετος, or unfruitful, but as it has been more truly called, the 'laboratory of continents'" (p. 100). This preference for a naturalistic description suggests that there are "truer" representations of nature, a theme that runs throughout *Cape Cod,* and these truths may indeed be dependent not only on the culture, but also on the moral character of the perceiver and the knowledge of the writer.

Yet, though Thoreau may criticize one report as less accurate than another, he often explains their differences as justifiable because of the specific conditions from which the representation or perception arose. Thus, the Pilgrims saw the Cape as fertile probably because they had seen so little vegetation for so long: "Everything appeared to them of the color of the rose, and had the scent of juniper and sassafras. Very different is the general and off-hand account given by Captain John Smith, who was on this coast six years earlier, and speaks like an old traveller, voyager, and soldier, who had seen too much of the world to exaggerate, or even to dwell long, on a part of it" (pp. 200–201). Representations of nature arise, then, not only from specific physical and cognitive conditions, but also from the peculiar "character" and experience of the perceiver. Placed next to each other, the filters used in the representations become obvious. In this sense, accounts of the Cape are accounts of "Human Culture." Thoreau is indeed serious in the opening pages of *Cape Cod* when he equates the two.

After Thoreau compiles representations of the ocean in chapter 6, he again addresses the reader: "Though we have indulged in some placid reflections of late, the reader must not forget that the dash and roar of the waves were incessant. Indeed, it would be well if he were to read with a large conch-shell at his ear" (p. 100). But to read with a "conch-shell" at one's ear is not to be one with the ocean scene, but to play with its absence. The shell, like the text, is different from the ocean's waves. At best we can sit in our chair, book in one hand and conch-shell in the other. The picture is again ironic and amusing.

Alongside the many observations in *Cape Cod* on the relativity of perception are specific comments on the relativity of words; they too arise out of specific contexts or points of view. In fact, the inhabitants of the lower Cape towns have different words for the same objects depending upon their position in relation to that object: "Standing on the western or larboard shore, and looking across to where the distant mainland looms, they can say, This is Massachusetts Bay; and then, after an hour's sauntering walk, they may stand on the starboard side, beyond which no land is seen to loom, and say, This is the Atlantic Ocean" (p. 115).

Thoreau is particularly aware of the "cultural" nature of representations when he extracts from historical accounts of Cape Cod. In the last chapter, "Provincetown," a chapter many critics read as anticlimactic, where numerous reports of the early settlements of Cape Cod are collected, Thoreau demonstrates how none of these accounts constitutes an accurate "history" of the place. The British begin their history of New England "only when it ceases to be *New France.*" The examples, of course, multiply—the Northmen have one history and the Spanish another. Boundaries of time and space are settled by politics and groups of people. History more than any other account becomes for Thoreau a reflector of human culture: "Consider what stuff history is made of,—that for the most part it is merely a story agreed on by posterity" (p. 197). As a guide to the "factual," history would be an abominable failure: "I believe that, if I were to live the life of mankind over again myself, (which I would not be hired to do), with the Universal History in my hands, I should not be able to tell what was what" (p. 197).

Unlike *A Week, Cape Cod* does not assert a "mythic" language and oppose it to history. Accounts of the Cape are completely secular, and the descriptions of geography are often a function of ideology and power. There is a persistent sense that one group's descriptions often eliminate or "forget" the experience of others in order to create cultural stories:

> It is not generally remembered, if known, by the descendants of the Pilgrims, that when their forefathers were spending

their first memorable winter in the New World, they had for
neighbors a colony of French no further off than Port Royal
(Annapolis, Nova Scotia), three hundred miles distant . . . (pp.
181–82)

Quoting frequently from Champlain's *Voyages,* Thoreau constructs
an "Ante-Pilgrim history of New England" and concludes that both
mediums of words and pictures, i.e., maps, render only relative
realities. Champlain is upset by the easy substitution of British
names for French on world maps whereby words like Acadie, Etch-
emins, and Almouchicois become Maine, New Brunswick, and
Massachusetts. And Thoreau registers his complaint by claiming
that Cabot's landing on Labrador "gave the English no just title to
New England, or to the United States" (p. 183). Maps and geographical descriptions become irrevocably intertwined with the
politics of possession. The rift between the word and the thing does
not result merely in a sense of failure for Thoreau, but in an opportunity to assert an increasingly complex analysis of human attempts at representation.

At the end of the book, Thoreau jokingly advises his audience
on how to read his puzzling text. He challenges his "townsmen" to
"step into the cars" and come to the scene of Cape Cod itself. He
notes that if the reader had started "when I first advised you, you
might have seen our tracks in the sand, still fresh, and reaching all
the way from the Nauset Lights to Race Point, some thirty miles,—
for at every step we made an impression on the Cape, though we
were not aware of it, and though our account may have made no
impression on your minds. But what is our account? In it there is
no roar, no beach-birds, no tow-cloth" (p. 212). Playing with the
language of both absence and presence, Thoreau dissociates the
word from the thing.

Also, the suggestion that the reader could catch up with him on
the beach invites the miraculous. As Thoreau continually points
out, the sand is often the great enemy of man, the eraser of culture
and the evidence of incessant change. Human footprints made in
the sand are washed away in a matter of minutes. Ironically, the
only way to read Thoreau's "account" is to leave the Cape behind.

*   *   *

In a later version of the text, after his lectures and the *Putnam's
Magazine* publications, Thoreau added a philological account of
the words *cape* and *cod:*

As for my title, I suppose that the word Cape is from the French *cap;* which is from the Latin *caput,* a head; which is, perhaps, from the verb *capere,* to take,—that being the part by which we take hold of a thing:—Take Time by the forelock. It is also the safest part to take a serpent by. And as for Cod, that was derived directly from that "great store of codfish" which Captain Bartholomew Gosnold caught there in 1602; which fish appears to have been so called from the Saxon word *codde,* "a case in which seeds are lodged," either from the form of the fish, or the quantity of spawn it contains; whence also, perhaps, codling ("*pomum coctile*"?) and coddle,—to cook green like peas. (pp. 3–4)

Sherman Paul interprets this section as a way to begin "with Cape Cod itself," with the name which for Thoreau "always stood for a thing."[25] A transcendentalist exercise, it is similar to what Emerson does in *Nature* where "every word which is used to express a moral or intellectual fact, if traced to its root, is found to be borrowed from some material appearance."[26] Premised upon a "unique linkage between the worlds of matter and spirit," as Philip Gura has pointed out, the description of nature necessarily conveys the spirit.[27] But Thoreau in his inventive and associative etymology is working from words that immediately refer material things to their place in the culture of naming and human activity. Captain Bartholomew Gosnold is, after all, not the "root" of the word in the Emersonian sense, but the cultural and historical context for the naming. Also, the relationship between cod and its root is based upon a resemblance of material form and does not symbolize a correspondence between matter and spirit. Thus, Thoreau's word-playing should be valued equally with the human inventiveness of naming and cultural activity, that is, cooking peas.

In *Cape Cod,* Thoreau is not merely an Emersonian etymologist. He freely associates with the Cape the human desire to "Take Time by the forelock" and stop its relentless passage. Perhaps this is the final aim of his representation of Cape Cod, an ever shifting landmass that, unlike Walden Pond and the Concord and Merrimack river systems, defies maps, pictures, and accounts. Like the artist of Kouroo at the end of *Walden,* Thoreau had imaginatively fashioned his own narrative that in a sense "made no compromise with Time." Ironically, however, his narrative takes into account the time-bound nature of representation and its uneasy relationship to natural "fact." More than ever, in *Cape Cod* we can watch Thoreau wrestling with the traditions of natural representation and the manner in which they reflect human culture as much as divine landscape.

*   *   *

The tragic sense of life, presented in the first chapter of *Cape Cod,* results, then, in a series of dissociations between matter and spirit and, consequently, between matter and language in the text as a whole, allowing Thoreau to play with the gaps created. The tragic environment of the sea, however, runs throughout the text but is continually mollified by the absurdity of representing Cape Cod accurately at all. For instance, in "The Sea and the Desert," Thoreau describes nature as the vision of death:

> It is a wild, rank place, and there is no flattery in it. Strewn with crabs, horse-shoes, and razor-clams, and whatever the sea casts up,—a vast *morgue,* where famished dogs may range in packs, and crows come daily to glean the pittance which the tide leaves them. The carcasses of men and beasts together lie stately up upon its shelf, rotting and bleaching in the sun and waves, and each tide turns them in their beds, and tucks fresh sand under them. There is naked Nature,—inhumanly sincere, wasting no thought on man, nibbling at the cliffy shore where gulls wheel amid the spray. (p. 147)

Echoing the description in "The Shipwreck," Thoreau purports to give us "naked Nature," finally the thing itself. But this sense of the natural world as graveyard and not the seed-house of regeneration is balanced against the futility of all human representations.

Thoreau, more acutely aware of the relativity of perception and words, does not withdraw from describing the natural world in *Cape Cod,* but he writes with a new ironic awareness that permits some of his most moving prose to emerge. He transforms a position of grief mixed with detachment into one of humor, acknowledging the limitations of human efforts to "see rightly" and to describe accurately what is seen. There are fewer absolutes in *Cape Cod* than in his other writings. But to evaluate this absence as a failure is to miss the insights into language and representation that Thoreau both playfully and seriously entertains in his writing. Laughter, after all, is a way of admitting our mortality, of recognizing the splits and going on with our lives; irony, a way of distancing ourselves from defeat.

FIVE

Terrestrial Rainbows

After the textual vagaries of *Cape Cod,* the fresh experimentation of the late *Journal* years (1857–1860) testifies to Thoreau's unflagging commitment to his methods. Never abandoning periodic composition, a renewed energy to record the perceptual events of nature takes place in these years. Strangely enough, Thoreau's journal writings composed after the publication of *Walden* in 1854 have received surprisingly little critical attention, perhaps because they have been judged inferior to his late nature essays. Described as a "repository of scientific facts," the late *Journal* has become a testament to the technical nature of Thoreau's observations on nature.[1] We know, however, that notational, that is, technical, notes pervade all of Thoreau's journal writings. From the late 1840s on, he consistently used technology to measure and observe, and he organized many of his natural descriptions in the journal entries as if they were verbal maps. Quite the opposite to the dictates of some criticism, the late *Journal* should be read as a continuation rather than a change in observations on nature and, in particular, his interest in perception.

Critics writing on Thoreau's relationship to luminism and nineteenth-century landscape painting have pointed out how Thoreau's descriptions of nature can be correlated with the painterly techniques so popular during his lifetime.[2] In particular, Thoreau's attention to light, color, and the organization of space have been essential to his descriptive techniques. The perceptual experimentation of his late journal entries needs careful analysis, rather than the emphasis on the technical aspects of Thoreau's late *Journal* that has been given. It would be inaccurate, however, to claim that Thoreau's late *Journal* was primarily color and light studies, or even sustained natural description. Lists of measurements, dates, and botanical names perforate the text along with extended passages of personal philosophy and moral concern, if not outrage, at political events.³ But those sections devoted to natural description are marked by an intense need to clarify the role of perception in historical knowledge.

In these later years, Thoreau recognizes even more acutely than before how dependent perception is on the material environment and not the world of "ideas." In 1854, he is disturbed by attempts to discuss the eye without the body, its site of materiality, and its connection to the mind. The eye as merely "visionary" is grotesque to him, an abstraction that happens when the viewer forgets the context in which the object is viewed; namely, the landscape, such conditions as atmosphere and light, and the human body/mind matrix. The descriptive passages of the late *Journal* focus increasingly on the *psychophysiology* of the eye,⁴ the process of the eye viewing the landscape, linking the moments of perception and shifting points of view with the effects of light and color and, then, with the affective reactions of the mind.

Such psychophysiological records are evident in the entries occurring in concentrated periods during the falls of 1857 and 1858 and during the springs of 1859 and 1860, particularly rich periods of observation for Thoreau. It is during this period that Thoreau becomes highly critical of John Ruskin's *Modern Painters,* asserting his own methods of first-person observation of nature as superior to Ruskin's descriptions of nature paintings. Thoreau finds that in Ruskin "much is written about Nature as somebody has portrayed her," but "little about Nature as she is" (10:69).

As if in response to Ruskin, Thoreau's journal entry, written the day after commenting on *Modern Painters,* resembles a guide to viewing the landscape. Organized as a mapped walk, the entry emphasizes the necessary attitude of the viewer. Thoreau requires that the observer "behold" the scene at his "leisure" and evoke a religious sensibility for sight. "It is always incredibly fair, but ordinarily we are mere objects in it, and not witnesses of it." With a renewed optimism, Thoreau implies that sight properly used and experienced continually reassures an edenic vision of natural history. The description Thoreau writes to illustrate his assertions, however, is a fusion of topographical precision with a new awareness of the demarcation of color bands. The changing colors of a fall landscape are described as follows:

I see, through the bright October air, a valley extending southwest and northeast and some two miles across,—so far I can see distinctly,—with a broad, yellow meadow tinged with brown at the bottom, and a blue river winding slowly through it northward, with a regular edging of low bushes on the brink, of the same color with the meadow. (10:73)

The eye sees through the medium of air and is bound by a grid of vision that extends for two miles across, but within the grid exist animated bands of color balanced and contrasted with lines of rivers and shapes of houses. At the bottom of the angle of vision is a base of brown and yellow forms with the movement of the river "northward," taking the eye away from the position of the viewer. As the eye travels out toward the horizon, the middle ground "on the hills around shoot up a million scarlet and orange and yellow and crimson fires amid the green." These explosive points are contrasted with "bright white or gray houses" and are finally set against a "dozen dark blue mountain-summits." But Thoreau does not order the description to end at the horizon, such as we would expect from the foreground/background arrangement of pictorial space, but returns it to the more immediate space of the viewer. "Large birds of a brilliant blue and white plumage are darting and screaming amid the glowing foliage a quarter of a mile below, while smaller blue birds warble faintly but sweetly around me" (10:73). The eye travels out within the grid to the horizon, but ends with a perception of sight and sound immediately surrounding the observer.

This descriptive entry epitomizes what Thoreau means by a record of the eye "beholding" the landscape. One watches the eye watching, notes the physical scope of its vision, and delineates the space within the view. The sensation of color and its effect are ordered and underscored by loosening the sense of color as a specific attribute of an object to a force in itself: "crimson fires amid the green." Sight is highly conditional and contextual. Yet within the confines of the grid of space, ordered shapes and colors emerge.

The passage clarifies Thoreau's objection to Ruskin. Descriptions of representations of nature, particularly those of painterly representations, are an illusory form of knowledge. For Thoreau, they reflect an endless subjectivity that preempts the natural landscape. His irritation with Ruskin betrays his desire to limit the constituting actions of the eye/mind and to use the object and its environment as restricting forces on vision. The eye tests its observations against nature and draws conclusions. To have a painting as an object is to lose the very ground for establishing the "truthfulness" of what the

eye sees, no matter how illusory that might be. For Thoreau, natural description, if it is to have the significance of witnessing *what
is* and of asserting both spiritual purpose and historical accuracy,
must not only contain a first-person account, but also an analysis
of the act of perception itself.

Coming after the ironies of *Cape Cod* and the doubts of *The Maine
Woods*, Thoreau's experiments with how the eye sees in his later
journal years mark a new commitment to solving the paradoxes of
perception. The landscape persists as the construction of a primal
artist which, once it is beheld properly, yields delight, knowledge,
and wisdom. Although Thoreau insists upon a contextual basis for
sight, anchored in the topos, the journal entry is a refined, almost
purified version of the contact between human seeing and the natural landscape. The self of the viewer is "transparent," yet a highly
structured consciousness; limited materially, but sensitive to the
designs of color and shape. Thoreau still wants to believe that,
unlike most modes of seeing, this sense of human seeing is not
molded by social institutions—what he labels the "church" or the
"village"—and therefore is capable of "beholding" the landscape.
Through precise and sensitive means of observation, Thoreau continues to think that he can outwit the ironies of cultural representation and once again assert a pure form of redemptive history.

Consequently, the signs of redemption on the landscape are
transformed in these later writings. Before, regenerative forms of
life, such as the first signs of spring in vegetation or their analogues
in water or sand, signalled the redeemed designs of nature. Now,
it is through the sensations of color and light as they delight the
eye that the promise of a paradisiacal sense of life on earth is revealed in historical time. Ostensibly, Thoreau requires a tradition-
ally religious basis for this form of seeing. On hearing the sound
of the funeral bell in the distance, Thoreau writes: "It suggests that
a man must die to his present life before he can appreciate his
opportunities and the beauty of the abode that is appointed him"
(10:74). But Thoreau's method of observing the landscape and descriptive style still demand a psychophysiology of seeing, a precision of measurement, and an admission of strict material limit for
any individual perception.

The preparation for this mode of seeing is not merely a psychological encounter with death; it involves a constant alertness, as we
have seen, to *how* the eye sees, not only *what* is seen. In this same
journal entry, Thoreau scrutinizes the way in which the eye perceives reflections. "As I sat on the high bank at the east end of

Walden this afternoon, at five o'clock, I saw, by a peculiar intention or dividing of the eye, a very striking subaqueous rainbow-like phenomenon" (10:74). Thoreau insists that the "passer-by," the idle viewer, not "on the alert for such effects," may fail "to perceive the full beauty of the phenomenon." Besides fostering psychological openness, the observer actively uses the mind and its intentionality to discover visual effects: "Unless you look for reflections, you commonly will not find them" (10:74–75). And only by focusing and refocusing on the scene can the distinct image in the reflection be seen as separate and different from the scene reflected.

Hence, the autumn landscape in the reflecting waters of Walden Pond is discovered to be a distortion by the exacting eye: "these reflections were not true to their height though true to their breadth, but were extended downward with mathematical perpendicularity, three or four times too far, forming sharp pyramids of the several colors, gradually reduced to mere dusky points" (10:75). Through measuring the landscape and its reflections, Thoreau can include even distortions into his general ideas about how the eye sees.

In the same journal description, color is shifted away from the object, here toward general shapes, and is seen as a strong reason why the scene has aesthetic significance: "The effect of this prolongation of the reflection was a very pleasing softening and blending of the colors, especially when a small bush of one bright tint stood directly before another of a contrary and equally bright tint" (10:75). In a modernist sense, Thoreau writes about the pleasure of the mere apprehension of color contrasts in a moment of lyric intensity. "It was just as if you were to brush firmly aside with your hand or a brush a fresh line of paint of various colors, or so many lumps of friable colored powders" (10:75). These pyramids of color exist in time and space for a second of aesthetic delight. Although tightly structured within the measured grid of space, they are highly animated and provide the basis of poetic vision. This further shift from the perception of objects to the effects of color and light does much to free Thoreau from the debilitating aspects of vision. As with the American luminist painters, the articulation of light is a means toward a synthesis of the real and the ideal and a paradisiacal sense of the landscape.[5]

By renewing his commitment to the processes of perception and shifting more emphatically to the observation of light and color, Thoreau rejoices in the perception of beauty as a sign of promise. Ironically, there are inherent dangers in this stance. Emerson says in *Nature* that "beauty is the mark God sets upon virtue,"[6] but he warns that "beauty in nature is not ultimate. It is the herald of inward and eternal beauty, and is not alone a solid and satisfactory good. It must therefore stand as a part and not as yet the last or highest expression of the final cause of Nature."[7] Thoreau, however, seems to compress together the delightful sensations of color and light as an experience of a redeemed vision of earth. In the temporal flux of nature, eden can be witnessed.

Also, in Thoreau's method of observation, the landscape of material objects can disappear beneath the record of sensation. In its most radical form, an abstract sense of color and light can invade Thoreau's vision of the landscape as it evolves during the 1850s, permeating the perception of single objects in nature.[8] For instance, a dandelion becomes a "conspicuous bright-yellow disk in the midst of a green space on the moist bank" (9:347). Once Thoreau begins to weave the effects of color into his mapped walks, he loosens further the attention to "objects" and focuses even more acutely on the conditional and atmospheric quality of seeing. In choosing reflections as the "object," the entire problem of substance and sight is in fact subsumed by the necessity to record the psychophysiology of seeing. Thoreau ends this section by writing: "The color seems to be reflected and re-reflected from ripple to ripple, losing brightness each time by the softest possible gradation, and tapering toward the beholder, since he occupies a mere point of view" (10:75–76). Again, the scene is pulled back into the grid of space emanating from the limited and distinct position held by the observer. No matter how intense the vision of color, the view is always confined within the limits of individual perception and consciousness.

In his reading of Ruskin during this period, Thoreau speculates that "the lover of art is one, and the lover of nature another, though true art is but the expression of our love of nature" (10:80). He insists on the problematics of viewing nature through pictorial representations and strongly favors the "word" as the accurate recorder of the eye/mind/landscape nexus. In this method of recording the first-person observations of the trained eye, description is never apart from the apprehension of beauty, with the hope that precise seeing fuses both truth and beauty. Thus, the description is a reflection or an echo, not the thing itself; a necessary distortion that does not repeat, but inspires, grapples with, and admits the material restraints of seeing, placing the reader within the "eyes" of the consciousness of the individual viewer.

Thoreau maintains the "usefulness" of his work by insisting that, unlike the farmer, his poetic effort consists of gathering from the landscape "scenes" that produce an apprehension of the beautiful. "I take all these walks to every point of the compass, and it is always harvest-time with me. I am always gathering my crop from these woods and fields and waters, and no man is in my way or interferes with me. My crop is not their crop" (10:93). The walk, then, provides a gathering ground for correct views that fuse the technological training of the eye with aesthetic delight.

In Thoreau's late *Journal*, then, redemptive history frequently becomes the temporal record of color and light as it produces pleasure. Rarely concerned with articulating a moral analogy for such moments, Thoreau simply affirms the perception of beauty as a sign both of a purified observer and a redeemed landscape. Eden exists, if only for a second, within the constantly fluctuating surfaces of natural history. At times, Thoreau even claims that it is our fate to be confined within surfaces: "We must not expect to probe with our fingers the sanctuary of any life, whether animal or vegetable. If we do, we shall discover nothing but surface still. The ultimate expression or fruit of any created thing is a fine effluence which only the most ingenuous worshipper perceives at a reverent distance from its surface even" (12:23). Locked within a point of view, the natural historian, however, reads in the surfaces of nature the promise of life. This "fine effluence," a phrase particularly associated with light, electricity, and magnetism in the nineteenth century,[9] permits a perfect mediation between the individual and the natural world.

* * *

Almost to guard against the celebratory nature of his rhetoric, during this period Thoreau continues, however, to describe the magic of surfaces through a mapped orientation toward space. The map in a sense becomes the coefficient of truth, helping to stabilize perception in order to speculate about the laws of nature. As in *Walden*, delight in the return of spring is not presented without measuring the pond and utilizing a technological grid in order to induce a natural law. For instance, by accurately viewing the objects in the landscape and their reflections, Thoreau can also generalize about *laws* that go unnoticed by many writers concerned with the pictorial representations of nature, whose work may reflect beauty but lacks truth. His absorption with the distorting effect of reflections leads him to the principle that "Nature avoids repeating herself" (10:96).

This problem of understanding reflections is transformed into a complex discussion of shifting points of view. The reflection of a hill, for instance, becomes what "*apparently*" the observer would see if his "eye were placed at that part of the surface of the pond where the reflection seems to be" (10:96). But Thoreau goes on to ask, "Is the reflection of a hillside, however, such an aspect of it as can be obtained by the eye directed to the hill itself from any single point of view?" (10:97). The answer begins to posit complex points of view within vision itself:

> It plainly is not such a view as the eye would get looking upward from the immediate base of the hill or water's edge, for there the first rank of bushes on the lower part of the hill would conceal the upper. The reflection of the top appears to be such a view of it as I should get with my eye at the water's edge above the edge of the reflection; but would the lower part of the hill also appear from this point as it does in the reflection? Should I see as much of the under sides of the leaves there? (10:97)

With these questions in mind, Thoreau begins to understand that a reflection involves multiple points of view and does not simply mirror the image reflected. If the reflection cannot be accounted for by a single point of view, then Thoreau concludes that "the reflection is never a true copy or repetition of its substance, but a new composition, and this may be the source of its novelty and attractiveness, and of this nature, too, may be the charm of an echo. I doubt if you can ever get Nature to repeat herself exactly" (10:97). Accordingly, Thoreau does not need to be scrupulous about the problem of exact representation. There are no mirrors, and the strongly mimetic philosophy of his earlier writings can be mollified. He justifies reflection, again, no longer as an ideal version of the object, but as a "new composition" with its own pleasure and charm.

Once Thoreau has established this principle, he can also discount Ruskin's claim in "Elements of Drawing" that a reflection is merely the image "reversed" or "topsy-turvy," maintaining the "true perspective of the solid objects."[10] Thoreau thereby legitimates first-person observation of nature with its precise regard for the technology of seeing and its insistence on the angle of vision as a limiting structure, while asserting that the viewer be affected by the landscape. He is also able to debunk the claims to truth of this prominent writer on perception.

Thoreau's discussion of poetic description, then, calls for a check on an exacting mode of viewing and emphasizes "effects" on the eye. He wants to loosen the technology of seeing: "Sometimes I would rather get a transient glimpse or side view of a thing than stand fronting to it,—as those polypodies. The object I caught a glimpse of as I went by haunts my thoughts a long time, is infinitely suggestive, and I do not care to front it and scrutinize it, for I know that the thing that really concerns me is not there, but in my relation to that. That is a mere reflecting surface" (10:164). Yet Thoreau carefully watches how an individual point of view fronting an object limits and constructs the view of it. The danger is that the effect on the watching eye will be lost. The eye is trained so well that it takes on a quality of abstraction and autonomy. The reader watches Thoreau watch his eye watch the scene.

In the fall of 1857, Thoreau berates the "men of science," again distinguishing his mode of viewing from the strictly scientific. The problem is one of "attitude." Scientific observation is based on the assumption that "[you] should coolly give your chief attention to the phenomenon which excites you as something independent on you, and not as it is related to you" (10:165). He recognizes clearly that vision depends not only on the materiality of the viewer within the context of a landscape conditioned by atmosphere and light, but also on the consciousness of the viewer, and that the "important fact" is the object's "effect on me."

He then claims not to care whether his "vision of truth is a waking thought or dream remembered, whether it is seen in the light or in the dark. It is the subject of the vision, the truth alone, that concerns me" (10:165). Such a tenet would be standard romantic epistemology but for the technology of seeing implied in the relationship between the eye and the object. When Thoreau writes that it is not the objects themselves that concern him, but that "the point of interest is somewhere *between* me and them . . ." (10:165), he is defending his rigorous method of seeing against an easy identification with scientific methods of observation. He insists on first-person analysis of the scene, but with a validation of aesthetic experience.

As with much of Thoreau's psychophysiology of the eye, however, the method involves the distorting quality of sight. His trip to the Franconia Mountains and in particular to the summit of Mount Washington becomes a lesson in the "tricks" of the eye. "The surface was so irregular that you would have thought you saw the summit a dozen times before you did, and in one sense the nearer you got to it, the further off it was" (11:52). This observation forms the basis of a discussion of the possible laws of sight:

> I suspect that such are the laws of light that our eye, as it were, leaps from one prominence to another, connecting them by a straight line when at a distance and making one side balance the other. So that when the summit viewed is fifty or a hundred miles distant, there is but very general and very little truth in the impression of its outline conveyed to the mind. (11:52)

These "laws" ironically do not lead to truth but apply to the mechanical functioning of the eye. They do not produce an "outline" that would, like a map, generate an accurate sense of shape and distance. Instead, they are mere surface gestures of an eye locked in an individual point of view.

Thoreau then speculates on the way in which the eye constructs shapes in the landscape: "It would seem as if by some law of light and vision the eye inclined to connect the base and apex of a peak in the horizon by a straight line" (11:53). Hence, the eye tends to view mountain peaks as pyramidal shapes, so that "you might think that the summit was a smooth inclined plane, though you can reach it only over a succession of promontories and shelves" (11:53). The eye and mind, then, take an active role in shaping what is seen. But Thoreau hardly offers this explanation for the way the eyes see mountainous shapes before recognizing that some summits appear not as pyramids, but as large "lumpish" shapes—a recognition which leads him to speculate that "the eye needs only a hint of the general form and completes the outline from the slightest suggestion" (11:53). Described functionally and hence physiologically, the eye completes and infers the outline perhaps innately. Potentially, then, vision should be understood not only as a religious experience or as a learned, cultural activity, but also as a complex, physiological function of the eye/mind.[11] This psychophysiological function of the eye is the source of many speculations in the later journal years. By examining the effects of light, color, and finally shape, Thoreau begins to see how greatly what is differs from what is seen. The mind becomes important not only as an affective source of reactions to objects, but also as a constructor of the very objects that are seen.

Thoreau does not develop systematically these "laws" about how the eye sees. In the fall of 1858, when he is taken by the colors of the landscape, he also posits an opposing scenario of how the eye functions to construct the scene. No longer the inescapable mediator between the real and the ideal, the eye sits apart from the scene:

> The November twilights just begun! It appeared like a part of a panorama at which I sat spectator, a part with which I was perfectly familiar just coming into view, and I foresaw how it would look and roll along, and prepared to be pleased. Just such a piece of art merely, though infinitely sweet and grand, did it appear to me, and just as little were any active duties required of me. We are independent on all that we see. The hangman whom I have *seen* cannot hang me. The earth which I have *seen* cannot bury me. Such doubleness and distance does sight prove. Only the rich and such as are troubled with ennui are implicated in the maze of phenomena. You cannot see anything until you are clear of it. (11:273)

In his late *Journal,* Thoreau does not hesitate to wander into the "maze of phenomena." The recognition of entrapment within surfaces of light and color often provokes a vision of beauty and, at times, order. But, as we have seen before, Thoreau, having inherited the transcendentalist world view, could not comfortably consider beauty the final cause of nature. The fluctuating world of sensation and perception is always in danger of becoming an illusion. Hence, in this entry, Thoreau's anxieties about his method result in a detachment from sight by positing a doubled vision in which the eye is both an active and a passive agent. As active, it constructs and determines the relationship between consciousness and the object in a highly interdependent, inseparable mode. But the more Thoreau understands the active role of the eye/mind in constructing sight, the greater the danger of entrapment in a physiological explanation of sight. As a result, Thoreau once again rejects vision and the phenomenal world. As a passive agent, the eye waits like a spectator of the scene and is freed from materiality and hence death. This doubleness, that Emerson in his later essays attributes to the self, Thoreau at times in his later years attributes to the eye.[12] Vision itself is split: as a passive dreamer it transcends all limits, bounded only by the imaginary and, hence, is freed of the threat of annihilation; but as active constructor of vision, it is always bound with the grid of space and time, locked into the materiality of contexts and conditions. The splitting we saw in *Cape Cod* and

The Maine Woods occurs not between the body and the mind, but internally within the mind/eye. As such, Thoreau again finds himself denying his own methods as an uncivil historian. As a professional observer of not only what the eye sees but also how it sees, he has developed his skills to read and describe the landscape. Perception as a means to discover redemption, however, is always a double-edged sword. To see is to die. This paradox Thoreau could not avoid.

*   *   *

Despite these anxieties and potential dangers, in March of 1859, Thoreau scrutinizes the landscape with renewed concentration and enthusiasm and reinvestigates the conditions of vision fused to delight. In the following entries, Thoreau writes successful uncivil history, capturing the effects of color and light in time without the loss of the object-world of nature. In so doing, he describes natural phenomena that are as significant as the sand-foliage passage in *Walden*. These observable moments, locked in time, yield fully a sense of redemption for the history of nature.

First, by observing white pines on the horizon, he recognizes that what "pleases" the eye is complex, involving a sense of form, a richness of detail, and an alertness to the effects of light. The eye/mind, as it is "charmed" by the presence of the tree, analyzes the causes of "delight":

> You not only see the regular bilateral form of the tree, all the branches distinct like the frond of a fern or a feather (for the pine, even at this distance, has not merely beauty of outline and color,—it is not merely an amorphous and homogenous or continuous mass of green,—but shows a regular succession of flattish leafy boughs or stages, in flakes one above another, like the veins of a leaf or the leafets of a frond; it is this richness and symmetry of detail which, more than its outline, charms us), but that fine silvery light reflected from its needles (perhaps their under sides) incessantly in motion. (12:63)

The eye/mind continually discriminates within its perceptual field, breaking down "masses" into a "succession" of shapes and shades of green, and finally seeing within the "needles" the dynamic quality of light. The solidity of shape is ultimately analyzed into the fluidity of light as the eye/mind reflects upon a sensation of delight.

Ultimately, the dynamic quality of light becomes the basis for understanding the proper, and hence the normative, angle of light on the pine as opposed to the "appearance" of light coming from the "base of the tree." What is seen, once the eye/mind focuses on the effect of light, can be described as a deception: "As a tree bends and waves like a feather in the gale, I see it alternately dark and light, as the sides of the needles, which reflect the cool sheen, are alternately withdrawn from and restored to the proper angle, and the light appears to flash upward from the base of the tree incessantly" (12:63). Eventually this combination of wind and light prevents the very apprehension of the object: "In the intervals of the flash it is often as if the tree were withdrawn altogether from sight."

Light creates, then, major conditions for seeing the pines, and this "seeing" is worth noting because it is not merely a physical perception, but an aesthetic experience. By following how the eye sees the pines, the description attempts to capture and name the quality of light that conditions the event:

> I see one large pine wood over whose whole top these cold electric flashes are incessantly passing off harmlessly into the air above. I thought at first of some fine spray dashed upward, but it is rather like broad flashes of pale, cold light. Surely you can never see a pine wood so expressive, so speaking. This reflection of light from the waving crests of the earth is like the play and flashing of electricity. (12:64)

Thoreau analogizes the effect of the light, but only after he has attempted to fix a sequence of causes for the event. The eye/mind must break down perception into conditions, distilling the context for seeing before the analogy has any significance in his description of the white pines.

Even after the analogy, Thoreau further draws attention to the conditions for this special seeing. The structural nature of the pines and their needles contribute to the effect: "No deciduous tree exhibits these fine effects of light" (12:64). The force of the wind also contributes to the quality of light: "The wind is making passes over them, magnetizing and electrifying them" (12:64). He even adds into the description the fact that the "flow of sap" in the pines might contribute to the effect. Hence, vision depends upon a multitude of factors in the landscape, the objects themselves, and the viewer.

The description of the pines is actually an analysis of the very conditions for seeing the pines and an attempt to articulate sequentially what contributes to the effect of light on the eye/mind. Only afterwards can a philosophy of the effects of light be developed. Vision itself becomes an open-ended phenomenon, capable of endless analysis.

Later in the entry, however, Thoreau indirectly castigates himself for being interested in the conditions of extraordinary effects of light. He balances the splendid display of light on the pines with the mundane reflection of light from "withered grass and bare hills." Seeing must include the most unspectacular events: "I was drawn toward and worshipped the brownish light in the sod . . . . I felt as if I could eat the very crust of the earth; I never felt so terrene, never sympathized so with the surface of the earth. From whatever source the light and heat come, thither we look with love" (12:67). But the mundane effect does not prompt an analysis of how the eye sees; it merely records an emotional response to the seeing.

Thoreau's desire to understand how the eye sees often dominates this emotional response. The white pines held his attention precisely because they challenged his ability to discern from the landscape the conditions for the vision. This process of analysis minimizes the emotional response while emphasizing the contextual nature of perception.

Yet Thoreau talks about his descriptions as if their primary concern were with "objects." In February 1860, he juxtaposes once again the difference between living in the world of ideas and in the world of things: "Surrounded by our thoughts or imaginary objects, living in our *ideas*, not one in a million ever sees the objects which are actually around him" (13:137). To offset his preoccupation with ideas, Thoreau writes the following passage as an antidote:

Above me is a cloudless blue sky; beneath, the sky-blue, i.e. sky-reflecting, ice with patches of snow scattered over it like mackerel clouds. At a distance in several directions I see the tawny earth streaked or spotted with white where the bank or hills and fields appear, or else the green-black evergreen forests, or the brown, or russet, or tawny deciduous woods, and here and there, where the agitated surface of the river is exposed, the blue-black water. That dark-eyed water, especially when I see it at right angles with the direction of the sun, is it not the first sign of spring? (13:137–38)

Thoreau names the objects and their colors in relation to his spatial position; if given the appropriate conditions for being seen, these objects signify spring or the promise of regeneration.

Color has now become indispensable to delineating the object, but it is also the most unstable attribute, changing with light, atmosphere, and the angle of perception. Therefore, to favor "things" over "ideas" in the description basically involves for Thoreau a record of a sensing presence among the flux of phenomena and of the constitutive force of the sensing presence upon the phenomena. The "dark-eyed water" that Thoreau describes in the journal entry becomes analogous to a "black artery" through the "snow-clad town": "These are the wrists, temples, of the earth, where I feel its pulse with my eye. The living waters, not the dead earth. It is as if the dormant earth opened its dark and liquid eye upon us" (13:138). Although the description is intent upon noting how the eye sees, it quickly moves to this additional rhetorical level where the object becomes an immanent force of meaning upon the observer. As in the thawing sand bank in *Walden,* the flow of the blue-black waters quickly turns into a source of power in itself.

Hardly has the observer been placed by Thoreau into a more passive, receptive stance than he is returned to an active, constituting role:

> But to return to my walk. I proceed over the sky-blue ice, winding amid the flat drifts as if amid the clouds, now and then treading on that thin white ice (much marked) of absorbed puddles (of the surface), which crackles somewhat like dry hard biscuit. Call it biscuit ice. (13:138)

The direction of the walker, the sights, and the sounds make it possible to describe and name the environment. The walk, however, continues in a much more visionary strain: "I thus find myself returning over a green sea, winding amid purple islets, and the low sedge of the meadow on one side is really a burning yellow" (13:140). Specific objects recede to the background as the sensations of color and singular shapes come to the fore, all held together by the presence of the walker.

Thoreau takes the description far into the imaginary while holding onto the materiality of the scene. Seeing is a continual negotiation between the forces of nature and those of the eye/mind. The eye sees from a particular point of view, but what it sees is conditioned by the structure of the object and the atmospheric conditions of the scene. The eye delineates specific colors, but they in turn acquire a forcefulness that impresses the eye. The mind weaves all these specifics into analogies and interprets the scene as part of a symbol system of promise and regeneration.

The entry of this February walk continues with a description of object reversals:

> I walk over a smooth green sea, or *aequor*, the sun just disappearing in the cloudless horizon, amid thousands of these flat isles as purple as the petals of a flower. It would not be more enchanting to walk amid the purple clouds of the sunset sky. And, by the way, this is but a sunset sky under our feet, produced by the same law, the same slanting rays and twilight. Here the clouds are these patches of snow or frozen vapor, and the ice is the greenish sky between them. Thus all of heaven is realized on earth. You have seen those purple fortunate isles in the sunset heavens, and that green and amber sky between them. Would you believe that you could ever walk amid those isles? You can on many a winter evening. I have done so a hundred times. The ice is a solid crystalline sky under our feet. (13:140–41)

The enchantment of the scene resides in both nature and the human viewer and serves as the basis of a sequence of reversals that insists that the far is near, that heaven is earth, that the sky is ice. These substitutions eventually force the apprehension of the landscape into a potential state of doubleness. The phenomenon of winter sunset, a display of light and color on the horizon, is reflected through the snow-covered fields. Because he walks on a middle ground between sky and earth, the observer is privileged to "behold" the enchantment of doubling.

Not present in the description is the potential of splitting the observer into separate functions. To write uncivil history now, Thoreau acts as if the landscape solves the riddles of spirit/matter, heaven/earth, mind/body. It expresses the paradox through the perceptual epiphany of sequences of mirrors that can be observed. The earth reflects the sky, until differences vanish and all is seen within the other. A tour de force of Thoreau's later nature writings, this entry is like the sand-flow passage in *Walden* where the perceptual event makes the inorganic organic. Both are visual paradoxes and, as such, are the essence of uncivil history. Seeing is not merely an act of fusing symbol and fact. It involves the triumph over a threatening contradiction. Can life be seen in all matter? Can nature yield a vision of redemption? For a moment to be observed and described, fitting Thoreau's expectations and addressing his anxieties, the moment must become a visual paradox. And, with Thoreau's later preoccupation with how light affects what the eye sees, it is appropriate that the epiphany is expressed as a play of reflected light.

If part of the transcendental mandate was to perceive sequences of correspondences in the natural world, then Thoreau's walks provide material evidence of visually apprehensible correspondences that are, however, visual paradoxes. Toward the end of this February walk, "the ice is a solid sky on which we walk" (13:142). Not only a doubleness, but also a complete identification and substitution of terms make it possible to hold together in one moment and in one space, the real and the ideal, the near and the far. Only in this way do Thoreau's methods as an uncivil historian reach their final goal.

The ability to perceive this "perceptual fact" in the landscape also involves a change of consciousness for the observer, a purification. "In winter we are purified and translated. The earth does not absorb our thoughts. It becomes a Valhalla" (13:142). Consciousness alone does not construct the scene. Once the eye is trained to see what *is there,* the brilliance of the landscape affects the eye/mind of the observer, cleansing him and allowing him to behold the vision of "Valhalla" on earth. Both sight and mind must undergo this purification process before the landscape can be translated into paradise.

But as we have seen, Thoreau's ability to hold onto these paradisiacal moments is briefly sustained, and his desire to order and discern "laws" in the natural world sometimes militates against the final visionary apprehension of Valhalla. For instance, on the excursion the following day, he writes: "The principal charm of a winter walk over ice is perhaps the peculiar and pure colors exhibited" (13:143). Thoreau then lists nine colors and the general objects associated with them. These colors have no exclusive relationship to the natural world; seven of the nine are attributes of the sky and clouds. In naming them, Thoreau seems almost to remind himself of the reality of each, though he does not extrapolate a symbolic significance for the quality of color in itself.

It is usually when the color becomes part of a description of a scene that its significance emerges. At various places in the spring of 1860, Thoreau constructs the narrative entry as if what is seen is primarily a painted map: "Looking across the Peninsula toward Ball's Hill, I am struck by the bright blue of the river (a deeper blue than the sky), contrasting with the fresh yellow green of the meadow (i.e. of coarse sedges just starting), and, between them, a darker or greener green next the edge of the river, especially where that small sand-bar island is,—the green of that early rank river-grass" (13:275). The fascination with shades of green continues as Thoreau connects certain species of vegetation with particular qualities of green within the mapped space. For instance, on May 9 he writes: "As I stand on Hunt's Bridge, I notice the now comparatively dark green of the canary grass (*Phalaris*), the coarse grass vigorously spring[ing] up on the muddy islands and edges, the glaucous green of *Carex stricta* tufts, and the light yellowish green of the very coarse sedges of the meadow" (13:287). His ability to delineate colors within a space increases as he ties the distinct hues to specific species and topographical location.

Perhaps the most extreme version of this technique, one that leads again to the observation of a visual paradox, appears on July 22, 1860:

> The next field on the west slopes gently from both east and west to a meadow in the middle. So, as I look over the wall, it is first dark-green, where white clover has been cut (still showing a myriad low white heads which resound with the hum of bees); next, along the edge of the bottom or meadow, is a strip or belt three or four rods wide of red-top, uncut, perfectly distinct; then the cheerful bright-yellow sedge of the meadow, yellow almost as gamboge; then a corresponding belt of red-top on its upper edge, quite straight and rectilinear like the first; then a glaucous-green field of grain still quite low; and, in the further corner of the field, a much darker square of green than any yet, all brilliant in this wonderful light. You thus have a sort of terrestrial rainbow, thus: —

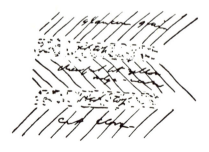

(13:414)

All the ingredients of mapped space wedded to color perception are present. The landscape is aestheticized, with the same attempt to wed opposites into one concept and perception. Like the figurative language of the "solid sky" on the winter walk, the final trope is an oxymoron, a "terrestrial rainbow." For Thoreau, the paradoxical relationship of earth and sky and the ability to see each as the other is equivalent to fusing the real and the ideal. The doubleness of sight leads to an apprehension of the landscape as a fusion of opposites.

Later in the summer of 1860, Thoreau again insists that the training for his specific mode of viewing is based not on "painterly" techniques, but on scientific knowledge and, in particular knowledge of classification systems and nomenclature. "No one but a botanist is likely to distinguish nicely the different shades of green with which the open surface of the earth is clothed,—not even a landscape-painter if he does not know the species of sedges and grasses which paint it" (14:3). Discrimination within the topographical field of vision depends upon the trained eye's ability to distinguish species within the landscape; "variety of color," therefore, depends upon the knowledge of "various species." First-person observation in this instance rests not merely on empirical methods of viewing the landscape but on cognitive categories within which the observer places visual discriminations. This point, one that occupies Thoreau's attention throughout his late nature essays, eventually leads him away from direct observation and toward a concern with language systems as a guide for vision.

Thoreau constructs in this entry, however, a description that perhaps better typifies his antipictorial technique in representing the landscape:

Again, I sit on the brow of the orchard, and look northwest down the river valley (at mid-afternoon). There flows, or rests, the calm blue winding river, lake-like, with its smooth silver-plated sides, and wherever weeds extend across it, there too the silver plate bridges it, like a spirit's bridge across the Styx; but the rippled portions are blue as the sky. This river reposes in the midst of a broad brilliant yellow valley amid green fields and hills and woods, as if, like the Nanking or Yang-ho (or what-not), it flowed through an Oriental Chinese meadow where yellow is the imperial color. The immediate and raised edge of the river, with its willows and button-bushes and polygonums, is a light green, but the immediately adjacent low meadows, where the sedge prevails, is a brilliant and cheerful yellow, intensely, incredibly bright, such color as you never see in pictures; yellow of various tints, in the lowest and sedgiest parts deepening to so much color as if gamboge had been rubbed into the meadow there; the most cheering color in all the landscape; shaded with little darker isles of green in the midst of this yellow sea of sedge. Yet it is the bright and cheerful yellow, as of spring, and with nothing in the least autumnal in it. How this contrasts with the adjacent fields of red-top, now fast falling before the scythe! (14:4–5)

The colors in the landscape that Thoreau names and positions within the mapped space cannot be imitated on canvas or reproduced by man, but they can be "beheld" and recorded in language. His description can help train the eye to see the landscape discriminately so that the beauty of these colors makes itself felt on the reader/observer. Thoreau wants this image-making quality of language to compete with pictorial representation.[13] The expression of what he calls the "delight which any natural object draws from us" is the end of his description. And because we cannot imitate its existence through matter, language becomes for Thoreau the only legitimate vehicle to express this "delight."

Contrary, then, to critical opinion that the late *Journal* is largely a compendium of "scientific" facts, in reality it argues against any strictly scientific description of natural phenomena which does not permit "delight." In these later years, color and light function as the catalyst in many entries to create this sense of beauty in beholding the landscape, which then leads to tropes that fuse physical fact with moral or spiritual purpose. In the fall of 1860, Thoreau writes that it is important to describe "the most familiar object with a zest and vividness of imagery as if [one] saw it for the first time, the novelty consisting not in the strangeness of the object, but in the new and clearer perception of it" (14:120). Color and light imagery wedded with topography—this combination becomes the rhetorical feature of Thoreau's description, which merges science with art. Hence, the accurate rendering of topographical space is one with delight; geometry and pleasure blend.

In these journal writings, then, the record of the temporal moment in nature takes on an increasingly complex understanding of perception, an understanding not without fear and doubt. The "maze of phenomena" can create a longing to split sight and to postulate a formidable detachment for the eye. The uncivil historian must therefore become the sentient observer whose constant attention to the fleeting visual effects of the landscape nonetheless captures an enduring sense of promise, beauty, and renewal. At their best, these historical visions express visual paradoxes in which the material world is indistinguishable from the immaterial. Spirit is indeed matter, if only for a second, and time is redeemed.

SIX

Regulating Eden

In Thoreau's late journal writings, perception continues to be the prevailing means for affirming redemptive history. Visual paradoxes can be seen and described, but these exemplary moments, embedded within the historical changes of nature, are both rare and fleeting. In the fall of 1860, somewhat abruptly, while Thoreau is still taken by the perception of beauty in the landscape, he begins to turn from the natural description of delight to observations about the succession of forest trees,[1] recording information in an attempt to articulate "laws" about pine and oak forests and to formulate principles of management for woodlots. Reading the *Journal* of 1860, one is struck by the shift in focus within a few weeks from beauty to usefulness and a new justification for writing uncivil history.

This movement from beauty to usefulness, from the epiphany to the catalogue, most dramatic in the fall of 1860, is not new to Thoreau's writings but occurs in practically all of them. On April 28, 1852, for instance, he lists flowers by date in their order of appearance,[2] and on June 24, 1852, in a list omitted by editors Torrey and Allen, he notes hundreds of flowers and birds in a strict time chronology.[3] Thoreau's practice of cataloguing increased through the 1850s and the early 1860s, as he collated natural events over periods of years,[4] perhaps in search of representative natural occurrences for individual months and entire years.[5] But toward the end of his life, he may have felt a growing need to impose order on the massive observations in his *Journal*.[6]

In his grand experiment of observation, Thoreau faces the dilemma of finding in the discrete moment of natural history a vision of redemption, or of extracting from sequences of perceived natural events a law or demonstrable pattern of redemptive growth. Although Thoreau is continually moved by the former method, the latter best suited his need to formulate a sustained vision of history. Currently, Thoreau's late nature essays, culled from journal entries and sequential observations, are receiving fuller critical attention. John Hildebidle observes: "Toward the end of his life he is still writing essays which, by their very titles and subjects, identify themselves as natural history, and which at the same time try to expand the form into myth and prophecy."[7] On a general level, Thoreau can be seen as following in the tradition of Puritan history writing in which history becomes prophecy.[8] However, this fusion of history and prophecy should not be understood in any way as a complete acceptance of Puritan attitudes toward historical time. In his late essays, Thoreau, while holding onto the need to preserve the sacredness of history, argues against a vision of providential history in particular.

Thoreau's catalogues and late nature essays are in many ways the keys to understanding what was at stake in his vision of history. On the most practical level, Thoreau had to answer the question of how much time is necessary to induce a law of natural history. He had at hand in the last months of his life up to ten years of journal entries from which he could correlate natural events. But is ten years adequate to display an accurate seasonal chart of growth, decay, and rebirth? On a more general level, Thoreau's laws of historical change must be poignant enough to persuade his readers to put aside both the inherited ideas of history and the emerging historical designs of contemporary naturalists.

In other words, through his careful notations, Thoreau hopes to defeat the historical sense of time he had inherited from the Puritans, namely, a providential history, and then to argue against the nineteenth-century's emerging materialistic explanation of the history of nature. Although the Puritan attitudes toward nature are complex and at times contradictory, it is clear that in providential history, God is always the first cause: "Sometimes in the world of nature He uses instrumental causes, which we can trace, but if the being of things be followed to the top, 'this will of God, is the First Cause of all things,' and we cannot understand it or trace its logic."[9] Religious scientists like Louis Agassiz who led the American opposition against Darwinism, faltered on the same distinction between first and instrumental causes. Agassiz "found it impossible to interpret the results of his research in such a fashion as to provide a positive role for 'physical agencies' in natural history." For instance, "he saw the glaciers as 'God's great plough,' destructive forces that yet signified supernatural intervention."[10]

Darwin, of course, argued for the "positive role" of material or instrumental causes and from one point of view eliminated divine intervention. Thoreau's challenge is how to keep his vision of natural history, which also eliminates divine intervention, from becoming secular, and instead to keep it sacred. His enemies are both the providential and materialistic histories. In his late nature essays and charts, Thoreau attempts to find over a period of time a temporal order that verifies a redemptive pattern, an order drawn from natural events and their conditions, thereby combining first and instrumental cause. In the process, Thoreau must banish any sense of interrupted time as the special place of supernatural action. Uncivil history must ultimately be argued on the basis of natural laws of succession. The epiphany of redeemed time, visible on the landscape, must be buttressed by an extensive polemic of laws and observations. Only in this way can history become prophecy.

The late nature essays are, then, highly individual attempts to present the historical plot of natural events. Each places the history of civilization, a story of conquest and betrayal, within the uncivil history of vegetation. The natural laws of pine trees, autumn foliage, wild apples, and huckleberries contain a rhetoric of historical change necessary for the continuation of the human species. As in *A Week*, Thoreau forces his reader to recognize a new sense of the historical and, hence, to realign the relationship between nature and civilization. In "The Succession of Forest Trees," Thoreau extracts a law of sequence that accurately explains the replacement of a pine forest by one of oak from a carefully repeated examination of the conditions of forest growth, thus documenting how the laws of nature are beneficent to man and society. In "Autumnal Tints," he describes the sequence of color change in fall foliage observed over the course of several years, indicating how scientific nomenclature permits greater accuracy for color terms and validates the need for mental, linguistic categories in order to see the patterns of redemption. In "Wild Apples" and "Huckleberries," individual species that are charted over the change of season yield their natural histories that warn man to either heed the ways of nature or face extinction.

Each essay posits a historical truth about the landscape that is accessible only to the trained observer who can induce laws from natural events, and who can use not only perception, but also mental categories and scientific nomenclature, to refine observations. In Thoreau's late essays, beauty is not forgotten, but it is subservient to the need to present logical, categorical evidence for the laws of redemptive history.

* * *

"The Succession of Forest Trees" begins with an apologia for the transcendentalist as scientist, then blends the two identities, and ends by dissociating them altogether. It is at once a vindication of the methods of observation that Thoreau has developed and a final assertion that the transcendentalist also sees redemptive design within the specific laws of the material universe. For example, Thoreau employs both the image and the fact of the seed as the principal agent of forest growth in a cogent explanation of forest succession and in a view of the universe that values human imagination. In so doing, however, he gives no ground to a theory of spontaneous generation, popular with scientists such as Agassiz and writers such as Emerson,[11] nor to a providential interruption of natural time to produce a forest. Like the human observer, the seed works in time and, given appropriate conditions for growth, will produce a tree. These conditions are not magical or mysterious; they can be observed, noted, and even reproduced by naturalists.

The problem Thoreau confronts in this essay is why, when a pine forest is cut down, an oak forest replaces it, a problem that "is no mystery to" one who has observed and studied it for years. Thoreau's method of viewing the landscape within a mapped space and hence always within a context finally merges with explanations of natural activity. The illustrative walk that Thoreau uses to "prove" his theory of succession proceeds as follows:

> . . . I walked the same day to a small but very dense and handsome white pine grove, about fifteen rods square, in the east part of this town. The trees are large for Concord, being from ten to twenty inches in diameter, and as exclusively pine as any wood that I know. Indeed, I selected this wood because I thought it the least likely to contain anything else. It stands on an open plain or pasture, except that it adjoins another small pine wood, which has a few little oaks in it, on the southeast side. On every other side, it was at least thirty rods from the nearest woods. Standing on the edge of this grove and looking through it, for it is quite level and free from underwood, for the most part bare, red-carpeted ground, you would have said that there was not a hardwood tree in it, young or

old. But on looking carefully along over its floor I discovered, though it was not till my eye had got used to the search, that, alternating with thin ferns, and small blueberry bushes, there was, not merely here and there, but as often as every five feet and with a degree of regularity, a little oak, from three to twelve inches high, and in one place I found a green acorn dropped by the base of a pine. (5:191–92) [12]

Apprehending the cartography of the scene is essential for arriving at a law that the inexperienced observer would overlook. A nursery of small oaks inhabits the floor of the pine forest, and its agents, the red squirrels, are hard at their tasks as Thoreau observes the miniature forest.

Far from being governed providentially, nature "is all the while planting the oaks amid the pines without our knowledge, and at last . . . we send a party of woodchoppers to cut down the pines, and so rescue an oak forest, at which we wonder as if it had dropped from the skies" (p. 194). Further, a reciprocal relationship exists between the mature pines and the oak seedlings: "But although these oaks almost invariably die if the pines are not cut down, it is probable that they do better for a few years under their shelter than they would anywhere else" (p. 192). English planters had used pines to protect oaks but, Thoreau implies, without recognizing that the method was originally found in nature. Nature is the laboratory where continuous tests and experiments have been advancing for millions of years. Only the observer who goes into that laboratory, who examines natural phenomena in context, can understand the cycles of growth and decay. A child of Darwin, Thoreau takes his theory of perception into the field of natural observation.

Leo Stoller has pointed out that the "succession of forest trees had been observed by New Englanders for many years before Henry Thoreau became a botanist." [13] In the nineteenth century, Americans were not, however, busy extracting conservation principles from these observations. Instead, "more typical was the discussion of forest lands in Tench Coxe's *A View of the United States of America*," whose purpose was to show how America's "vast forests might be used to supply exports to Europe and thus earn money for investment in industry while at the same time freeing more earth for farming." [14] But Thoreau's uncivil history of forest succession ultimately complicates any easy directive for civilized progress and radically undermines this simplistic commercial view of forest production.

In addition, the "Succession" essay does not fully demonstrate how committed Thoreau was to disproving the naturalist theory of "spontaneous generation."[15] Rather, in a long, unpublished document entitled "The Dispersion of Seeds,"[16] Thoreau writes with less tact that "it is a vulgar prejudice that such forests are 'spontaneously generated,' but science knows that there has not been a sudden new creation in their [this?] case, but a steady progress according to existing laws, that they come from seeds, i.e., are the result of causes still in operation, though we may not be aware that they are operating."[17] Like Asa Gray, who voiced his opinion of Darwin in the famous *American Journal of Science*,[18] Thoreau argues in the "Dispersion of Seeds" that "the development theory implies a greater vital force in Nature—because it is more flexible and accommodating—and equivalent to a sort of constant new creation."[19] This theory of "constant new creation" has significant implications for Thoreau's concept of uncivil history. For instance, Agassiz, following the writings of Baron Georges Cuvier, believed that the "finite individuals of animate nature were forever linked to the immaterial forms in which they participated, as represented by the divinely inspired identity of structural plan."[20] Not only did the supernatural interrupt time, but the "structural plan" of the divine existed outside of time. Thoreau, of course, flips what Agassiz considered without to within. Laws, therefore, must come from temporal sequence. Like Gray, Thoreau finds nothing objectionable to the claims of both religion and science in these instances. Though the world of matter could threaten identity, as in "Ktaadn," and shock belief in the "afterlife," as in *Cape Cod*, Thoreau basically holds onto the laws extracted from chronological observations to prove redemptive history. Thoreau does not share Darwin's agnosticism and increasing skepticism about the correlation between law and intelligence in the 1859 "Dispersion of Seeds" document. The structure of the "Succession" essay does betray, however, doubt about any simple adherence to the development theory. Within the double image of the seed, Thoreau's uneasy vision of redemptive history emerges.

A new appraisal of the function of the seed accompanies the insistence on context as a crucial element of perception. For Thoreau as well as for British and American romantics, the seed has been a recurring metaphor of regeneration, renewal, and infinite potential. Coleridge's *Biographia Literaria* is woven with the image of the seed as the romantic imagination, always ready to generate new ideas that signify the growth of the human mind. But in the "Succession" essay the seed is demetaphorized into a natural cause. No tree can grow without a seed, the bedrock of the material cause. "No such tree has ever been known to spring from anything else. If any one asserts that it sprang from something else, or from nothing, the burden of proof lies with him" (p. 186).

All reasoning must proceed, then, from the simple but irrefutable cause of the seed. Hence, the seed is redefined as a transient source of vitality, not a permanent source of generating power; only under certain conditions and within a restricted period of time can it function. "The stories of wheat raised from seed buried with an ancient Egyptian, and of raspberries raised from seed found in the stomach of a man in England, who is supposed to have died sixteen or seventeen hundred years ago, are generally discredited, simply because the evidence is not conclusive" (pp. 200–201). Apocryphal stories that could point to the infinite resources of the potential of life, as represented by the seed, Thoreau now coolly discounts. Fragile and dependent upon conditions for germination, the seed has lost its power to represent the human imagination. But with a condition, "I am prepared to believe that some seeds, especially small ones, may retain their vitality for centuries under favorable circumstances" (p. 201). "Favorable circumstances," context, and conditions, therefore, become the dominant factors in understanding generation.

Thoreau ends the essay by dissociating the seed as natural cause from the seed as metaphor. Hitherto in pursuit of natural explanation, he now adds a countermanding postscript that claims a range of knowledge beyond natural observation. "Other seeds I have which will find other things in that corner of my garden, in like fashion, almost any fruit you wish, every year for ages, until the crop more than fills the whole garden" (p. 204). The seed produces a fruit of endless productivity in the imaginary garden, unhindered by the structures of the material universe. The problem of value is redefined. Whereas knowledge of the law of succession for forest trees can profit the Concord farmer who wisely manages his woodlots, the products of the imagination are not so easily "sold" to the agricultural society. Implicit in Thoreau's positing separate seeds for the imagination and the material universe is the possibility of separate systems for the two realms, precisely what he was trying to avoid by his vision of uncivil history. By the end of the essay, however, the synthesis of natural causes and of imaginative associations appears impossible.

Thoreau is also keenly aware that his observations on succession are highly regarded because they may profit his audience. His discomfort with the ironies of this position can be seen in another passage in the "Dispersion of Seeds" manuscript, an anecdote about a local farmer whose greed was exceeded only by his ignorance. After cutting down a pine forest,

> . . . he thought it would be clear gain if he could extract a little rye from it in the meanwhile. What a fool! Here nature had got everything ready for this emergency—kept them ready for many years—oaks half a dozen years old with fusiform roots full charged and tops already pointing skyward, only waiting to be touched off by the sun—and he thought he knew better and would get a little rye out of it first which he could feel at once between his fingers, and so he burned it and dragged his harrow over it.
>
> He has got his dollars for the pine timber, and now he wishes to get his bushels of grain, and finger the dollars that they will bring—and then, Nature—you may have your way again—a greediness that defeats its own ends—for nature can not now pursue the way she had entered upon.—As if oaks would bide his time—or come at his bidding—or as if he preferred to have a pine or a birch wood here, possibly, 30 to 50 years hence—rather than an oak wood at once—[21]

This is a form of abuse that Thoreau had hoped his argument would prevent, but he is acutely aware that human greed also motivates change.

Thoreau closes the "Succession" essay less harshly, warning his audience that there are other seeds beyond profit and amusement: "Yet farmers' sons will stare by the hour to see a juggler draw ribbons from his throat, though he tells them it is all deception. Surely, men love darkness rather than light" (p. 204). A more generalized criticism, the pursuit of truth and not deception, a truth which can be pursued in both the fields and the mind, becomes Thoreau's final message to the agricultural society.

In this essay, however, Thoreau is caught in the dilemma of his sense of history. While he wants the laws of natural phenomena to "plot" a redemptive truth about natural history, he cannot trust the manipulative use of these laws for societal gain. Knowledge of nature might increase the greed of men who are without moral character. In order to prevent such abuse, Thoreau must redefine the seed as beyond matter and as part of the imagination, and hence for a transcendentalist, part of a system of moral principles. The laws of history are, then, suspended within the pressing demands of moral order.

*   *   *

"Autumnal Tints" depends as heavily as "Succession of Forest Trees" on the description of natural phenomena "in the order in which they present themselves" (p. 251), but here color is the indexing device to measure position in a time sequence and therefore functions as a classification term—not merely as a component of perception and aesthetic pleasure, as in his late *Journal*. Hence, color terms become the means to pinpoint redemptive design. Thoreau did, of course, throughout his writings use color symbolically. As Richard Colyer points out, he "was probably scientist enough to know the relationship between light rays and natural color phenomena. Certainly he was transcendentalist enough to see the implications for his symbolic system, and artist enough to recognize the wide range of sensory appeal inherent in color."[22] So color functions symbolically in "Autumnal Tints" too. But here that role is less important than that of signaling change in a particular historical sequence. Thoreau takes us through the changes in color from the purple grasses to the scarlet oaks, spinning an elaborate moral from the fall foliage. Eventually, the catalogue of change serves as a base for a Thoreauvian thanatopsis in which color becomes "evidence" of ripeness and proof of the positive message of decay and death.

The desire to separate species of vegetation and recount in sequential order the change in color substantiates Thoreau's commitment to the distinguishing power of the human eye. Once the viewer can connect color with individual species, its gradations expand, just as the color green separates into ten or twelve shades in his late *Journal*. Likewise, the perception of the fall foliage as a "simple mass of color" can expand into a perception of "different trees being of different colors and hues" (p. 262). Again, Thoreau identifies a subtlety of vision beyond the power of the "painter"— where the correct seer is a trained naturalist who knows the names of different species and can identify them in the landscape. Purple grasses, red maples, elms, sugar maples, and scarlet oaks become the grid used to inventory color succession and hue differentiation. The identification of species with its linguistic code goes hand in hand with the increased perception of varieties of color.

Color terms themselves are a topic of discussion in this essay. Contemporary linguists and philosophers of language are still debating the relationship between color and language. In a recent article, Paul Kay and Chad K. McDaniel refute the theory of the relativity of color perception among cultures, a hypothesis commonly attributed to Edward Sapir and Benjamin Whorf, in preference for a "biologically based understanding of basic color-term semantics."[23] Do we see universal perceptions of color, or do we see what each language imposes upon the array of perceptions? To Thoreau, the species code is important because, being transient and highly dependent upon conditions, color itself is an unstable variable in perception. He notes, for instance, that the "burning red" of the scarlet oaks is not contained within the substance of the oaks. "The focus of their reflected color is in the atmosphere far on this side. Every such tree becomes a nucleus of red, as it were, where, with the declining sun, that color grows and glows. It is partly borrowed fire, gathering strength from the sun on its way to your eye. . . . You see a redder tree than exists" (p. 283). It is not a matter of whether we all see red, but the relationship between "redness," matter, and the eye/mind. The conditions of sight, then, create illusions that must be noted, but beneath the flux of color and its fleeting appearance in time lie the names of the species that order the phenomena in sequential development. Like the map and the discernible law, color terms compensate for the illusiveness of perception.

Naming color helps unite the range of color perception with a stable system of signifiers. The species code serves Thoreau in other ways. Ideologically similar to his use of the map, it offers an alternative to the popular color terms that he associates with decadent or materialistic cultural values. Thoreau disdains the tendency to name colors after "obscure foreign localities" and "trivial articles of commerce" (p. 273). He is particularly critical of the vogue in contemporary writing to allude to precious jewels when attempting to image color to the reader, a practice that both Emily Dickinson and Elizabeth Barrett Browning found so imaginatively suggestive.[24] Instead, Thoreau offers the "names of some of our trees and shrubs, as well as flowers" to be the linguistic grid for color terms because the natural landscape in its differentiation into categories of species contains for him an infinitely richer scale of color. As usual, he elevates the observer of the landscape over the painter and the poverty of his methods: "Our paint-box is very imperfectly filled. Instead of, or beside, supplying such paint-boxes as we do, we might supply these natural colors to the young" (p. 273). And the way to catalogue "these natural colors" is by the names of species. Color still functions in relation to a specific grid, but instead of jewels, items of trade, and foreign localities, species of American vegetation dominate the references.

Thoreau associates this shift in naming with a nationalistic motive. America, the land of truly spectacular fall foliage, much more "brilliant" than its European or British counterpart, is the fitting locale for referencing color. American species *should* supply the names of colors, and the beauty of the American landscape *should* become the major linguistic code for color terms. Instead of "Prussian blue," we should name crayons, paint tubes, and dress fabrics "Indian-grass blue." Such new names will suggest a different value system. Instead of profit and aristocratic pretensions, they will signal the presence of "a race capable of wild delight" (p. 275), a race of careful observers who not only have the "knowledge of the names and distinctions of color," but also possess the "joy and exhilaration which these colored leaves excite" (p. 274). The names, then, signal not only observable categories, but also pleasurable sensations. The ideologies of both science and poetry are wedded in these new names.

Thoreau's catalogue of color also underpins the ode of consolation for the death and decay that follows, resulting again in a triumph of redemptive history. The fallen leaves of all these species provide the "muck" that nature needs to go on reproducing. The leaves themselves represent the scientific economy of the natural world. But this economy is also an aesthetic moment: "How beautifully they [the leaves] go to their graves! how gently lay themselves down and turn to mould!—painted of a thousand hues, and fit to make the beds of us living. . . . They teach us how to die. One wonders if the time will ever come when men, with their boasted faith in immortality, will lie down as gracefully and as ripe,—with such an Indian-summer serenity will shed their bodies, as they do their hair and nails" (pp. 269–70). The beauty and economy of natural phenomena, fixed within the cycle of growth and decay, are strictly understood only through the evolving techniques of observation that Thoreau advocates in "Autumnal Tints." He ends the essay with these general remarks on perception:

Objects are concealed from our view, not so much because they are out of the course of our visual ray as because we do not bring our minds and eyes to bear on them, for there is no power to see in the eye itself, any more than in any other jelly. . . . The actual objects which one man will see from a particular hilltop are just as different from those which another will see as the beholders are different. The scarlet oak must, in a sense, be in your eye when you go forth. We cannot see anything until we are possessed with the idea of it, take it into our heads,—and then we can hardly see anything else. . . . I have found that it required a different intention of the eye, in the same locality, to see different plants, even when they were closely allied, as *Juncaceae* and *Gramineae:* when I was looking for the former, I did not see the latter in the midst of them. How much more, then, it requires different intentions of the eye and of the mind to attend to different departments of knowledge! How differently the poet and the naturalist look at objects! (pp. 285–86)

In his later years, taking perceptual subjectivity and illusion as absolute principles of fact, Thoreau concedes that the mind must structure perception before correct observation can occur. His *Journal* of 1858 echoes these sentiments, advocating a parallel intentionality of both eye and mind before correct seeing can take place. In "Autumnal Tints," the grid of species' names becomes a sorting processor by which the observer collects discrete observations and experiences beauty and moral value. The poet always goes beyond the grid to questions of wider value, but without the grid he or she is lost in the labyrinth of subjectivity. In this instance, natural science provides the necessary nomenclature not only for careful observation, but for moral and aesthetic truth.

The last paragraph of "Autumnal Tints" makes the method very clear. "When you come to observe faithfully the changes of each humblest plant, you find that each has, sooner or later, its peculiar autumnal tint; and if you undertake to make a complete list of the bright tints, it will be nearly as long as a catalogue of the plants in your vicinity" (p. 289). This agreement between the variety of color and vegetation validates the grid of scientific nomenclature as the reference for color observation. Without it, color only signals illusion and instability in the natural world; with it, the law of temporal sequence is revealed and nature's redemptive message decoded.

* * *

In "Wild Apples," a cleverly written essay, Thoreau reintroduces the story of sequential development along the familiar civil versus uncivil opposition. The wild apple is itself a hybrid of the civil and uncivil. Like Thoreau, it represents one who does not belong "to the aboriginal race" but has "strayed into the woods from the cultivated stock" (p. 301). The naming of its many species should challenge the traditional names that refer back only to culture. "We should have to call in the sunrise and the sunset, the rainbow and the autumn woods and the wild-flowers, and the woodpecker and the purple finch and the squirrel and the jay and the butterfly, the November traveler and the truant boy, to our aid" (p. 315). The naming of wild apples would go beyond scientific Latin nomenclature that means so much in stabilizing color terms in "Autumnal Tints." Now the grid functions in a new way to reflect the significance of an individual species. Thoreau manipulates it, playfully introducing both natural and cultural events until even mythology serves to name objects: there are blue-jay apples, partridge apples, truant's apples, railroad apples, and "also the Apple where hangs the Forgotten Scythe; Iduna's Apples, and the Apples which Loki found in the Wood; and a great many more I have on my list, too numerous to mention,—all of them good" (p. 317). The list reflects, then, the departments of knowledge in the human mind, as much as the objects referenced, and these departments are no longer constituted by nineteenth-century science. They include the unwieldy categories of personal experience and local terminology, causing one to sense the arbitrary ordering of all natural phenomena and, perhaps, to smile at the high seriousness of scientific nomenclature.

"Wild Apples" does more, however, than parody scientific nomenclature. Ending with a quote from the Book of Joel, this essay, similar in form to the jeremiad,[25] by instructing the reader on his concept of uncivil history, is as close as Thoreau comes to blending prophecy and history. The essay combines natural description and pointed social criticism and warns against the destruction of the land.

The history of the apple, like the history of man, has taken a bifurcated route. The civil apple, a product of the civilizations in the north temperate zone, is in danger of losing its enchantment. The profit-minded New England farmer who sees apples as "pomace" destroys agriculture, much as agricultural avarice blights the land in the "Succession of Forest Trees." Unlike that essay, however, Thoreau invents no method to save the cultivated apples, but merely juxtaposes them with the history of the wild or uncivil apple, turning its fate into an emblem of the fate of civilization. In this way the history of the uncivil apple contains within it the story of civilization.

Like the early Puritan and the oxen grazing on his claimed lands, the wild apple was a fellow emigrant from the Old World. The wild apple's history of growth and reproduction was shaped by the new environment of North America and, in particular, by the habits of the domesticated cow that feasted upon its vegetation:

> The cows continue to browse them thus for twenty years or more, keeping them down and compelling them to spread, until at last they are so broad that they become their own fence, when some interior shoot, which their foes cannot reach, darts upward with joy: for it has not forgotten its high calling, and bears its own peculiar fruit in triumph. (p. 305)

This method of "cultivation," invented by what Thoreau calls the "system of Van Cow," yields almost a moral analogy for man, since "only the most persistent and strongest genius defends itself and prevails, sends a tender scion upward at last, and drops its perfect fruit on the ungrateful earth" (p. 307). Because man's fate is akin to that of the wild apple, it is necessary to understand the wild apple's history. Again, Thoreau's version of history downplays supernatural or human intervention, but demonstrates how historical time proceeds along the line of conditional restraints and necessitates a highly contextual understanding of life. No living thing can be taken out of the web of conditions without damaging the redemptive designs of nature's historical continuum.

This sense of time stands in opposition not only to civilized progress, but to the biblical myth of creation and its ensuing myth of redemption. Though Thoreau ends this essay by quoting from the Old Testament, he consistently revises and modifies the biblical version of Genesis. On one level, as many critics have pointed out, Thoreau's need for an earthly paradise resembles that of the American Adam.[26] In "Wild Apples," he entreats the reader to taste the apple and gain the "new" knowledge that will promise redemption. An inversion of the Genesis story, the history of the wild apple becomes the means to truth: "To appreciate the flavor of these wild apples requires vigorous and healthy senses, *papillae* firm and erect on the tongue and palate, not easily flattened and tamed" (p. 313). Tasting the apple and its "ambrosia" becomes the test of regeneration. "What a healthy out-of-door appetite it takes to relish the apple of life, the apple of the world, then!" (p. 313). This is truly Iduna's apple; one eats it and is restored.

By its ignorance of the wild apple's history, human society disregards this ritual of consummation and wastes its fruit. Even worse, by manipulating the vegetation of the wild, humans doom their own species. Only by recognizing that the history of the wild apple and the history of man are one "in time" can redemption be attained.

In this sense, Thoreau rewrites a biblical or providential sense of time, where only a supernatural act can restore the Garden of Eden. To one who perceives the garden as already present, the rest of mankind appears blind, since any attempt to change the ecological conditions of nature's interdependent system will end in a violation of historical time. Thoreau arrives at his logical conclusion that the wild apple's end is at hand. He even prophesies it:

> The era of the Wild Apple will soon be past. It is a fruit which will probably become extinct in New England. You may still wander through old orchards of native fruit of great extent, which for the most part went to the cider-mill, now all gone to decay. I have heard of an orchard in a distant town, on the side of a hill, where the apples rolled down and lay four feet deep against a wall on the lower side, and this the owner cut down for fear they should be made into cider. Since the temperance reform and the general introduction of grafted fruit, no native apple trees, such as I see everywhere in deserted pastures, and where the woods have grown up around them, are set out. I fear that he who walks over these fields a century hence will not know the pleasure of knocking off wild apples. Ah, poor man, there are many pleasures which he will not know! (p. 321)

Thoreau dramatizes this bleak prediction of a twentieth century devoid of wild fruit and a sensual relationship to nature by concluding the essay with a quotation from the Book of Joel describing the decay of the land: "'The vine is dried up, and the fig tree languisheth; the pomegranate tree, and palm tree also, and the apple tree, even all the trees of the field are withered: because joy is withered away from the sons of men'" (p. 322). Unlike the usual American form of the jeremiad which offered the means to regain the kingdom and used a language of crisis to spur the nation to greater effort, Thoreau's essay merely ends with a warning of doom. But implicit within the essay is the means to regain Eden, though not through traditional biblical means. "To call on the name of the Lord" translates, in Thoreau's vision of redemptive history, as gaining knowledge of the historical continuum of nature as it is lived through species other than the human. One must eat of the wild apple to gain this knowledge, a knowledge of both truth and pleasure.

In a sense, this knowledge exists beyond language for Thoreau. In "Wild Apples," the natural abundance of the wild extends beyond linguistic codes. Adapting the writings of Bodaeus, Thoreau quotes: "'Not if I had a hundred tongues, a hundred mouths, / An iron voice, could I describe all the forms / And reckon up all the names of these *wild apples*" (p. 317). Human speech, whether in the form of scientific nomenclature or mythological allusion, merely approximates the fertility of the earth. Only by a lived interdependence and an existential sense of historical continuity between all living things can Thoreau's vision of redeemed time emerge.

* * *

In "Huckleberries," nomenclature is also important, not because it stabilizes perception or spurs creative naming, but because it also testifies to fertility and wildness. The total of fourteen species of the whortleberry on New England's soil as opposed to the two species commonly noted in England proves the landscape's prolificacy. Like Whitman's grass, the berry symbolizes vegetation stretching out over the North American continent: "In short the whortleberry bushes in the Northern States and British America are a sort of miniature forest surviving under the great forest, and reappearing when the latter is cut, and also extending northward beyond it" (p. 14).[27]

For Thoreau, the "word berry has a new significance in America" (p. 10). Its name draws the naturalist and the observer of the landscape into the culture of the native Americans, to an understanding of their gathering, naming, and cooking practices. In particular, the huckleberry which Thoreau seeks to "celebrate" is "very nearly coterminous with what has been called the Algonquin Family of Indians" (p. 15). Indians harvested the fruit and relied upon it as a major source of sustenance. Thoreau attempts to generalize beyond the Northeast and draws together the practices of many North American Indians under the ritual of gathering wild berries: "Hence you see that the Indians from time immemorial, down to the present day, all over the northern part of America—have made far more extensive use of the whortleberry—at all seasons and in various ways—than we—and that they were far more important to them than to us" (p. 20).

The huckleberry's significance to America resides not only in its presence on the land, but in its function within a culture that draws food from uncultivated sources. Unlike the Indians who followed the economy of nature, whites substituted an economy that destroys wild fruits. The berry "grows wild all over the country— wholesome, bountiful and free, a real ambrosia. And yet men, the foolish demons that they are, devote themselves to the culture of tobacco, inventing slavery and a thousand other curses for that purpose—with infinite pains and inhumanity go raise tobacco all their lives, and that is the staple instead of huckleberries" (p. 22). The rejected berry, then, stands as proof of America's corrupt agricultural practices. Societies that cannot "use" it are detached from the economic systems of the natural world. In their greed for crops of "value" rather than sustenance, they "invent" labor practices that enslave thousands of human lives. Crops as commodities become an insidious part of the American landscape and a symbol of the decadence of its society.

Contrasted to the agricultural practices of the nineteenth century is Thoreau's vision of the landscape as a new Eden, a utopian society that exists on the food nature provides. Because nature is a good mother who "does her best to feed her children" (p. 22), humans should depend on natural food systems. "Man at length stands in such a relation to Nature as the animals which pluck and eat as they go. The fields and hills are a table constantly spread" (p. 23). If man does likewise, then his harvest becomes a sacrament and not a tasting of the fruit of good and evil. "We pluck and eat in remembrance of her. It is a sort of sacrament—a communion— the *not* forbidden fruits, which no serpent tempts us to eat. Slight and innocent savors which relate us to Nature, make us her guests, and entitle us to her regard and protection" (p. 23).

The way to become gods on earth, redeeming the tragic sense of history, then, is to redesign human culture in such a way that it is dependent upon the wild economies of natural productivity. Agriculture has abandoned the original innocence of the garden and has ended in the corrupt production of crops for profit. The essay is filled with nostalgic glimpses of a time that is vanishing. Thoreau remembers the "sense of freedom and spirit of adventure" he possessed as a youth roaming the hills and swamps in search of wild fruit. He sees the end of this freedom on a level not only personal but national: "The wild fruits of the earth disappear before civilization, or only the husks of them are to be found in large markets" (p. 28). Like Cooper's Hawkeye and Twain's Huckleberry Finn, he sees civilization as antithetical to the freedom of the hunter and the youth. Sustenance from the wild crops of the land, therefore, symbolizes health and freedom. It also marks the extent to which a common vision for culture has been lost. With agriculture comes the perception of space and crops as private property. "What sort of a country is that where the huckleberry fields are private property? When I pass such fields on the highway, my heart sinks within me. I see a blight on the land. Nature is under a veil there. I make haste away from the accursed spot. Nothing could deform her fair face more. I cannot think of it ever after but as the place where fair and palatable berries are converted into money, where the huckleberry is desecrated" (p. 28).

Unlike the "Succession of Forest Trees," this essay urges the user of the land to integrate himself into wild crop cycles. The woodlots that local farmers sought to make more profitable through Thoreau's suggestions have no place in the Edenic vision of the American landscape Thoreau longs for here. The pursuit for profit becomes a downward spiral of greed. "It is true, we have as good a right to make berries private property, as to make wild grass and trees such—it is not worse than a thousand other practices which custom has sanctioned—but that is the worst of it, for it suggests how bad the rest are, and to what result our civilization and division of labor naturally tend, to make all things venal" (pp. 28–29). The landscape becomes a commodity, valuable only to make money. Civilization becomes a labor camp, functioning to maximize profit for the owners.

Juxtaposed to this vision of the landscape as commodity and private property is that of the landscape as communal storehouse in which the Indian is the true exemplar of life, as opposed to the corrupt Puritan divine: "Among the Indians, the earth and its productions generally were common and free to all the tribe, like the air and water—but among us who have supplanted the Indians, the public retain only a small yard or common in the middle of the village, with perhaps a grave-yard beside it, and the right of way, by sufferance, by a particular narrow route, which is annually becoming narrower, from one such yard to another" (p. 30). The greed of the "fathers" is the major legacy of the Puritans: "If they were in earnest seeking thus far away 'freedom to worship God,' as some assure us—why did they not secure a little more of it, when it was so cheap and they were about it? At the same time that they built meeting-houses why did they not preserve from desecration and destruction far grander temples not made with hands?" (p. 31).

The New England village emerges as a utilitarian force that exerts a particular ideology on the landscape. Not understanding how to "use" the economies of nature, the town corporations "utilize" the commodity value of the land. In an increasingly industrialized environment, Thoreau cautions that America, if it is to stay free, must make "a wary use of the city" and "preserve as far as possible, the advantages of living in the country" (p. 31). He then constructs an ideal vision of the country and the landscape that affirms communal ownership of wilderness. Unlike the answer of *Walden,* which asserts the culture of one placed within the natural setting, Thoreau now advocates a town, or communal group, adjacent to a commonly shared tract of wilderness: "I think that each town should have a park, or rather a primitive forest, of five hundred or a thousand acres, either in one body or several—where a stick should never be cut for fuel—nor for the navy, nor to make wagons, but stand and decay for higher uses—a common possession forever, for instruction and recreation" (p. 35). Here the wild serves the group, not the individual. Culture, modeled after Indian tribal society, becomes a way station in the midst of an expanse of nature.

According to Robert Sayre in *Thoreau and The American Indians,* later in life Thoreau moved "beyond savagism," the fashionable romantic doctrine of the nineteenth century that glamorized the individual Indian as warrior and hunter, and "came to recognize the amazing social qualities of Indians, both from his reading and his times in Maine." Eventually, "the image of 'the Indian' as solitary rebel had to give way."[28] Perhaps a companion text to "Huckleberries" is Thoreau's "Indian Notebooks," eleven volumes of compiled notes on the cultural life of diverse Indian groups. Considered by Richard F. Fleck as the "largest body of knowledge on American Indian culture in the nineteenth century,"[29] these notes demonstrate how difficult it would be for Thoreau to equate the daily life of North American Indians with a belief in radical individualism. Intent on understanding the history, tradition, and language of many Indian cultures, Thoreau recorded extensive notes on how Indians built their houses, planted fields, ate, recreated, and practiced traditional religious beliefs. Drawing heavily from colonial and nineteenth-century sources, Thoreau was particularly impressed by the observations of John Heckewelder in his *History of the Indian Nations* in which creation myths, linguistic practices, and social mores are described with a genuine respect for the cultural practices of American Indians. Although obviously intrigued by the various creation myths and oral traditions of Indians, he was equally concerned with their labor customs, governments, and tribal organizations. The Indian as lone "savage" without community is unthinkable considering the massive weight of Thoreau's "Indian Notebooks."

Although it is questionable that this recognition of the communal basis of Indian life implied for Thoreau a return to the "village street," it did give him an alternative model to his culture of one at Walden Pond, which faltered against the ideal of the lone wanderer in the woods. Ever skeptical of village culture, Thoreau merges the tribal image and that of the village to produce a final model for the synthesis of nature and culture.

Roderick Nash asserts: "Previously most Americans had revered the rural, agrarian condition as a release both from wilderness and from high civilization. They stood, so to speak, with both feet in the center of the spectrum of environments. Thoreau, on the other hand, arrived at the middle by straddling."[30] This straddling becomes less awkward, however, when nature and culture are synthesized with an underlying historical continuum. Once we adopt Thoreau's vision of history, a history steeped in the religious tradition of redemption, nature and culture cannot exist apart.

In "Huckleberries," the Puritan settler emerges as the enemy who justifies his destructive agricultural practices according to a sense of historical and religious mission. In his study of Puritan attitudes toward the wilderness, Peter N. Carroll concludes that from "the beginning of colonization, the Puritans emphasized the importance of transforming the wilderness into cultivated acreage."[31] To some extent, the historical vision of settling a New World kingdom was harmonious with their agricultural practices. It is precisely this historical mission that Thoreau attacks in "Huckleberries." If the history of collective groups is consistently viewed as a cultural phenomenon, then the history of nature remains a mere backdrop for the actions of individuals and groups. But once the sense of historical mission is fused with natural history, the same religious commitment to establish a New World kingdom must rest upon the laws and perceptions of redemptive history.

Only by recognizing the relationship between the cycles of natural and cultural time can health and wisdom be acquired. "Live in each season as it passes; breathe the air, drink the drink, taste the fruit, and resign yourself to the influences of each. Let these be your only diet-drink and botanical medicines" (p. 36). In such a relationship between nature and culture, nature serves the redemptive designs of life. "For all nature is doing her best each moment to make us well. She exists for no other end. Do not resist her. With the least inclination to be well we should not be sick. Men have discovered, or think that they have discovered the salutariness of a few wild things only, and not of all nature. Why nature is but another name for health" (p. 36). But to realize this dream demands a total belief in the inseparableness of human and natural time.

These final essays, then, bring to a culmination Thoreau's method as a historian. They testify to the persuasiveness with which he sustains the language of historical mission, inherited from the Puritan religious tradition. Fight he would to preserve the continuum of natural and cultural events. In this way, he differs remarkably from the figure R. W. B. Lewis described in *The American Adam:*

> . . . an individual emancipated from history, happily bereft of ancestry, untouched and undefiled by the usual inheritances of family and race; an individual standing alone, self-reliant and self-propelling, ready to confront whatever awaited him with the aid of his own unique and inherent resources. It was not surprising, in a Bible-reading generation, that the new hero (in praise or disapproval) was most easily identified with Adam before the Fall. Adam was the first, the archetypal, man. His moral position was prior to experience, and in his very newness he was fundamentally innocent. The world and history lay all before him.[32]

Quite the opposite, to Thoreau—history lay all around. The burden of historical knowledge, gleaned from the observation of natural events, was awesome and never-ending. The Fall, in a sense, was the inability to conceive more widely of our place in this historical reality.

Stone Fruit

When describing the view of Mount Monadnock in "A Walk to Wachusett," Thoreau notices that the valleys are "teeming with Yankee men along their respective streams," but it is unclear for "what destiny."[1] The growth of civilization amid nature is not necessarily a story of triumph and progress; it could as easily become a tragedy. The plot appears too unstable, pointing toward disaster or triumph in a disturbingly erratic manner. Instead, Thoreau turns to a deliberate record of the natural laws of succession and perceptual events in nature to form the basis for a continuing belief in the possibility of redemption on earth. A history above the destinies of both groups and nations, this story, Thoreau hopes, will replace the elaborate justifications for communities designed by both the New England settlers and the nineteenth-century industrial planners whose true motives spring from greed and profit.

With the tools of cartography and the methods of natural science, this new history places the burden of truth on individual perception. Through the act of perceiving and describing nature, the riddle of time is finally comprehended: "The process that goes on in the sod and the dark, about the minute fibres of the grass,— the chemistry and the mechanics,—before a single green blade can appear above the withered herbage, if it could [be] adequately described, would supplant all other revelations" (5:69). This revelation combines both history and prophecy; it directs men and women to live in accordance with the acts of nature and tells them to place faith in the history of natural processes and build their societies based upon observable natural laws.

This study presents Thoreau's quest for redemptive history as an attempt to rescue history from the hands of the falsifiers, those writers who proclaimed the advancement of civilization at the expense of nature. But Thoreau's uncivil history can also be seen as the beginning of the demise of history as a persuasive tool to reassure us of our place in the world. The chronological code that Thoreau enforces is precisely that of individual life. Almost as a reaction to the reach of time into distant geological periods and extinct human societies, the perspective from which one must view time is made proportionately narrow. One result of insisting on first-person observation as the means to gather historical evidence for a new vision of time is that history becomes interdependent with questions about perception and language. Locked into a particular perspective of time and place, Thoreau must continually guard against the inevitable illusiveness and subjectivity of his method.

Can one man's life, no matter how assiduous the effort, capture and collect enough observations to describe an accurate version of redemptive history? Thoreau himself raised this question; and his nature-charts alone, page after page of recorded natural events, testify to his belief in the legitimacy of his method of collecting individual observations. Like Darwin, who spent years noting the minute variations of barnacles, Thoreau's methods of observation imply his belief that an individual life could comprehend the plot and laws of natural history. Time was encased in natural events, and an enormous effort was necessary to unpack its meaning: "Nature never lost a day, nor a moment. As the planet in its orbit and around its axis, so do the seasons, so does time, revolve, with a rapidity inconceivable. In the moment, in the aeon, well employed, time ever advances with this rapidity" (4:350). How then can the individual observer begin to capture adequately nature's history?

Thoreau's writings chart his drive both to refine the methods of history and to guard against their potential failure. On one level, his anxiety about his method can be traced to the Puritan religious tradition. Although Thoreau rejects the historical explanations of the Puritans, he participates in their tradition of history writing through the chronicling of individual life. The trained observer of nature is, after all, the Puritan saint. Tracing the language of soteriological history in the early Puritans, Sacvan Bercovitch claims that the effort to write auto-American-biography involves significant risk: "All evidence indicates that an enormous private anxiety underlies the affirmation of national identity."[2] For instance, in Cotton Mather's biography of John Winthrop, Winthrop is a "saint who never leaves behind his historicity." But although he is a historical person at the core, his identity mirrors the *typus Christi:* sainthood and nationality blend. Mather's Winthrop is an exemplary figure not only because he was a *typus Christi* and lived in historical time, but also because he lived in a unique geographical setting: New England, the New World, America. To maintain this vision is to invite a condition of self-doubt.

As various critics of American culture have pointed out, with nineteenth-century American writers, overt biblical metaphors fade before a direct hermeneutics of the American landscape. The text of nature replaces the scriptural text; the observer replaces the Puritan. What the observer finds in the landscape should not be his invention, but an accurate record of regeneration and promise. In this rhetoric, subjectivity must be overcome so that the text of nature can be correctly seen. As with the Puritan writers, if the observer cannot see spiritual evidence in the landscape of the promise, it is not because that evidence does not exist; it is because the observer is imperfect. Discrepancies between "promise and ful-fillment" were explained as errors in perception. The task was not to invent new interpretations of the Scripture or the landscape, but to devise methods that would sustain belief in the promise.

The simple need to rid perception of error resulted, however, in elaborate strategies within the writings of Thoreau. Most of these involve a play on doubling either the self, the eye, or the landscape. If perception does not see evidence of promise in the American landscape, then splitting necessarily occurs. On Saddleback Mountain and the shipwrecked coast of Cape Cod, the natural landscape is negated and substituted by a counter-landscape transcendent of earth and without the texture of its vestiges. This alternate landscape is, however, incapable of description, and is asserted as equivalent to the mind and imagination. It is possible, then, for the artist to dream forever the golden dream of promise without the pressure to connect this vision to the description of the natural world.

On Mount Katahdin, doubling increases when both the landscape and the self are presented as split. Nature is both good mother and cruel stepmother; the self is both matter and spirit, leaving in abeyance the possibility of having the perceiver see directly a hermeneutics of the landscape that results in the promise. Likewise, in the Walden cabin, where the constraints of material and cultural structures are affirmed, the self emerges with an essential doubleness, leading to the assertion of the imagination and the work of art as transcendent forces over the world of history and culture.

In the *Journal*, all these strategies are found, but as Thoreau examines the processes of perception he even goes so far as to insert doubleness into the eye itself. The eye can become trapped in physiological restraints, and consequently an alternative eye is imagined and connected to the free play of the mind. For Thoreau, doubling always involves a move toward transcendence and away from the dialectical processes of perceiving and describing the promise in the natural landscape. If Eden cannot be seen, then splitting inevitably becomes the method to account for error.

*   *   *

On March 28, 1859, three years before his death, Thoreau set out to search for arrowheads. He describes how he has spent "many hours every spring gathering the crop which the melting snow and rain have washed bare" (12:88), and how his "eyes rest on the evidences of an aboriginal life which passed here a thousand years ago perchance" (12:88). Civil history as practiced in the nineteenth century would turn its back on the significance of these documents. To Thoreau, however, arrowheads as historical vestiges combine a perception of both surface and depth; these fossils testify to a form of human history found immediately on the surface of the earth and illuminate the distant presence of the human mind in cultural objects:

> They are sown, like a grain that is slow to germinate, broadcast over the earth. Like the dragon's teeth which bore a crop of soldiers, these bear crops of philosophers and poets, and the same seed is just as good to plant again. It is a stone fruit. Each one yields me a thought. I come nearer to the maker of it than if I found his bones. His bones would not prove any wit that wielded them, such as this work of his bones does. It is humanity inscribed on the face of the earth, patent to my eyes as soon as the snow goes off, not hidden away in some crypt or grave or under a pyramid. No disgusting mummy, but a clean stone, the best symbol or letter that could have been transmitted to me.

> *The Red Man, his mark*

At every step I see it, and I can easily supply the "Tahatawan" or "Mantatuket" that might have been written if he had had a clerk. It is no single inscription on a particular rock, but a footprint—rather a mind-print—left everywhere, and altogether illegible. No vandals, however vandalic in their disposition, can be so industrious as to destroy them. (12:90–91)

"Chiefly made to be lost," these arrowheads are permanent re-minders of uncivil history. Stone fruit, like the visible paradoxes of terrestrial rainbows or sand foliage, the arrowheads indicate that the earth, particularly the natural landscape of America, is not dead but bears the "footprint, the mind-print of the oldest men."

Ironically, however, the arrowhead described as "stone fruit" be-comes an elaborate trope that hides as much as it reveals. For in-stance, the bones of the Indian would not have been an appropriate term on which to build a figure of speech: hidden away in the earth, they act like a "disgusting mummy," merely signifying death and decay. The arrowhead, a product of human culture and labor, bears within it the action of the human mind. As "a clean stone," purified by the action of the human artist, matter becomes a symbol of regeneration. The arrowhead defined as "stone fruit" becomes an oxymoron, resolving the tension between life and death, spirit and matter. Hence, the Indian is not dead; his presence is found throughout the New World. True to the dictums of uncivil history, the arrowhead proves that significant human experience exists out-side the narrow strictures of civilization. By making the arrowhead a mind-print, not a footprint, Thoreau claims the arrowhead as positive proof of a larger order for historical time.

But, unlike the sand foliage of *Walden* that decodes a specific story of redemption through time, Thoreau claims that the stone fruit are "illegible"; they cannot be deciphered. Thoreau sees them in the landscape and defines their presence paradoxically, but he cannot build from them a vision of redemption. He finally draws the mark of the Indian into the text where it sits as both symbol and letter. Like the *A* in *The Scarlet Letter*, the doubloon on the mast in *Moby-Dick*, and the cryptograms of *The Narrative of Arthur Gordon Pym*, the text ultimately presents back to the reader the puzzle of interpretation.

By making the arrowhead illegible, Thoreau silences the docu-ments of the past. The arrowhead may be a "clean stone," and as such may testify to the presence of mind, but as a cultural symbol it is also evidence of a vanished and defeated society caught in the tragic destructiveness of civilized progress. The existence of the arrowhead on the surface of the American landscape means that this distinct geography cannot suppress the violence of its past. Thoreau, however, does not draw this inference here, though he does elsewhere in his writings. In this passage, the cultural symbol of the arrowhead is silent, incapable of interpretation, yet memorialized within the text. It points to an expanded sense of the human mind, but cannot tell the story of continuity between human cultures. The interpretation of the cultural artifact is rendered mute in the text, a riddle left to generations of Americans to hold up before their historical stories of national identity.

As evidence of mind, however, the arrowhead is able to defeat time: "Time will soon destroy the works of famous painters and sculptors, but the Indian arrowhead will balk his efforts and Eternity will have come to his aid" (12:91). Stating that arrowheads "are not fossil bones, but, as it were, fossil thoughts, forever reminding me of the mind that shaped them" (12:91), Thoreau remains a genuine transcendentalist committed to the universality of the human mind and the transparency of language. Left without a vision of progress in the stories of civilized men and women, Thoreau clings to the events of the natural world to revive the possibility of historical redemption. Fraught with danger, this attempt to rescue history often leads to the maze of perception and the doubling of self, landscape, and eye. At its worst, it suppresses historical evidence and retreats into dreams. The hope, however, remains. By describing a slice of natural time, all time is revealed. Once this story becomes language, an entirely unique world is formed of perfect proportions, one that hopefully will not fall prey to the ravages of time. Outside of chronology, this New World signifies not only a constant regeneration, but creativity itself, where description finally turns into revelation, and history participates in the sacred.

NOTES

Introduction

1. Quoted in Carl E. Pletsch, "History and Friedrich Nietzsche's Philosophy of Time," *History and Theory* 16 (1977): 33. Also, Hayden White, in "The Burden of History" (in *Tropics of Discourse: Essays in Cultural Criticism* [Baltimore: Johns Hopkins Univ. Press, 1978]), states that "Nietzsche hated history even more than he hated religion. History promoted a debilitating voyeurism in men, made them feel that they were latecomers to a world in which everything worth doing had already been done, and thereby undermined that impulse to heroic exertion that might give a peculiarly human, if only transient, meaning to an absurd world," p. 32.

2. Nathaniel P. Willis, *American Scenery; or, Land, Lake, and River Illustrations of Transatlantic Nature*, 2 vols. (London: George Virtue, 1852), 1:2.

3. Roderick Nash writes in chapter 4 of *Wilderness and the American Mind* (New Haven: Yale Univ. Press, 1982) that romantic attitudes toward nature became a source of national pride in nineteenth-century America, often evoking a sense of the future glory of civilization, pp. 67–83.

4. Thomas Cole, "Essays in American Scenery," in *American Art: 1700–1960 Sources and Documents*, ed. John W. McCoubrey (Englewood Cliffs, N.J.: Prentice-Hall, 1965), p. 109.

5. Sacvan Bercovitch, *The American Jeremiad* (Madison: Univ. of Wisconsin Press, 1978), p. 15.

6. Sacvan Bercovitch writes in chapter 2, "The Vision of History," of *The Puritan Origins of the American Self* (New Haven: Yale Univ. Press, 1975) that for his purpose, "the most convenient terms are those now in use: soteriology and secular history, where secular history designates the providential view (not the humanists' a-religious, empirical realism) and soteriology the mode of identifying the individual, the community, or the event in question within the scheme of salvation," p. 43.

7. *The Works of Anne Bradstreet*, ed. Jeannine Hensley (Cambridge: Harvard Univ. Press, Belknap Press, 1967), p. 209, ll. 121–27.

8. Stephen Toulmin and June Goodfield, *The Discovery of Time* (Chicago: Univ. of Chicago Press, 1965), pp. 142–43. See also Hans Eichner, "The Rise of Modern Science and the Genesis of Romanticism," *PMLA* 97 (1982): 8–30; and Barbara Maria Stafford, *Voyage into Substance: Art, Science, Nature, and the Illustrated Travel Account, 1760–1840* (Cambridge: MIT Press, 1984), pp. 59–65.

9. John Hildebidle, *Thoreau: A Naturalist's Liberty* (Cambridge: Harvard Univ. Press, 1983), p. 25.

10. See in particular Asa Gray, "Evolutionary Teleology," in *Darwiniana: Essays and Reviews Pertaining to Darwinism*, ed. A. Hunter Dupree (Cambridge: Harvard Univ. Press, Belknap Press, 1963); and Edward Hitchcock, *The Religion of Geology and Its Connected Sciences* (Boston: Phillips, Sampson, and Co., 1851).

11. Asa Gray, "Review of Darwin's Theory on the Origin of Species by Means of Natural Selection," *The American Journal of Science and Arts* 29, no. 86 (1860): 176.

12. Paul F. Boller, Jr., in *American Thought in Transition: The Impact of Evolutionary Naturalism, 1865–1900* (Chicago: Rand McNally & Co., 1969), pp. 7–11, notes that Asa Gray and Charles Darwin thought they agreed for years, only to find that the massive evidence of laws that Darwin had accumulated testified to the tenacious power of matter, not to the redemptive vision of God. The subtle gradations of species pointed less to a form of divine intelligence than to a network of natural causes. Gray, the representative religious scientist, held onto the theological argument from design, despite Darwin's frustration and eventual anger at his thinking.

13. White, "Fictions of Factual Representation," in *Tropics of Discourse*, p. 125. See also Hayden White, *Metahistory: The Historical Imagination in Nineteenth-Century Europe* (Baltimore: Johns Hopkins Univ. Press, 1973), pp. 1–42.

14. Bercovitch, *Puritan Origins*, p. 152.

15. Harold Bloom, "The Internalization of Quest-Romance," in *Romanticism and Consciousness*, ed. Harold Bloom (New York: W. W. Norton & Co., 1970), pp. 3–24. The great exception, of course, is Goethe. See also Willy Hartner, "Goethe and the Natural Sciences," in *Goethe: A Collection of Critical Essays*, ed. Victor Lange (Englewood Cliffs, N.J.: Prentice-Hall, 1968), pp. 145–60.

16. Ralph Waldo Emerson, *The Collected Works of Ralph Waldo Emerson*, vol. 1, ed. Alfred R. Ferguson et al. (Cambridge: Harvard Univ. Press, Belknap Press, 1971), p. 40; and "The Uses of Natural History," in *The Early Lectures of Ralph Waldo Emerson*, ed. Stephen E. Whicher and Robert E. Spiller (Cambridge: Harvard Univ. Press, Belknap Press, 1966), 1:8. For a good discussion of Emerson's interest in and use of natural science, see David Robinson, *Apostle of Culture: Emerson as Preacher and Lecturer* (Philadelphia: Univ. of Pennsylvania Press, 1982), pp. 71–94.

17. Emerson, *Collected Works*, 1:40.

18. Ibid., p. 37.

19. Ibid., p. 39.

20. Ibid., p. 36.

21. Ibid., p. 45.

22. Northrop Frye, "The Drunken Boat: The Revolutionary Element in Romanticism," in *Romanticism: Points of View*, 2nd ed., ed. Robert F. Gleck-

ner and Gerald E. Enscoe, (Detroit: Wayne State Univ. Press, 1975), pp. 304–5.

23. Emerson, *The Collected Works of Ralph Waldo Emerson*, vol. 2, ed. Joseph Slater et al. (Cambridge: Harvard Univ. Press, Belknap Press, 1979), p. 6.

24. Terence Martin, *The Instructed Vision: Scottish Common Sense Philosophy and the Origins of American Fiction* (Bloomington: Indiana Univ. Press, 1961), p. 73.

25. Critics particularly concerned with Thoreau's contradictory strategies in representing nature are Walter Benn Michaels, "Walden's False Bottoms," in *Glyph: Johns Hopkins Textual Studies* (Baltimore: Johns Hopkins Univ. Press, 1977), 1:132–49; and James McIntosh, *Thoreau as Romantic Naturalist* (Ithaca, N.Y.: Cornell Univ. Press, 1974). Richard Lebeaux, in *Young Man Thoreau* (Amherst: Univ. of Massachusetts Press, 1977), as well as in his *Thoreau's Seasons* (Amherst: Univ. of Massachusetts Press, 1984), and Richard Bridgman, in *Dark Thoreau* (Lincoln: Univ. of Nebraska Press, 1982) both explore the psychological tensions and frustrations in Thoreau's life and writings.

26. McIntosh, *Thoreau as Romantic Naturalist*, p. 34.

27. David Scofield Wilson (*In the Presence of Nature* [Amherst: Univ. of Massachusetts Press, 1978]) uses this phrase to describe the tradition of nature reportage in America since the colonial period. He writes that "the nature reporter was more than a scientist. He legitimated and domesticated as well as described American nature," p. 29.

28. The most direct example of this approach appears in Raymond D. Gozzi, "Some Aspects of Thoreau's Personality," in *Henry David Thoreau: A Profile*, ed. Walter Harding (New York: Hill and Wang, 1971), pp. 150–71. In this essay, Gozzi writes that "a final reason for thinking of Thoreau as an obsessional personality is that he shows elements of unconscious libidinal regression to what is termed the 'anal-sadistic' level. Such regression is typical of obsessional neurotics. Perhaps the most dramatic evidence of this regression in Thoreau is provided by his interest in and literary descriptions of sand-and-clay banks having an excrementitious appearance," p. 165.

29. F. O. Matthiessen, *American Renaissance: Art and Expression in the Age of Emerson and Whitman* (New York: Oxford Univ. Press, 1941), p. 174.

30. Sherman Paul, *The Shores of America: Thoreau's Inward Exploration* (Urbana: Univ. of Illinois Press, 1972), p. 395.

31. Thoreau's quarrel with science is continually debated among critics. For instance, Nina Baym ("Thoreau's View of Science," *Journal of the History of Ideas* 26 [1965]) thinks that even though Thoreau in his later writings remains scientific, he basically experiences the failure of science and the inappropriateness of his writings to it. Baym writes that the "growth of the number of strictures against science in the late journals records his realization that science was not what he had taken it to be, and is a separate

development from the private collapse of his 'anticipation' enterprise," p. 234. John Hildebidle (*Thoreau: A Naturalist's Liberty*) disagrees with Baym, stating that "in 1860 Thoreau still unashamedly claimed for himself a scientific investigation, and a scientific result," p. 94.

32. Philip F. Gura, "The Transcendentalists and Language: The Unitarian Exegetical Background," *Studies in the American Renaissance: 1979* (Boston: Twayne Publishers, 1979), p. 11.

33. Textual quotations from the *Journal* in the Introduction are from *The Journal of Henry D. Thoreau*, ed. Bradford Torrey and Francis H. Allen, 14 vols. printed in two folio vols. (1906; reprint, New York: Dover Publications, 1962). References are to volume and page.

34. Warner Berthoff, "Fiction, History, Myth: Notes toward the Discrimination of Narrative Forms," in *The Interpretation of Narrative: Theory and Practice*, ed. Morton W. Bloomfield (Cambridge: Harvard Univ. Press, 1970), p. 270.

35. It is interesting that in the final section of *Nature*, entitled "Prospects," Emerson exhorts the reader: "Build, therefore, your own world. As fast as you conform your life to the pure idea in your mind, that will unfold its great proportions. A correspondent revolution in things will attend the influx of the spirit. So fast will disagreeable appearances, swine, spiders, snakes, pests, mad-houses, prisons, enemies vanish; they are temporary and shall be no more seen. The sordor and filths of nature, the sun shall dry up, and the wind exhale" (*Collected Works*, 1:45). The unpleasant details of the natural landscape are erased by the contemplative mind.

36. Georg Lukacs, *Writer and Critics*, trans. and ed. Arthur Kahn (London: Merlin Press, 1970), p. 139.

Chapter One. Mapping New Worlds

1. Russel B. Nye, Introduction to *The History of the United States of America from the Discovery of the Continent*, by George Bancroft (Chicago: Univ. of Chicago Press, 1966), p. xxvi.

2. George Bancroft, *History of the United States of America, from the Discovery of the Continent*, 6 vols. (New York: D. Appleton and Co., 1895), 6:474.

3. Henry D. Thoreau, "The Commercial Spirit of Modern Times," in *Early Essays and Miscellanies*, ed. Joseph J. Moldenhauer et al. (Princeton: Princeton Univ. Press, 1975), p. 118.

4. Quoted in Toulmin and Goodfield, *The Discovery of Time*, p. 144.

5. David Levin, *History as Romantic Art: Bancroft, Prescott, Motley, and Parkman* (New York: Harcourt, Brace & World, 1959). See also C. Harvey Gardiner, Introduction to *The History of the Conquest of Mexico*, by William H. Prescott (Chicago: Univ. of Chicago Press, 1966); and George H. Callcott, *History in the United States: 1800–1860* (Baltimore: Johns Hopkins Univ. Press, 1970).

6. For a recent discussion of the literary models Thoreau used in *A Week*, see Linck C. Johnson, *Thoreau's Complex Weave: The Writing of 'A Week on the Concord and Merrimack Rivers' with the Text of the First Draft* (Charlottesville: Univ. Press of Virginia, 1986), pp. 3–40.

7. All textual quotations are from Henry D. Thoreau, *A Week on the Concord and Merrimack Rivers*, ed. Carl F. Hovde (Princeton: Princeton Univ. Press, 1980).

8. At this time, in 1841, Emerson thought that all history could be read *as if* it were autobiography: "I can find Greece, Asia, Italy, Spain, and the Islands, the genius and creative principle of each and of all eras in my own mind." ("History," in Emerson, *Collected Works*, 2:6).

9. White, "Interpretation in History," in *Tropics of Discourse*, p. 54.

10. Johnson, in *Thoreau's Complex Weave*, ultimately interprets Thoreau's use of historical materials in *A Week* as part of an extended commentary on Indian-white relations in which even "the historical destruction of the Indians" changes "into a powerful scene in the drama of life, death, and rebirth in *A Week*," p. 162. Thoreau's motives are interpreted as primarily literary: "history was thus not useful to Thoreau insofar as it remained past, but only insofar as it could be made present, could be revivified in his own life and writings," p. 122. The conventions of contemporary history writing and the implications for historical knowledge are not developed, and, hence, Johnson interprets less ambiguity and tension in the use of these sources than this study.

11. Periodically, throughout *A Week*, Thoreau claims that the sacred text, whether myth, fable, dream, or literary classic, communicates what is "universal" about human history. In essence, these are transcendent scripts for Thoreau, and they are the only texts exempt from the demands of first-person form.

12. Emile Benveniste, in *Problems in General Linguistics* (Coral Gables, Fla.: Univ. of Miami Press, 1971), writes that "it is by identifying himself as a unique person pronouncing *I* that each speaker sets himself up in turn as the 'subject,'" p. 220.

13. White, in *Metahistory*, writes: "Providing the 'meaning' of a story by identifying the *kind of story* that has been told is called explanation by emplotment," p. 7.

14. Nye, Introduction to *History of the United States*, p. xiii.

15. Levin, *History as Romantic Art*, p. 12.

16. Christopher Hussey, in *The Picturesque: Studies in a Point of View* (New York: G. P. Putnam's Sons, 1927), characterizes the picturesque as a late eighteenth-century mode of viewing nature as if it were a sequence of subjects for painting. As a convention, the "picturesque" was very popular among the Knickerbocker writers during the first half of the nineteenth century. See James T. Callow, *Kindred Spirits: Knickerbocker Writers and American Artists 1807–1855* (Chapel Hill: Univ. of North Carolina Press, 1967); Blake Nevius, *Cooper's Landscapes: An Essay on the Picturesque Vision* (Berkeley: Univ. of California Press, 1976); and Donald A. Ringe, *The Pictorial*

Mode: Space and Time in the Art of Bryant, Irving, and Cooper (Lexington: Univ. of Kentucky Press, 1971).

17. "Every literary description is a *view.* It could be said that the speaker, before describing, stands at the window, not so much to see, but to establish what he sees by its very frame: the window frame creates the scene." Roland Barthes, *S/Z,* trans. Richard Miller (New York: Hill and Wang, 1974), p. 54.

18. Donald M. Lowe, in *The History of Bourgeois Perception* (Chicago: Univ. of Chicago Press, 1982), writes that the "new dominant field of perception in bourgeois society was constituted by the predominance of typographic media, the hierarchy of sensing which emphasized the primacy of sight, and the epistemic order of development-in-time. Typography promoted the ideal that knowledge could be detached from the knower to become impartial and explicit. The primacy of sight made possible scientific verification of that knowledge," p. 18.

19. "Musings," in *Early Essays and Miscellanies,* ed. Moldenhauer et al., pp. 14–15.

20. Perry Miller, ed., *Consciousness in Concord: The Text of Thoreau's Hitherto "Lost Journal" (1840–41)* (Boston: Houghton-Mifflin, 1958), pp. 161–62.

21. "A Walk to Wachusett," in *The Writings of Henry David Thoreau,* 20 vols. (1906; reprint, New York: AMS Press, 1968), 5:145. See also the historical introduction to *A Week,* ed. Hovde, p. 445.

22. "A Walk to Wachusett," p. 147.

23. "Thomas Carlyle and His Works," in *Early Essays and Miscellanies,* ed. Moldenhauer et al., p. 234.

24. See John W. McCoubrey's remarks on Puritanism and graven images in *American Art: 1700–1960 Sources and Documents* (Englewood Cliffs, N.J.: Prentice-Hall, 1965), pp. 3–5.

25. Albert F. McLean, Jr., "Thoreau's True Meridian: Natural Fact and Metaphor," *American Quarterly* 20 (1968): 567–79. See also *A Catalog of Thoreau's Surveys in the Concord Free Public Library,* ed. Marcia Moss, Thoreau Society Booklet 28 (Geneseo, N.Y.: Thoreau Society, 1976).

26. Barbara Novak, "The Meteorological Vision: Clouds," in *Nature and Culture: American Landscape and Painting 1825–1875* (New York: Oxford Univ. Press, 1980), pp. 78–100.

27. E. H. Gombrich, *Art and Illusion: A Study in the Psychology of Pictorial Representation* (Princeton: Princeton Univ. Press, 1969), p. 49.

28. It is hardly surprising to note that in the 1840s the first-person observation of nature was an American pastime. See Donald Zochert, "Science and the Common Man in Ante-Bellum America," in *Science in America since 1820,* ed. Nathan Reingold (New York: Science History Publications, 1976), pp. 7–32.

29. Kenneth Burke, in *A Grammar of Motives* (Berkeley: Univ. of California Press, 1969), points out that "Act" refers to things in *energia,* p. 227.

30. "Natural History of Massachusetts," in *Writings of Henry David Thoreau*, 5:107.

31. Frederick Garber, in *Thoreau's Redemptive Imagination* (New York: New York Univ. Press, 1977), writes that the "landscape radiates from Thoreau wherever he is ('wherever I sat'), and all points of the compass start from him as center ('all things are up and down, east and west to *me*')," p. 6.

32. In this respect, it is clear why Thoreau's uncivil history was not the story Americans wanted to hear. David D. Van Tassel, in *Recording America's Past: An Interpretation of the Development of Historical Studies in America 1607–1884* (Chicago: Univ. of Chicago Press, 1960), writes that the American romantic historians "took on faith the idea of progress and the existence of an underlying pattern of laws which gave order to the chaos of history. Their immediate and primary concern was an inquiry into the nature of the Republic. That the nation had a character, a 'spirit' and 'idea,' they did not question," p. 114. See also Harvey Wish, *The American Historian: A Social-Intellectual History of the Writing of the American Past* (New York: Oxford Univ. Press, 1960), pp. 70–87.

33. There has been much critical debate about whether *A Week* should be read as a tragedy or a romance. Paul David Johnson ("Thoreau's Redemptive *Week*," *American Literature* 49 [1977]: 22–33) thinks that *A Week* is "carefully structured around the quest for self-liberation." Earlier, Sherman Paul, in *Shores of America*, had stated that *A Week* was Thoreau's "most contemplative book." Lawrence Buell, in *Literary Transcendentalism: Style and Vision in the American Renaissance* (Ithaca, N.Y.: Cornell Univ. Press, 1973), modifies this view somewhat, but he also finds in Thoreau's attempt to reach transcendence an "inevitable return, which amounts to a defeat as well as the completion of a cycle," p. 237. Jonathan Bishop ("The Experience of the Sacred in Thoreau's *Week*," *ELH* 33 [1966]: 66–91) also charts a cyclical process for the quest. Walter Hesford ("'Incessant Tragedies': A Reading of *A Week on the Concord and Merrimack Rivers*," *ELH* 44 [1977]: 515–25), like Bishop, explicates the tragic voice but finds ultimately that Thoreau's art is the final means for the redemption of time and history. My position is that Thoreau uses the tragic voice to undermine the "progressive" stories of the American historians, but he hopes to discover in his methods of observation a redeemed vision of time. When he is unable to do so, he backs off from empirical description and posits a transcendent reality beyond history.

34. Jamie Hutchinson, in "'The Lapse of the Current': Thoreau's Historical Vision in *A Week on the Concord and Merrimack Rivers*" (*ESQ: A Journal of the American Renaissance* 25 [1979]: 211–23), argues that Thoreau does not reject the historical perspective "in favor of timeless, transcendental illumination," even though he often rebels against it.

35. Vestiges are, hence, in Burke's terminology, "Acts," and as such they have an unstable relationship to the question of motive. Thus, it is often

necessary for Thoreau to look "outside" the vestige for its "plot." Frequently Thoreau needs to decipher the vestige according to a symbolic or metaphysical code. It is also interesting that various critics have noted how dangerously close transcendentalism was to naturalism. For if the motive of the act is in the "scene" or the environment, then transcendentalism becomes a naturalistic philosophy. See Frederick Ives Carpenter, "Transcendentalism," in *American Transcendentalism: An Anthology of Criticism*, ed. Brian M. Barbour (Notre Dame, Ind.: Univ. of Notre Dame Press, 1973), pp. 25–26.

36. John Carlos Rowe, in "'The Being of Language: The Language of Being' in *A Week on the Concord and Merrimack Rivers*" (*boundary 2* 7 [1979]: 91–115), also discusses Thoreau's fascination with time and its implications for language, but does so within the philosophical tradition of Heidegger.

Chapter Two. Framing Time

1. Claude Lévi-Strauss, *The Savage Mind* (Chicago: Univ. of Chicago Press, 1966), p. 258.

2. Daniel B. Shea, Jr., in *Spiritual Autobiography in Early America* (Princeton: Princeton Univ. Press, 1968), uses the phrase "periodic in composition" to distinguish autobiographical writing from journal writing, p. x.

3. The aesthetic value of the *Journal* has been consistently debated. Laurence Stapleton, editor of *H. D. Thoreau: A Writer's Journal* (New York: Dover Publications, 1960), writes:

> The journal is Thoreau's principal, if not his greatest work. It provided the motif and much of the substance of his books. Yet we must prefer *A Week on the Concord and the Merrimack,* and *Walden,* to any section of the journal with which they may be compared. The significance of the journal is that in it Thoreau practiced: practiced his ways of observing, his laments, his methods of composition, and his sentences. (p. ix)

This paradoxical response to the *Journal,* evaluating it as Thoreau's "greatest work" yet denigrating it to the status of a workbook, is fairly common among critics. Charles R. Anderson, editor of *Thoreau's World: Miniatures from his Journal* (Englewood Cliffs, N.J.: Prentice-Hall, 1971), considers individual entries "extraordinary 'miniatures'" but still writes that the "most satisfactory definition of Thoreau's *Journal* . . . is that it was a writer's workbook, serving all the purposes included in that comprehensive term," p. 9. Recently, Sharon Cameron, in *Writing Nature: Henry Thoreau's 'Journal,'* (New York: Oxford Univ. Press, 1985), asserts that the *Journal* is "not (only) draft material for the writings Thoreau himself published." Further, *Walden* and the *Journal* are "not just complementary, but make competitive claims," and "it may be the *Journal* which Thoreau understood to be the primary work," p. 22.

It cannot be debated that Thoreau used the *Journal* as a source for his other writings, yet this fact has often obscured what advantages Thoreau gained by the use of periodic composition as a literary form. Usually, the main advantage is given as a truer means to give a sincere account of his days. As such, this point is irrelevant to my study. What is significant is how the form of periodic first-person discourse amplifies questions of time, perception, and language for Thoreau. What is it about the form that intrigued him his entire adult life and seemed so responsive to his particular mode of observing and recording both human consciousness and natural phenomena?

4. All textual quotations are from *The Journal of Henry D. Thoreau*, ed. Torrey and Allen, except where noted.

5. I am using the term "index" here to refer to time and space notations that are in the text to evoke "factual" representation as opposed to a sign which represents or points to a truth greater than itself.

6. Thoreau is both concerned with how dates signal time for the reader and how the process of relating thoughts violates form. He writes, "I do not know but thoughts written down thus in a journal might be printed in the same form with greater advantage than if the related ones were brought together into separate essays" (3:239). But he is also concerned with what happens once the journal is used as a writer's workbook: "How will you ever rivet them together without leaving the marks of the file?" (3:239). The language of the journal is implicitly "purer" for Thoreau.

7. The extent of Thoreau's revising in the *Journal* is still problematic. Miller, in *Consciousness in Concord,* considers the *Journal* a fairly self-consciously crafted document that is a work of the study, not the fields. However, more recently, in the general introduction to Henry D. Thoreau, *Journal Volume One: 1837–1844,* ed. Elizabeth Hall Witherell et al. (Princeton: Princeton Univ. Press, 1981), it is stated that the changes Torrey and Allen made to the text "convey an impression of the Journal as a more polished and final work than it actually is; in their original form, Thoreau's thoughts are frequently tentative, provisional, and hastily noted," p. 589.

8. *Journal Volume One,* p. 53.

9. Jonathan Culler, in *Structuralist Poetics: Structuralism, Linguistics, and the Study of Literature* (Ithaca, N.Y.: Cornell Univ. Press, 1975), writes that the novel (and I would include Thoreau's prose discourse) can contain a level of "descriptive residue" to assert the representational or mimetic value of the language. Culler defines this "descriptive residue" as:

> . . . items whose only apparent role in the text is that of denoting a concrete reality (trivial gestures, insignificant objects, superfluous dialogue). In a description of a room items which are not picked up and integrated by symbolic or thematic codes (items which tell us nothing about the inhabitant of the room, for example) and which do not have a function in the plot produce what Barthes calls a 'reality effect'. . . . (p. 193)

To assist in the reading of passages that exemplify Thoreau's developing descriptive techniques, I have selected the following sections from the middle *Journal* years: 2:106–08 (Nov. 21, 1850); 2:234–48 (June 11, 1851); 2:248–54 (June 13, 1851); 2:254–66 (June 15, 1851); 2:266–70 (June 22, 1851); 2:297–302 (July 11, 1851); 2:370–75 (Aug. 5, 1851); 2:378–82 (Aug. 8, 1851); 2:383–89 (Aug. 12, 1851); 2:467–80 (Sept. 7, 1851); 3:47–52 (Oct. 6, 1851); 3:97–98 (Nov. 8, 1851); 3:131–32 (Nov. 30, 1851); 3:270–76 (Feb. 3, 1852); 3:339–41 (March 7, 1852); 3:369–77 (April 1, 1852); 3:377–86 (April 2, 1852); 4:1–7 (May 1, 1852); 4:8–9 (May 2, 1852); 4:10–15 (May 3, 1852); 4:17–24 (May 5, 1852); 4:24–29 (May 6, 1852); 4:98–105 (June 15, 1852); 4:129–38 (June 23, 1852); 4:147–54 (June 26, 1852); 4:172–76 (July 2, 1852); 4:179–85 (July 4, 1852); 4:204–10 (July 9, 1852); 4:230–32 (July 17, 1852); 4:232–39 (July 18, 1852); 4:282–87 (Aug. 6, 1852); 4:308–10 (Aug. 22, 1852); 4:310–13 (Aug. 23, 1852); 4:440–44 (Jan. 2, 1853); 4:458–61 (Jan. 9, 1853); 5:60–71 (March 29, 1853); 5:132–42 (May 10, 1853); 5:215–20 (June 2, 1853); 5:247–55 (June 14, 1853); 5:270–81 (June 18, 1853); 5:390–96 (Aug. 23, 1853); 5:442–47 (Oct. 22, 1853); 5:519–21 (Nov. 25, 1853); 6:114–21 (Feb. 12, 1854); 6:271–78 (May 17, 1854); 6:285–91 (May 22, 1854); 6:291–95 (May 23, 1854); 6:328–30 (June 5, 1854); 6:415–19 (Aug. 2, 1854); 6:453–57 (Aug. 19, 1854); 7:37–42 (Sept. 14, 1854).

10. White, in "Fictions of Factual Representation," in *Tropics of Discourse,* writes that Darwin

> . . . does not wish to suggest, as many of his contemporaries held, that all systems of classifications are arbitrary, that is, mere products of the minds of the classifiers; he insists that there is a *real* order in nature. On the other hand, he does not wish to regard this order as a product of some spiritual or teleological power. The order which he seeks in the data, then, must be manifest in the facts themselves but not manifested in such a way as to display the operations of any transcendental power. In order to establish this notion of nature's plan, he purports, first, simply to entertain "objectively" all of the "facts" of natural history provided by field naturalists, domestic breeders, and students of the geological record. . . . (p. 130)

11. See in particular the following entries of the *Journal:* 7:410; 7:420; 9:74; 13:298.

12. Michel Foucault, in *The Order of Things: An Archaeology of the Human Sciences* (New York: Vintage Books, 1970), writes that Cuvier was responsible for the shift from classical analysis of natural phenomena in which "the organ was defined by both its structure and its function" to one in which function takes "prominence over the organ." Cuvier "subjects the arrangement of the organ to the sovereignty of function. He rejects, if not the individuality of the organ, at least its independence. . . . Now, these functions are relatively few in number: respiration, digestion, circulation, locomotion . . ." p. 264. Foucault also claims that from "Cuvier onward, function, defined according to its non-perceptible form as an effect to be attained, is to serve as a constant middle term and to make it possible to

relate together totalities of elements without the slightest visible identity," p. 265.

13. The example from Charles Darwin's text is from *The Voyage of the Beagle* (New York: E. P. Dutton, 1967), pp. 154–56.

14. Emerson, *The Collected Works of Ralph Waldo Emerson,* vol. 3, ed. Joseph Slater et al. (Cambridge: Harvard Univ. Press, Belknap Press, 1983), p. 22.

15. Perry Miller, *Errand into the Wilderness* (New York: Harper and Row, 1956), p. 185.

16. Cameron, in *Writing Nature,* finds radical discontinuity in Thoreau's journal language: "In the *Journal* analogies do not inaugurate connections between nature and the mind. They rather call attention to the impossibility of such connection," p. 46. My reading addresses both Thoreau's techniques of synthesis and his moments of disrupture, finding an ongoing dialectic between the demands of perception and language.

17. William Ellery Channing, *Thoreau: The Poet-Naturalist (With Memorial Verses),* ed. F. B. Sanborn (1902; reprint, New York: Biblo and Tannen, 1966), pp. 65–66.

18. Barbara Novak, in *American Painting of the Nineteenth Century: Realism, Idealism, and the American Experience* (New York: Praeger Publishers, 1969), p. 93, discusses the "dual need for the real and the ideal" as an aesthetic necessity of mid-nineteenth-century Americans. She finds the luminist landscape painters, such as Fitz Hugh Lane, Arthur B. Durand, and John F. Kensett, trying to express the ultraclarity of the phenomena of nature and the ideal embodied in the overall conception of the landscape.

19. Thoreau, "Of Keeping a Private Journal," in *Early Essays and Miscellanies,* p. 8.

20. As Bercovitch, in *Puritan Origins,* pp. 136–86, has pointed out, with several nineteenth-century artists, the text of nature replaced the scriptural text, and the perceiver replaced the Puritan. What the perceiver found in the landscape must not be the result of his invention, but an "accurate" description of perceived "facts," which, in turn, signify regeneration and promise. In this rhetoric, subjectivity must be overcome so that the text of nature can be rightly seen and its value as spirit described. As with Puritan writers, the perceiver who cannot see spiritual evidence in the landscape of promise is morally imperfect.

Chapter Three. Views from the Walden Settlement

1. John Stuart Mill, *On Bentham and Coleridge* (New York: Harper and Row, 1950), p. 132.

2. Raymond Williams, *Culture and Society: 1780–1950* (New York: Harper and Row, 1958), p. 34.

3. More than a spiritual autobiography, *Walden* conforms to colonial writings that attempt to justify the establishment of communities in the

New World. Stanley Cavell, in *The Senses of Walden* (New York: Viking Press, 1972), writes that the day Thoreau settled Walden pond was a reenactment of the national event "to discover and settle this land, or the question of this land, once for all," p. 8. Richard Slotkin, in *Regeneration Through Violence: The Mythology of the American Frontier, 1600–1860* (Middletown, Conn.: Wesleyan Univ. Press, 1973), states that *Walden* is a "unique synthesis of several genres of Colonial writing." It is both a "personal narrative of conversion" and a "discovery narrative, complete with the traditional paraphernalia of surveyor's measurements and lists of plants and animals," p. 526. The discovery narrative, however, does not imply the building of a house and the cultivation of soil, two activities that *Walden* describes in depth. *Walden* is a nineteenth-century justification of a "plantation."

4. R. Jackson Wilson, *In Quest of Community: Social Philosophy in the United States, 1860–1920* (New York: Oxford Univ. Press, 1968), pp. 8–9.

5. William Drake, "Walden," in *Thoreau: A Collection of Critical Essays,* ed. Sherman Paul (Englewood Cliffs, N.J.: Prentice-Hall, 1962), p. 72. This attitude toward *Walden,* which views the text as a symbolic or mythic account of "awakening," is also shared by critics such as Sherman Paul, Charles R. Anderson, Lawrence Buell, Walter Harding, and Frederick Garber.

6. All textual quotations are from Henry D. Thoreau, *Walden,* ed. J. Lyndon Shanley (Princeton: Princeton Univ. Press, 1971).

7. Martin Heidegger, *Poetry, Language, Thought,* trans. Albert Hofstadter (New York: Harper and Row, 1971), p. 149.

8. Sherman Paul, *Shores of America,* p. 293.

9. In particular, what Thoreau called the "telegraph harp" was like the aeolian lyre, transmitting the wild music of the wind ironically through the wires of an industrializing landscape.

10. Gaston Bachelard, *The Poetics of Space,* trans. Maria Jolas (Boston: Beacon Press, 1964), p. 32.

11. J. Lyndon Shanley, in *The Making of Walden* (Chicago: Univ. of Chicago Press, 1957), writes that the "greatest growth in Thoreau's conception of *Walden* resulted, however, from his seeing how he might fill out his account of the progress of the seasons and describe the changes they had brought in his daily affairs and thoughts . . ." p. 67.

12. This process is, of course, a fictional device of the text since most of the description of the pond and its environment comes after Thoreau has returned to his home in the village. Biographically speaking, the house in Concord became the base from which he gathered his observations on nature.

13. By pursuing laws, Thoreau is trying to hold onto a concept of the mind that encompasses both consciousness and reason. Richard Rorty, in *Philosophy and the Mirror of Nature* (Princeton: Princeton Univ. Press, 1979), points out that the "sensory grasp of particulars" or how one defines sense as opposed to imagination, often determines whether one considers the "mind-as-reason" or the "mind-as-consciousness," p. 54. By inferring from

sense data progressive laws of the seasons, Thoreau gathers additional evidence for his version of historical time.

14. In a sense, the book can be seen as moving toward a sequence of surveys from which a law emerges.

15. I do not mean to assert that *Walden* was a failed utopian experiment, but that the persuasive appeal of Thoreau's vision of culture was often doubted within the text. The excursion model then reappears as a cultural mythos in America, beckoning the inhabitants of rigidified town-life to adventure into unexplored space.

16. Bachelard, *Poetics of Space,* p. 78.

17. Thoreau's study of color increases throughout his later writings and is indicative of his concern about the psychological processes of perception.

18. See Joseph Allen Boone, "Delving and Diving for Truth: Breaking through to Bottom in Thoreau's *Walden,*" *ESQ: A Journal of the American Renaissance* 27 (1981): 135–46; and Walter Benn Michaels, "*Walden's* False Bottoms," in *Glyph: Johns Hopkins Textual Studies* (Baltimore: Johns Hopkins Univ. Press, 1977), 1:132–49.

19. The map occurs not only as a description but as an illustration and hence becomes a dominant rhetorical technique. Robert F. Stowell, in *A Thoreau Gazetteer,* ed. William L. Howarth (Princeton: Princeton Univ. Press, 1970), writes that the map was designed to "face page 307 of the 1854 edition," p. 8; although some editors dropped the illustration, and "a few even thought it was included for humorous reasons," p. 9.

20. Paul, *Shores of America,* p. 297, and Robert D. Richardson, Jr., *Myth and Literature in the American Renaissance* (Bloomington: Indiana Univ. Press, 1978), p. 133.

21. Charles Coulston Gillispie, in *Genesis and Geology: A Study in the Relations of Scientific Thought, Natural Theology, and Social Opinion in Great Britain, 1790–1850* (Cambridge, Mass.: Harvard Univ. Press, 1951), comments that Robert Chambers, author of *Vestiges of Creation,* a popularized account of developmental creation theory, also "had very little sense of the limitations of illustrative analogy; the accident that frosted vapor on a windowpane often crystallizes in designs reminiscent of fern leaves, he thought an illustration of the identity of organic and inorganic matter," p. 156.

22. Shanley, *The Making of Walden,* pp. 207–8.

23. The cyclical language of rebirth seems to disappear under the pressures of a more extravagant vision of death that in its bravado seems to trivialize the fact of death itself.

24. Charles Feidelson, Jr., *Symbolism and American Literature* (Chicago: Univ. of Chicago Press, 1953), pp. 52–57.

25. Paul, *Shores of America,* pp. 188–91.

26. Richardson, *Myth and Literature in the American Renaissance,* p. 136.

27. "Walking," in *Writings,* 5:240.

28. Ibid.

29. Ibid., p. 247–48.

30. Ibid., p. 242. Also, in "Walking," the use of cultural grids such as the map is associated more with metaphor than with measurement and is a product of intuition, not intention. The points of Thoreau's compass are bereft of scientific objectivism. "My needle is slow to settle,—varies a few degrees, and does not always point due southwest, it is true, and it has good authority for this variation,' but it always settles between west and south-southwest" (ibid., p. 217). The direction of west suggests a larger sociopolitical geography. In the west is freedom; in the east, force. In the west is the wilderness; in the east, the city. "I must walk toward Oregon, and not toward Europe. And that way the nation is moving, and I may say that mankind progress from east to west" (ibid., p. 218).

31. Nelson Goodman, *Ways of Worldmaking.* (Indianapolis: Hackett Publishing Co., 1978), p. 7.

Chapter Four. Tracks in the Sand

1. All textual quotations are from Henry D. Thoreau, *Cape Cod,* ed. Joseph J. Moldenhauer (Princeton: Princeton Univ. Press, forthcoming).

2. See in particular Paul, *Shores of America,* pp. 379–88; McIntosh, *Thoreau as Romantic Naturalist,* pp. 216–35; Martin Leonard Pops, "An Analysis of Thoreau's *Cape Cod,*" *Bulletin of the New York Public Library* 67, no. 7 (1963): 419–28; Mario L. D'Avanzo, "Fortitude and Nature in Thoreau's *Cape Cod,*" *ESQ: A Journal of the American Reniassance* 20, no. 2 (1974): 132. An exception to this position is the work of Mitchell Robert Breitwieser, "Thoreau and the Wrecks on Cape Cod," *Studies in Romanticism* 20 (Spring 1981): 3–20. He comments on the ironic pose of Thoreau as a writer: "Having rejected not only specific books, but also the idea of the Book— reality premorse, between covers, the idea that writing can be so well-made that it is an adequate substitute for the thing at its extremity—he writes a book," p. 14.

3. See in particular McIntosh, in *Thoreau as Romantic Naturalist,* who writes that "the overriding strain is not a wandering naturalist's optimism but a threatened private pessimism," p. 205. See also William Howarth, *Thoreau in the Mountains: Writings by Henry David Thoreau* (New York: Farrar, Straus and Giroux, 1982); Howarth writes that many critics think that the experience on the summit was "Thoreau's first recognition of a brutal force in nature. Clearly, his idyllic dreams do give way to a tempered, observant realism," pp. 86–87.

4. Howarth, in *Thoreau in the Mountains,* writes that Mount Katahdin "had been climbed only by a few surveyors and scientists. In August 1845, Thoreau saw a story in the Boston *Daily Advertiser* of an ascent by two young Harvard men, Edward Everett Hale and William Francis Channing. One year later, Thoreau headed north on a similar expedition," p. 85.

5. *The Maine Woods,* ed. Joseph J. Moldenhauer (Princeton: Princeton Univ. Press, 1972), p. 16.

6. Ibid., p. 64.

7. Ibid., p. 64.

8. Ibid., pp. 70–71.

9. Ibid., p. 71.

10. Emerson, *Collected Works*, 1:8.

11. Moldenhauer, *Maine Woods*, p. 81.

12. Ibid., p. 81. Moldenhauer writes in the "Textual Introduction" that Thoreau "revised 'Ktaadn,' expanding the text with several footnotes and major insertions" before he died. It is possible that this passage was inserted during these last revisions.

13. Moldenhauer, *Maine Woods*, p. 81.

14. The Norse legends were of particular interest to Thoreau. He even entertained the idea that perhaps his name was connected with the Thors of Norway. In his *Journal*, Thoreau writes: "Perhaps I am descended from that Northman named 'Thorer the Dog-footed.' Thorer Hund—'he was the most powerful man in the North'—to judge from his name belonged to the same family," (3:304).

15. The dialectical synthesis of nature and soul that Barry Wood discusses in "The Growth of the Soul: Coleridge's Dialectical Method and the Strategy of Emerson's *Nature*" (*PMLA* 91 [May 1976]: 385–97) refines the relationship between the me and the "Not Me," but as long as nature includes the body, the evolving synthesis can be conceptualized as occurring within the self.

16. Paul, *Shores of America*, p. 379.

17. Ibid., p. 380.

18. Ibid., p. 381.

19. Pops, "An Analysis of Thoreau's *Cape Cod*," p. 423.

20. McIntosh, *Thoreau as Romantic Naturalist*, p. 219.

21. Walter Harding, *The Days of Henry Thoreau* (New York: Alfred A. Knopf, 1965), p. 359.

22. D'Avanzo, "Fortitude and Nature in Thoreau's *Cape Cod*," p. 132.

23. Richard J. Schneider, "Reflections in Walden Pond: Thoreau's Optics," *ESQ: A Journal of the American Renaissance* 21, no. 2 (1975): 70. See also his article, "*Cape Cod*: Thoreau's Wilderness of Illusion," *ESQ: A Journal of the American Renaissance* 26, no. 4 (1980): 184–95.

24. Gordon V. Boudreau, "H. D. Thoreau, William Gilpin, and the Metaphysical Ground of the Picturesque," *American Literature* 45 (1973): 369.

25. Paul, *Shores of America*, p. 381.

26. Emerson, *Collected Works*, 1:18.

27. Philip F. Gura, *The Wisdom of Words: Language, Theology, and Literature in the New England Renaissance* (Middletown, Conn.: Wesleyan Univ. Press, 1981), p. 94.

Chapter Five: Terrestrial Rainbows

1. Paul, *Shores of America*, p. 395.

2. John Conron, in "'Bright American Rivers': The Luminist Land-

scapes of Thoreau's *A Week on the Concord and Merrimack Rivers*" (*American Quarterly* 32: no. 2 [1980]), writes that in *A Week* "each of the seven chapters begins with an evocation of the morning light; each ends with evocations of dusk, twilight, the night sky. Light, as we have seen, graces every significant detail of the landscape—the scales and fins of the bream, the coat of a fisherman, the face of a boatman, the walls of a house—kindling in each an apprehension of the causes and spirits that inform them," p. 161. See also Barton Levi St. Armand, "Luminism in the Work of Henry David Thoreau: The Dark and the Light," *The Canadian Review of American Studies* 11, no. 1 (1980): 13–30.

3. For instance, a heated discussion of John Brown dominates the *Journal* in the winter of 1859.

4. Nicholas Pastore, in *Selective History of Theories of Visual Perception: 1650–1950* (New York: Oxford Univ. Press, 1971), writes that "empiristic explanations of acquired perceptions from the time of Locke and Berkeley were 'psychological.' Although there had been much discussion of the way in which the 'mind' or the 'intellect' formed associations and perceptions, no attempt was made to relate them to the physiology and anatomy of the brain," p. 146. I am not claiming by using the term psychophysiology that Thoreau postulated a strict physiological explanation, but that his interest in illusion led him to speculate about mental laws of perception that could result in material explanations of vision.

5. A significant amount of material has emerged since John I. H. Baur's pioneering article, "American Luminism: A Neglected Aspect of the Realist Movement in Nineteenth-Century American Painting," *Perspectives U.S.A.*, no. 9 (Autumn 1954): 90–98. See also Barbara Novak, *American Painting of the Nineteenth Century*, and her later volume, *Nature and Culture: American Landscape and Painting 1825–1875* (New York: Oxford Univ. Press, 1980). *American Light: The Luminist Movement: 1850–1875*, ed. John Wilmerding (New York: Harper and Row, 1980), also contains a good selection of essays.

6. Emerson, *Collected Works*, 1:15.

7. Ibid., p. 17.

8. Color as an attribute of an object, and hence a means to know the object world, is qualitatively different from a modernist sensibility about color. For instance, in 1911, Wassily Kandinsky writes that "color directly influences the soul. Color is the keyboard, the eyes are the hammers, the soul is the piano with many strings. The artist is the hand that plays, touching one key or another purposively, to cause vibrations in the soul." *Theories of Modern Art: A Source Book by Artists and Critics*, ed. Herschel B. Chipp (Berkeley: Univ. of California Press, 1968), pp. 154–55.

9. Electric fluid and electric light were also terms used to describe the physical effect Thoreau was observing.

10. Here again we see an eroding of the object world from description.

11. The discussion of vision according to an inference from the part to

the whole was not fully developed until the gestalt theory of perception. In particular, the study of camouflage and the perception of an object in motion facilitated field theories of perception, resulting in laws about brain processes. See Nicholas Pastore, *Selective Theories of Visual Perception*, pp. 268–319.

12. For instance, Stephen E. Whicher, in *Freedom and Fate: An Inner Life of Ralph Waldo Emerson* (Philadelphia: Univ. of Pennsylvania Press, 1953), writes that in the essay "Experience," Emerson "finds that the self on which he would rely is governed by an incongruous set of conditions which he can neither reconcile nor control," p. 111.

13. The use of the term "image" justifies the use of language as the most significant means to capture the relationship between the eye and the world. Image is in both the eye and the mind and, as part of consciousness, becomes embedded in language for him.

Chapter Six: Regulating Eden

1. As early as 1851, Thoreau was noting how oaks were interspersed among pine woods. Leo Stoller, in *After Walden: Thoreau's Changing Views on Economic Man* (Stanford: Stanford Univ. Press, 1957), also comments that in April 1856, "the hitherto unrelated pieces of information lying dormant in Thoreau's mind were precipitated into a synthesis," p. 81. But it is not until 1860 that an argument about forest succession is fully developed in the *Journal*.

2. Journals of natural phenomena noted in their order of appearance were a fairly common practice in nineteenth-century America.

3. See the journal manuscript at the Pierpont Morgan Library, New York. Citation: *Journal* [vol. 11], MA 1302:17, title: April 28th, 1852.

4. Thoreau's nature notes often list phenomena from up to ten years of the *Journal* during one particular month. See William L. Howarth, *The Literary Manuscripts of Henry David Thoreau* (Columbus: Ohio State Univ. Press, 1974), pp. 306–31.

5. The movement from the unique event to the representative event is a constant struggle for Thoreau. His indexes, appendixes to the *Journal*, and nature notes demonstrate the laborious process he used to extract from the discrete observation a representative description.

6. Howarth, in *The Literary Manuscripts of Henry David Thoreau*, states that "during the last six years of his life Thoreau spent many hours compiling tables, indexes, and other notes on the natural phenomena described in his *Journal* between 1851 and 1861. These 'nature notes' fall into four general categories: the seasons, plant life, animal life, and miscellanea. Exactly why he compiled all this data is uncertain. His notes on fruits and seeds were clearly part of intended publications, and some observers believe that his seasonal notes were for a projected 'Calendar' (or 'Kalendar'), a book about an archetypal year in the Concord region," p. 306. John

Hildebidle, however, thinks that "neither the 'Calendar' which Sherman Paul assumed was in progress nor the 'book on the Indians' which F. B. Sanborn suggested, was the goal that Thoreau had in mind" (*Thoreau: A Naturalist's Liberty*, p. 70).

7. Hildebidle, *Thoreau: A Naturalist's Liberty*, p. 93.

8. Sacvan Bercovitch, in *The American Jeremiad* (Madison: Univ. of Wisconsin Press, 1978), writes that the "Puritans' concept of errand entailed a fusion of secular and sacred history. The purpose of their jeremiads was to direct an imperiled people of God toward the fulfillment of their destiny, to guide them individually toward salvation, and collectively toward the American city of God," p. 9.

9. Perry Miller, *The New England Mind: The Seventeenth Century* (Boston: Beacon Press, 1939), p. 16.

10. Louis Agassiz, *Essay on Classification*, ed. Edward Lurie (Cambridge: Harvard Univ. Press, Belknap Press, 1962), p. xiv.

11. Edward Lurie, editor of *Essay on Classification*, states that "Emerson was one of Agassiz's greatest admirers, applauding the nobility of his cultural purposes, the virtue of his social democracy, and the validity of his natural religion," p. xvi.

12. Textual quotations for "Succession of Forest Trees," "Autumnal Tints," and "Wild Apples" are from *The Writings of Henry David Thoreau*, vol. 5.

13. Stoller, *After Walden*, p. 77.

14. Stoller, *After Walden*, pp. 77–78. See also William Cronon, *Changes in the Land: Indians, Colonists, and the Ecology of New England* (New York: Hill and Wang, 1983), pp. 108–26, for an account of deforestation in colonial New England.

15. In "Succession," Thoreau appears fairly cautious in his undermining of "spontaneous generation." His audience, perhaps, would not have responded so readily to his ideas if he had made this debate dominate his presentation.

16. This manuscript is in the Berg Collection, New York Public Library. Citation: Nature Notes; Berg: 70B; title: The Dispersion of Seeds. Howarth, in *The Literary Manuscripts,* notes that this "project, divided into chapters, appears to be a massive revision and expansion of 'The Succession of Forest Trees' (C19) into a book-length ms.," p. 327.

17. The pagination of the "Dispersion of Seeds" manuscript follows the Berg Collection annotation, given in the following format: "Dispersion of Seeds": Berg-32v.

18. To underscore how the battle lines in American intellectual circles were drawn, Oliver Wendell Holmes applauded "Agassiz's Natural History" in the *Atlantic Monthly* 1 (January 1858): 320–23.

19. "Dispersion of Seeds": Berg-225.

20. Edward Lurie, ed., *Essay on Classification*, p. xi.

21. "Dispersion of Seeds": Berg-398-399.

22. Richard Colyer, "Thoreau's Color Symbols," *PMLA* 86, no. 5 (1971): 999.

23. Paul Kay and Chad K. McDaniel, "The Linguistic Significance of the Meanings of Basic Color Terms," *Language* (1978): 611.

24. Rebecca Patterson, in *Emily Dickinson's Imagery* (ed. Margaret H. Freeman [Amherst: Univ. of Massachusetts Press, 1979]), registers Thoreau's protest "against this fad of using precious stones as color names," p. 80.

25. Bercovitch, in *The American Jeremiad*, defines the classic seventeenth-century form of the jeremiad as follows: "first, a precedent from Scriptures that sets out the communal norms; then, a series of condemnations that details the actual state of the community (at the same time insinuating the covenantal promises that ensure success); and finally a prophetic vision that unveils the promises, announces the good things to come, and explains away the gap between fact and ideal," p. 16.

26. R. W. B. Lewis, in *The American Adam: Innocence, Tragedy, and Tradition in the Nineteenth Century* (Chicago: Univ. of Chicago Press, 1955), writes that "Hawthorne had articulated the need he detected in the atmosphere of the day for a purgatorial action—preceding, as it were, the life of the new Adam in the new earthly paradise. Thoreau, alert to the ritual aspects of human behavior and the primitive energy of words, gave voice to the same instinctive need while he was reflecting on 'the essential facts of life' at Walden Pond," p. 14.

27. Textual quotations for "Huckleberries" are from *Huckleberries*, ed. Leo Stoller (New York: Windhover Press of the Univ. of Iowa and New York Public Library, 1970).

28. Robert F. Sayre, *Thoreau and the American Indians* (Princeton: Princeton Univ. Press, 1977), p. 146.

29. *The Indians of Thoreau: Selections from the Indian Notebooks*, ed. Richard F. Fleck (Albuquerque: Hummingbird Press, 1974), p. 3.

30. Roderick Nash, *Wilderness and the American Mind* (New Haven: Yale Univ. Press, 1967), p. 94.

31. Peter N. Carroll, *Puritanism and the Wilderness: The Intellectual Significance of the New England Frontier, 1629–1700* (New York: Columbia Univ. Press, 1969), p. 128.

32. Lewis, *American Adam*, p. 5.

Conclusion. Stone Fruit

1. *The Writings of Henry David Thoreau*, 5:147.

2. Sacvan Bercovitch, *Puritan Origins of the American Self* (New Haven: Yale Univ. Press, 1975), p. 178.

INDEX

Agassiz, Louis, 124, 126, 128, 168
Allen, Francis H., 159
Anderson, Charles R., 158, 162

Bachelard, Gaston, 64
Bancroft, George, 15, 20
Barthes, Roland, 20, 42, 156
Baur, John I. H., 166
Baym, Nina, 153, 154
Benveniste, Emile, 155
Bercovitch, Sacvan, 6, 55, 146,
    151, 161, 168, 169
Berkeley, George, 166
Berthoff, Warner, 12
Bishop, Jonathan, 157
Bloom, Harold, 6, 152
Bodaeus, Johannes, 138
Boller, Paul F., Jr., 152
Boone, Joseph Allen, 72
Bradford, William, 60
Bradstreet, Anne, 3
Breitwieser, Mitchell Robert, 164
Bridgman, Richard, 153
Briggs, Rev. Ephraim, 93
Brown, John, 166
Browning, Elizabeth Barrett, 132
Buell, Lawrence, 157, 162
Burke, Edmund, 95
Burke, Kenneth, 23, 156, 157

Cameron, Sharon, 158, 161
Carlyle, Thomas, 21, 59, 84
Carpenter, Frederick Ives, 158
Carroll, Peter N., 142
Cavell, Stanley, 162
Chambers, Robert, 163
Channing, William Ellery, 51–53,
    92
Channing, William Francis, 164
Clemens, Samuel. See Twain, Mark

Cole, Thomas, 2
Coleridge, Samuel Taylor, 39, 129
Conron, John, 165
Cooper, James Fenimore, 140
Coxe, Tench, 127
Cronon, William, 168
Culler, Jonathan, 159
Culture, 59–61, 63, 67–68, 78–80,
    83, 90, 96–97, 100, 142–43,
    149–50
Curtis, George William, 93–94
Cuvier, Baron Georges, 28, 128,
    160

Darwin, Charles, 4, 14, 42, 43–46,
    124–25, 127–28, 146, 152,
    160
D'Avanzo, Mario L., 91, 94, 164
Death, 24, 30, 32, 38, 55–57, 76–
    79, 84, 86–91, 104, 131, 133,
    149
de Champlain, Samuel, 98
Dickinson, Emily, 132
Doubling, 64, 74, 111, 116–17,
    119, 147–48, 150
Durand, Arthur B., 161

Edwards, Jonathan, 6, 51
Emerson, Ralph Waldo, 6, 8, 9–14,
    26, 32, 36, 47, 51, 84, 86, 99,
    105–6, 111, 126, 152, 154,
    155, 167
Epiphany, 9, 14, 35, 40–41, 49–50,
    74–75, 80, 116–17, 123, 125

Feidelson, Charles, Jr., 80
Field, John, 66–67
Fleck, Richard F., 141
Foucault, Michel, 160

Frye, Northrop, 8
Fuller, Margaret, 88

Garber, Frederick, 157, 162
Gillispie, Charles Coulston, 163
Gilpin, William, 20, 95–96
Goethe, Johann Wolfgang von, 20, 39, 152
Gombrich, E. H., 22
Goodfield, June, 4
Goodman, Nelson, 81
Gosnold, (Captain) Bartholomew, 99
Gozzi, Raymond D., 153
Gray, Asa, 4–5, 43, 128, 152
Gura, Philip, 11, 99

Hale, Edward Everett, 164
Harding, Walter, 162
Hawthorne, Nathaniel, 8, 49, 149
Heckewelder, John, 142
Heidegger, Martin, 61, 158
Henry, Alexander, 28
Hesford, Walter, 157
Hildebidle, John, 4, 12, 124, 154, 167–68
History: civil, 1–2, 5, 15–19, 25–29, 34, 59, 135–36, 145, 148; and evidence, 3–4, 12–13, 17–18, 24, 29, 76–77, 87, 148; vs. fiction, 8–9; first-person discourse, 5, 9–10, 17–19, 22, 36–38, 90, 106, 108–9, 119, 146, 155; natural, 1–5, 12–14, 19, 43–44, 46, 76–77, 96, 123–25, 128, 146; Puritan, 2–3, 8–10, 51, 124, 143, 146–47; and redemption, 5, 19, 26, 35, 38, 43, 49–51, 59–60, 83–84, 87–90, 104, 125–26, 128, 133–34, 136–38, 142, 145–46; romantic, 15–19, 24–26, 36–37; and time, 3–5, 9, 13–17, 22, 29–31, 33, 36–39, 54, 79, 136–37, 145–46, 149–50; and truth, 5, 35–37, 56–57, 125–26, 145; uncivil, 1, 16–17, 19, 22, 25–30, 37, 51, 55–57, 60,

65–66, 77–78, 83, 89–91, 116–17, 120–30, 135–37, 145–46, 149
Hitchcock, Edward, 4
Holmes, Oliver Wendell, 168
Homer, 95
Hovde, Carl F., 156
Howarth, William, 163, 164, 167, 168
Hussey, Christopher, 155
Hutchinson, Jamie, 157

Indians, See Native Americans
Irony, 10, 14, 83, 87, 90, 92, 95, 97–98, 100, 130

James, William, 14
Jeremiad, 135, 137
Johnson, Linck C., 155
Johnson, Paul David, 157

Kandinsky, Wassily, 166
Kay, Paul, 132
Kensett, John F., 161

Laing, Samuel, 88
Landscape: American, 2, 10, 22, 29, 34, 57, 96, 133, 139–40, 147, 149; painting, 2, 20, 22, 101, 103–6, 119, 131–33, 161
Lane, Fitz Hugh, 161
Language, 32–33, 51–57, 60, 69, 90, 95, 97–100, 119–20, 142, 150
Lebeaux, Richard, 153
Leclerc, Georges Louis, 16
Levi St. Armand, Barton, 166
Lévi-Strauss, Claude, 35
Levin, David, 19
Lewis, R. W. B., 143, 169
Locke, John, 7–8, 166
Lowe, Donald M., 156
Lukacs, Georg, 14
Lurie, Edward, 168

McCoubrey, John W., 156
McDaniel, Chad K., 132
McIntosh, James, 10, 12, 91, 153, 164
Martin, Terence, 8
Mather, Cotton, 10, 146
Melville, Herman, 8, 49, 149
Michaels, Walter Benn, 72, 153
Mill, John Stuart, 59
Miller, Perry, 51, 159
Moldenhauer, Joseph J., 165
Montaigne, Michel Eyquem de, 36
Morality, 49, 60, 73, 131, 134, 136, 140–41
Motley, John Lothrop, 20

Nash, Roderick, 142, 151
Native Americans, 18–19, 25–29, 33, 85, 138–42, 148–49, 155
Natural science, 3–4, 8–9, 12, 19, 25, 29, 87, 119–20, 133–34, 145
Nature: and culture, 27, 61, 63, 65, 67, 81–82, 139–40, 143; and description, 2, 5, 11, 13–14, 27, 35, 43, 54, 71, 78, 84, 96, 102, 106, 123; and Emersonian transcendentalism, 32, 86; laws of, 14–15, 65–66, 70–74, 76, 78, 107, 117, 123–28, 145; and the pictorial code, 20, 39, 106; and regeneration, 29–34, 77–79, 82–84, 87, 100, 104, 115, 128, 147, 150; and representation, 94, 100; and splitting, 85–86; and succession, 13–14, 71, 75–76, 123, 125–32, 134, 145; as text, 11, 77, 147, 161
Nietzsche, Friedrich, 1, 151
Novak, Barbara, 161, 166
Nye, Russel B., 19

Ovid, 28

Paradox, 9, 38, 56, 61, 62, 75, 104, 112, 116–19, 121, 123, 149; in

Journal entry structure, 38; in relation between nature and culture, 61; in perception, 9, 62, 104, 112; visual, 75, 116–19, 121, 123, 149; in writing, 56
Pastore, Nicholas, 166, 167
Patterson, Rebecca, 169
Paul, Sherman, 11, 91, 99, 157, 162, 164, 168
Perception, 9, 14, 42, 61, 104; and color, 105–7, 163, 166; and consciousness, 38; contextual basis of, 62–63, 96–97, 102, 108–9, 113–18, 128; and description, 10, 43, 145–48; dialectics of, 24, 43, 45–47, 50–51, 81, 148; and language, 52–57, 132–33; as mirage, 40, 94; moving perceiver, use of, 38–39, 43–44; psychological process of, 60, 68–70, 81, 163, 167; psychophysiology of seeing, 102, 104, 109–11, 148, 166; and redemption, 66, 112, 120, 123; and splitting, 84, 111, 150; theories of, 22, 132, 166
Plutarch, 36
Poe, Edgar Allan, 8, 49, 149
Pops, Martin Leonard, 91, 164
Price, Udevale, 95
Putnam's Magazine, 98

Rhetorical motifs: map, 21, 23–26, 39–42, 69, 73, 95, 102, 107, 117–18, 120, 126, 132, 163; mind-machine, 54–55, 62; picture, 19–20, 22, 25, 34, 39, 95; theater, 19–22, 25, 34; vestige, 27, 28–33, 75, 87, 89, 148, 157; visual reflection, 52–53, 105
Robinson, David, 152
Romanticism, 3, 6, 8–9, 12, 80, 93, 95, 128–29
Rorty, Richard, 162
Rowe, John Carlos, 158
Ruskin, John, 20, 102–3, 106, 108

Sapir, Edward, 132
Sayre, Robert, 141
Schneider, Richard J., 94
Scott, Sir Walter, 17
Self, 64, 85–87, 90, 104, 111, 147, 165
Shanley, J. Lyndon, 162
Shea, Daniel B., Jr., 158
Slotkin, Richard, 162
Smith, (Captain) John, 96
Stapleton, Laurence, 158
Stoller, Leo, 12, 127, 167
Stowell, Robert F., 163

Technology, 21, 25–26, 34, 49, 74, 78–79, 101, 107–8; cartography, 22, 127, 145; of seeing, 22, 24, 69, 109; surveying, 22, 72, 81
Thoreau, Henry David: "Autumnal Tints," 125, 131–34; *Cape Cod*, 9, 14, 83–101, 104, 111, 128; "The Commercial Spirit of Modern Times," 15; "The Dispersion of Seeds," 128–30, 168; "Huckleberries," 125, 138–43; "Indian Notebooks," 141–42; *Journal*, 10, 12, 59–60, 73, 123, 147–48, 158, 159, 161; *Journal*, pre-1850, 20, 39; *Journal*, 1850–54, 13–14, 35–38, 40–57, 65, 75, 88–89, 160, 165; *Journal*, post-1854, 101–21, 123, 131, 134, 148–49, 167; "Of Keeping a Private Journal," 54; "Ktaadn," 84–86, 128, 165; *The Maine Woods*, 104, 112; "Musings," 20; "Natural History of Massachusetts," 23–24; "Slavery in Massachusetts," 50; "The Succession of Forest Trees," 125–31, 135, 140, 168; "Thomas Carlyle and His Works," 21; *Walden*, 11–13, 58–82, 83, 94, 99, 101, 107, 112, 115–16, 141, 149, 158, 161, 162, 163; "A Walk to Wachusett," 21, 145; "Walking," 80–81, 164; *A Week on the Concord and Merrimack Rivers*, 11, 15–36, 39, 41, 50, 59–60, 63, 69, 90, 94, 96–97, 125, 155, 157, 158, 166; "Wild Apples," 125, 135–38
Torrey, Bradford, 159
Toulmin, Stephen, 3
Transcendentalism, 11–12, 32, 83, 89, 95, 99, 111, 117, 126, 131, 150
Treat, Rev. Samuel, 92–93
Twain, Mark, 93, 140

Van Tassel, David D., 157

Whicher, Stephen E., 167
White, Hayden, 151, 155, 160
Whitman, Walt, 138
Whorf, Benjamin, 132
Willard, Mr., 92
Williams, Raymond, 59
Willis, Nathaniel P., 2
Wilmerding, John, 166
Wilson, David Scofield, 153
Winthrop, John, 60, 146
Wish, Harvey, 157
Wood, Barry, 165
Wordsworth, William, 8
Worldmaking, 79–81, 83

Zochert, Donald, 156